The critics

"It's a bracing, irreverent, worl

"Mr. Rybczynski is particularly good at describing the effects, and sometimes the surprising ineffectuality, of invention—whether water closet, gas jet, electric lamp, window sash, or whatever."
—*The New York Times Book Review*

"*Home* is serious, historically minded, and exquisitely readable. It is a triumph of intelligence."
—*The New Yorker*

"Exceptionally interesting and provocative"
—*Washington Post Book World*

"Rybczynski takes the reader on a chatty, informal yet scholarly stroll."
—*The Village Voice*

"A warm, erudite book aglow with common sense"
—*Kirkus Reviews*

"If we're lucky, it will become required reading at architectural schools throughout the land."
—*USA Today*

"After reading *Home* you may never take your domicile quite so for granted again."
—*Pittsburgh Post-Gazette*

"Provocative and engaging . . . His book suggests a history of the human spirit conceived in terms of its lodgings."
—*Los Angeles Times*

PENGUIN BOOKS

HOME

Witold Rybczynski, of Polish parentage, was born in Edinburgh in 1943, raised in Surrey, and attended Jesuit schools in England and Canada. He received Bachelor of Architecture (1960) and Master of Architecture (1972) degrees from McGill University in Montreal, where he is a Professor of Architecture. He is the author of more than fifty articles and papers on the subject of housing, architecture, and technology, including the books *Taming the Tiger* and *Paper Heroes*. He lives with his wife, Shirley Hallam, in rural Quebec, in a house of their own construction.

Home

A Short History of an Idea

Witold Rybczynski

PENGUIN BOOKS

PENGUIN BOOKS

Viking Penguin Inc., 40 West 23rd Street,
New York, New York 10010, U.S.A.
Penguin Books Ltd, Harmondsworth,
Middlesex, England
Penguin Books Australia Ltd, Ringwood,
Victoria, Australia
Penguin Books Canada Limited, 2801 John Street,
Markham, Ontario, Canada L3R 1B4
Penguin Books (N.Z.) Ltd, 182–190 Wairau Road,
Auckland 10, New Zealand

First published in the United States of America by
Viking Penguin Inc. 1986
Published in Penguin Books 1987
Reprinted 1987 (twice)

LIBRARY OF CONGRESS CATALOGING IN PUBLICATION DATA
Rybczynski, Witold.
Home.
Bibliography: p.
Includes index.
1. Dwellings—Psychological aspects. 2. Personal
space—Psychological aspects. 3. Architecture and
society. I. Title.
NA7125.R9 1987 728′.01′9 86–30398
ISBN 0 14 01.0231 0

Printed in the United States of America by
R. R. Donnelley & Sons Company, Harrisonburg, Virginia
Set in Sabon

To my parents, Anna and Witold

Foreword

During the six years of my architectural education the subject of comfort was mentioned only once. It was by a mechanical engineer whose job it was to initiate my classmates and me into the mysteries of air conditioning and heating. He described something called the "comfort zone," which, as far as I can remember, was a kidney-shaped, crosshatched area on a graph that showed the relationship between temperature and humidity. Comfort was inside the kidney, discomfort was everywhere else. This, apparently, was all that we needed to know about the subject. It was a curious omission from an otherwise rigorous curriculum; one would have thought that comfort was a crucial issue in preparing for the architectural profession, like justice in law, or health in medicine.

I write, then, from ignorance. I do not apologize for this, for, as Milan Kundera once said, "To be a writer does not mean to preach a truth, it means to *discover* a truth." This book is not intended to convince, it is an attempt, rather, to discover—first of all for myself—the meaning of comfort. I thought that this would be relatively easy, or at least straightforward. That was my first mistake. I also thought, having recently finished a book on technology, that mechanical devices would play a major role in the development of the home. Here, also, I was mistaken, for domesticity proved to be an idea that had almost nothing to do with technology, or at least an idea in which technology was a distinctly secondary consideration.

I had designed and built houses, and the experience was sometimes disturbing, for I found that the architectural ideals *vii* that I had been taught in school frequently disregarded—if they did not altogether contradict—my clients' conventional notions of comfort. I was not a willful designer, and attempted to accommodate my clients' demands, but I usually did so with a vague sense of unsettled compromise. It was only when my wife and I built our own home that I discovered at first hand the fundamental poverty of modern architectural ideas. I found myself turning again and again to memories of older houses, and older rooms, and trying to understand what had made them feel so right, so comfortable. I also began to suspect, and in this I was not mistaken, that women understand more about domestic comfort than do men.

This is not a book about interior decoration. It is not so much the reality of the home that is my subject as the idea of the home, and although history is here, it is the present that concerns me. As far as history is concerned, I have relied on the work of many scholars, mentioned in the notes, but I should like to single out two texts to which I owe a special debt of gratitude: Mario Praz's extraordinary excursion into the past *An Illustrated History of Interior Decoration* (London, 1964), and Peter Thornton's *Authentic Decor* (New York, 1984), whose erudition I could never hope to match.

I would like to acknowledge the advice and assistance of the following: my wife Shirley Hallam—the first to read and comment on what I have written—John Lukacs for his encouragement when this book was only an idea, my agent John Brockman, and my editors Stacy Schiff and William Strachan. McGill University was gracious enough to allow me a six-month sabbatical to complete this book. The staff of McGill's Blackader-Lauterman Library of Art and Architecture and of the McLennan Graduate Library offered invaluable assistance, as always.

W.R.
THE BOATHOUSE
Hemmingford, Québec

Contents

Foreword   vii

Chapter One   1
NOSTALGIA

Chapter Two   15
INTIMACY AND PRIVACY

Chapter Three   51
DOMESTICITY

Chapter Four   77
COMMODITY AND DELIGHT

Chapter Five   101
EASE

Chapter Six   123
LIGHT AND AIR

Chapter Seven   145
EFFICIENCY

Chapter Eight   173
STYLE AND SUBSTANCE

Chapter Nine   195
AUSTERITY

Chapter Ten   217
COMFORT AND WELL-BEING

Notes   233

Index   245

H O M E

Kate Greenaway, *Two Little Girls
at Tea* (1879)

Nostalgia

However, insofar as there is such reference to a historic past, the peculiarity of "invented" traditions is that the continuity with it is largely factitious.

—ERIC HOBSBAWM

THE INVENTION OF TRADITION

We've all seen this comfortable man; his face looks out from the advertising pages of magazines. His graying hair, which is close-cropped, belies his age—he is only forty-three—just as his frayed shirt and faded Levi's belie his eight-figure income. The latter is barely hinted at by the silver Rolex discreetly half-hidden by the jacket sleeve, and by the hand-made cowboy boots. What he does for a living is not immediately clear. Well, we do know that despite his worn work clothes he doesn't pick lettuce; migrant workers don't wear muted wool-and-mohair sport jackets. He could be a professional athlete—a purveyor of light beer and deodorant—but his clothes are too low-key, and in any case he lacks a mustache. Still, whatever he does do, it seems to agree with him—a half-smile crosses his tanned face. But his glance is neither the vacuous stare of the professional clotheshorse nor the self-satisfied grin of the celebrity; this man looks content. "Look at me," he is saying, "I could dress any way I want, but I don't need to impress anyone, not even you. I feel good just like this." Since all ads, whether for cigarettes or for cancer research, are selling something, we can only conclude that what this man is selling is comfort.

Of course, this man is comfortable. Why shouldn't he be? 1

He owns 90 percent of a business whose annual sales total a billion dollars. His personal after-tax income in 1982 was said to be fifteen million dollars. He has all the perks that success of this kind brings: an upper Fifth Avenue duplex (more about that later), an estate in Westchester, another on Jamaica, a beach house on Long Island, a ten-thousand-acre ranch in Colorado, and a private jet to travel among them.[1]

What does he do, this business mogul, this multimillionaire, this comfortable man? He thinks up ways for people to dress. Fifty years ago he might have been a tailor or a dressmaker; if he had lived in France he would have been called a couturier. But to call Ralph Lauren a tailor is like calling the Bechtel Corporation a builder. The word does not convey the sheer size or the international scale of the operation. A tailor makes clothes; Lauren's corporation franchises manufacturers on four continents who turn out products that are sold in more than three hundred shops carrying his name, as well as in specialty boutiques in department stores in the United States, Canada, England, Italy, Switzerland, Scandinavia, Mexico, and Hong Kong. As it has grown, his business has also diversified. It started modestly, with neckties, but soon expanded to men's wear, then clothes for women, lately a special line for children. Now perfumes, soaps, cosmetics, shoes, luggage, belts, wallets, and eyeglasses all bear his imprimatur. Lauren's is that most modern of professions: he is the total fashion designer.

The first thing that strikes us about Lauren's clothes is how American they look. They are based on recognizable homegrown images: the western ranch, the prairie farm, the Newport mansion, the Ivy League college. The feeling of déjà vu is intentional: Lauren is an orchestrator of images. Although his clothes are not faithful replicas of period dress, their appearance does reflect popular ideas about various romantic periods of American history. We have seen them all before, in paintings, in photographs, on television, and, especially, in films.

Lauren understands films. One of his early designs for men's evening wear consisted of a black dinner suit, wing-collared shirt, white gloves, and a white silk muffler. Reporting on the show, *The New York Times* described this outfit as having "stepped out of a Leslie Howard movie"; Lauren himself appeared in black pinstripes and reminded the reporter of Douglas Fairbanks.[2] The cinematic simile was appropriate, since Lauren had just designed the men's costumes for a film version of *The Great Gatsby*. For a brief time, Twenties-influenced fashion became popular; dress-for-success, Lauren called it. A few years later, many of his designs were featured in the film *Annie Hall*; the comfortable, relaxed clothes worn by its stars, Woody Allen and Diane Keaton, became the look of the year. This inclination to be a costumer, along with a career built as much on advertising as on fashion shows and *Vogue* magazine, has not assured Lauren a secure position in the fashion world. It is unlikely that there will ever be a Ralph Lauren retrospective at the Metroplitan Museum, as there was in 1984 for Yves Saint Laurent.

Whether or not fashion design is an art is arguable, but there is no doubt that today it is a very big business. It all started in 1967, when Yves Saint Laurent, the boy wonder of haute couture who had succeeded Christian Dior as Paris's leading dressmaker, opened Rive Gauche, a chain of shops that sold expensive but mass-produced clothes with the now-famous YSL label. Rive Gauche proved to be a great success (there are now more than 170 outlets around the world), and soon other couturiers such as Courrèges and Givenchy were lending—that is, selling—their talents to the *prêt à porter* trade. Even the conservative Chanel succumbed to this trend, although the house did so only after the death of its founder.

Haute couture had provided the fashion industry with

glamour, but ready-to-wear clothing now became its bread and butter.* In the process many designers acquired a distinctly commercial relationship to the products that they endorsed; if you've seen athletes peddling golf clothes or tennis shoes you get the idea. It is difficult to believe that Pierre Cardin, for instance, would ever be caught dead wearing much of the perfume or the clothing (made in a Bombay sweatshop) that carries his cachet. It is obvious that the fashion pates often have little, if anything, to do with the design of "their" products; in any case, their reputations, like those of Arnold Palmer or Bjorn Borg, are made elsewhere. In that sense, at least, mass marketing, lucrative though it may be, is only a sideline.

Unlike Cardin and Saint Laurent, whose careers were founded in the exclusive dress salons, Lauren was never a couturier; from the beginning he was concerned with mass-produced clothing, and so he acquired an understanding of popular instead of elite tastes. His renown as a designer has been the result of his commercial success, not vice versa. His influence on the way that Americans dress is often overlooked, precisely because it has been indirect. Most of the women who copied Diane Keaton's loose tweed jackets or oversized men's shirts in 1977 were unaware that they were imitating Lauren originals. The 1980s fashion for Ivy League clothes— the so-called preppy look—was also Lauren-inspired.

What does this have to do with domestic comfort? In 1984, Ralph Lauren announced that he was entering the home fur-

----

* The dressmaker Charles Frédéric Worth invented the term "haute couture" in 1858. For a long time it could only be used by fashion houses that were recognized by the French government Office pour Art et Création. Curiously, haute couture was *not* the highest accreditation; the work of the most select fashion houses was referred to as "couture création."

nishings field. The only surprise is that it took him so long. The relationship between clothing and interior decoration is venerable. Look at a Hogarth painting of an early Georgian interior. The soft curves of the carved furniture were a counterpart to the rich costumes of the time and complemented the voluminous gowns of the women and the lace fronts and elaborate wigs of the men. The slightly pompous interiors of the nineteenth century also reflected clothing fashions; skirted chairs and gathered draperies imitated the details of how cloth was used in skirts and gowns, and wallpaper copied the designs used in fabrics. The richness of Art Deco furniture mirrored its owners' luxurious costumes.

And how does Ralph Lauren intend to dress the modern home? The line of furnishings—it is called a Collection—provides everything needed to decorate the home. The Collection is meant to be, in the words of Lauren's publicists, a total home environment. You can now put on a Lauren dressing gown, slip on a pair of Lauren slippers, shower with Lauren soap, dry with a Lauren towel, walk across a Lauren rug, glance at the Lauren wallpaper, and slip between Lauren sheets, beneath a Lauren comforter, to sip warm milk from a Lauren glass. You can now be a part of the ad.

It is doubtful, however, that this is "the next plateau of life-style marketing," as one enthusiastic distributor has called it.[3] For one thing, the Collection will have a limited clientele. The Lauren furnishings, which are not mass-produced, are expensive, and are being sold only in fashionable department stores in major cities like Chicago, Dallas and Los Angeles. For another, despite Lauren's long list of products the Collection is limited and does not include a full range of furniture—thus far only a few wicker pieces are available. Nevertheless, it is worthwhile examining how a corporation whose success is based on understanding the public's taste for clothing interprets popular images of the home.

I go to Bloomingdale's, New York's store for the upper-middle-class consumer, to witness this next plateau. "Fashion is a function of life-style," a voice says as I get off the escalator. Startled, I turn. There he is, the comfortable man, star of his own furnishings video. Across from the television monitor is the entrance to the Ralph Lauren Home Furnishings boutique, which consists of a number of rooms displaying the Lauren products. They remind me of the Shelburne Museum, in Vermont, where furnishings and objects are displayed in actual houses as part of recreated room settings. This gives the historical rooms the impression of being inhabited. In Bloomingdale's, the Lauren rooms are also fully recreated, with walls, ceilings, even windows, and look more like movie sets than store displays.

It turns out that the Collection is not one line but four. The four have names: "Log Cabin," "Thoroughbred," "New England," and "Jamaica." The walls of the "Log Cabin" are chinked with white plaster, and the ceiling is supported by rough-hewn beams. Buffalo Check and Woodsman Plaid blankets cover the massive pegged timber bed. The bedclothes are soft brushed flannel with matching pillow shams, sheets, and bedskirts. The rugged furniture is obviously handmade, and goes nicely with the American Indian hearth rug on the floor. A pair of Bean boots stands by the bed; on the side table is a copy of everyone's favorite summer-cottage reading, the *National Geographic* magazine. The general effect is one of moneyed rusticity, the furnishings equivalent of designer jeans.

"Jamaica" is across the aisle. It is obviously designed for the Sunbelt. A giant bamboo four-poster bed, draped with what looks like voile but could be mosquito netting, stands in the center of a cool white room. The colors of the Italian linens, Swiss embroidery, and chambray comforters are feminine—pink and blue. The bedclothes and table linens are trimmed with ruffles and embroidered with floral bouquet designs. If the inhabitant of "Log Cabin" is out shooting moose, the owners of this home must be on the verandah sipping Planter's Punch.

The decor of "Thoroughbred" is equally genteel—a country gentleman's room of dark colors highlighted by the polished brass of the bedstead and the gleaming mahogany wall paneling. Pheasant and hunting motifs abound, as do paisley prints and tartans.* Wall coverings are checks, tattersalls, and foulards. The effect is a bit overwhelming, like being caught inside Rex Harrison's closet. At the foot of the bed are a pair of riding boots. The publicity stills showed two beagle hounds dozing among the tweeds. I look for them in the cozy setting, but that must be where Bloomingdale's drew the line. "Thoroughbred" includes a distinctly anglophile table setting: teapots, egg cups, and a covered muffin dish, as well as plates ornamented with scenes of mounted polo players. "A dream England filtered through preppy America," an uncharitable British journalist called it.[5]

"New England" contains staid Early American furniture; this could be the bedroom of a restored Vermont country inn. The colors are muted, the wall fabrics are solid and candy-striped to match the Oxford-cloth bedclothes. It is the least theatrical of the four; Yankee sobriety doesn't lend itself to dramatization.

The four themes have a lot in common. They are inspired

---

* Lauren is certainly unaware, as are most people, of the recent origin of the "traditional" Scottish tartan. The idea of associating specific tartans with different families occurred during the first part of the nineteenth century—not in the mists of Celtic antiquity—and, like the kilt itself, was a modern invention. The introduction of tartans was the result of Queen Victoria's cult of the Highlands, as evidenced at Balmoral Castle, her Scottish country home, and of a sales campaign by cloth manufacturers who were seeking to develop larger markets for their products.[4]

by Lauren's own homes—the Jamaican hideaway, the ranch, the New England farm.* They are aimed at the growing number of people who have second, and even third, homes—by the lake, next to the ski slope, or on the beach—and so they follow rural models. At the same time, the comfortable informality of these furnishings is likely to be just as appropriate to apartments and townhouses as to weekend retreats. The furnishings are also an extension of Lauren's clothing designs, which have been called "western and outdoorsy or conservative and tweedy."[7] In that sense these are settings, for which the costumes have already been designed. This tendency to coordinate clothes and furnishings is to be continued in two other themes not featured in Bloomingdale's—"Mariner" and "Safari." The former is to establish an appropriately yachtsmanlike setting; the latter will convey, according to the designer, the feeling "of a hunter getting out of his Range Rover and aiming his elephant gun."[8]

The settings have something else in common, something which has become the hallmark of the Lauren look. One of his early and more extravagant outfits for men consisted of a Donegal tweed jacket with back belt and bellows pockets, worn with white flannel trousers, and complete with collar pin and English shoes of saddle leather. "You just know that the gentleman wearing it belongs to a private club and drives a Rolls-Royce (or at least wants to give that impression)," wrote a fashion reporter, who dubbed this the "Vanderbilt look."[9] In much of his recent clothing designs, Lauren has managed to restrain a tendency to evoke the symbols and the style of turn-of-the-century wealth, but the major influence

---

* According to Lauren's wife, "The places we live are sort of dreams of Ralph's that have come true. But once there, he sets about making things perfect. He designs for the place. If we didn't have the house in Jamaica, perhaps he might still have designed a Jamaica look. But having it gave him the stimulation."[6]

on the treatment of the furnishing themes continues to be what an associate calls the look of "old money."* Old, in most cases, means falling between 1890 and 1930. The log cabin setting, for instance, has the affected, cedar-stump rusticity that used to characterize rich men's hunting lodges at the end of the last century—although Lauren, a supporter of wildlife preservation, has carefully omitted the stuffed animal heads mounted on the wall. The "old world elegance and refinement" of the Jamaican furnishings brings to mind the relaxed pace of life in the white porticoed homes of the island during its colonial period. The country gentleman's retreat evoked by "Thoroughbred" could be Lord Sebastian Flyte's room in Evelyn Waugh's *Brideshead Revisited*. But this is not period decor in the conventional sense—it lacks the consistent and specific details of neo-Georgian or French Antique, to name two popular styles. Lauren is not so much interested in recalling the authentic appearance of a historical period as he is in evoking the atmosphere of traditional hominess and solid domesticity that is associated with the past.

This acute awareness of tradition is a modern phenomenon that reflects a desire for custom and routine in a world characterized by constant change and innovation. Reverence for the past has become so strong that when traditions do not exist, they are frequently invented. There are other examples than the Scottish tartan. After England adopted a national anthem in the mid-eighteenth century, most European nations quickly followed suit. The results were sometimes curious. Denmark and Germany, for instance, simply set their own words to the English music. Switzerland still sings "Ruft die,

---

* The friction between new and old money took a bizarre turn recently, when it was reported that Lauren had brought legal action for infringing on "his" corporate symbol against an organization that had the temerity to use the figure of a man on a horse swinging a mallet as its insignia. The object of his suit was the United States Polo Association, founded in 1900.[10]

mein Vaterland" to the strains of "God Save the King," and until Congress adopted an official national anthem—in 1931—Americans sang "My Country 'Tis of Thee" to the same regal music. The "Marseillaise" is original, and authentic; it was written during the French Revolution. But Bastille Day was first celebrated in 1880, a hundred years after the actual event.

Another example of invented tradition is the popular fashion for so-called Early American or Colonial furniture. In most people's imagination it represents a link to the values of the Founding Fathers, the Spirit of '76, an integral part of the national heritage. The truth is that the Colonial style owes its existence not to an unbroken continuity passed from colonial father to republican son, but to the much more recent Centennial celebrations of 1876.[11] The Centennial encouraged the founding of many so-called patriotic societies, such as the Sons (now defunct) and the Daughters (still active) of the American Revolution, the Colonial Dames of America, and the Society of Mayflower Descendants. This new interest in genealogy was due partly to the Centennial itself, and partly to efforts by the established middle class to distance itself from the increasing number of new, predominantly non-British immigrants. This process of cultural authentification was fortified by furnishing homes in the so-called Colonial style, thus underlining the link to the past. Like most invented traditions, the Colonial revival was also a reflection of its own time—the nineteenth century. Its visual taste was influenced by the then current English architectural fashion—Queen Anne—which had nothing to do with the Pilgrim Fathers, but whose cozy hominess appealed to a public sated by the extravagances of the Gilded Age.

Lauren's invented traditions are derived from the literary and cinematic imagination. The English country life suggested by "Thoroughbred" was already in decline when Waugh wrote about it, forty years ago. Today, where fox-hunting still exists, it is practiced almost in secret, to avoid the attacks of various environmental and animal-welfare groups. "Mariner" conjures up the Newport of F. Scott Fitzgerald, but although his blazer-clad sailors lolled about on sixty-foot teak-decked ketches—crewed by hired help—most of us have to be content with a car-topped fiberglass dinghy. "Safari" recalls a time when wealthy Americans and Europeans could go to Africa and shoot their hearts out; today, if they go they are less likely to be carrying a Mannlicher—as Hemingway did—than a Minolta. The real postindependence Jamaica is less old-world charm than packaged tours, dope, and threatening Rastafarians. As for the simple fireside pleasures implicit in "Log Cabin," these have been replaced, or at least augmented, by hang gliders and mountain bikes.

What is also striking about these handsome interiors is the absence of so many of the things that characterize modern life. We look in vain for clock-radios, electric hair dryers, or video games. There are pipe racks and humidors in the bedrooms, but no cordless telephones, no televisions. There may be snowshoes hanging on the cabin wall, but there are no snowmobile boots by the door. In the tropical setting we glimpse an overhead fan instead of an air-conditioning unit. The mechanical paraphernalia of contemporary living has been put away, and replaced by brass-cornered gun boxes, silver bedside water carafes, and leather-bound books.

Admittedly, these tableaux are not real interiors but only backdrops designed to set off the fabrics, tableware, and bedclothes that form the Furnishings Collection; it is unlikely that anyone would ever furnish his or her home to look like the Lauren publicity brochures. But that is beside the point; advertisements often represent a not altogether real, stylized world, but one which does reflect society's view of how things *ought* to be. These themes have been chosen to evoke popular images that are informal and comfortable, reminiscent of wealth, stability, and tradition. What they leave out is as revealing as what they include.

There is little doubt that these carefully arranged rooms would be compromised by the introduction of modern objects. Like a director filming a costume epic who blanks out the telephone wires and the drone of the overhead jet, Lauren has kept the twentieth century at bay. There is no polypropylene thermal underwear drying in front of the stone fireplace, no electric toaster on the table, to intrude on the traditional coziness of "Log Cabin," just as there is no personal computer on the desk in "Thoroughbred." How do we fit reality into this dream world? One way is to not even try. The headquarters of Estée Lauder Incorporated, a large cosmetics corporation, are located in the General Motors Building in New York. The main offices are conventional; the chairman's office is not—it resembles the small drawing room of a Loire château. Estée Lauder's desk is Louis XVI, as are two of the side chairs. The two wing chairs are Second Empire, the couch is Belle Epoque, and the lamp holder is French Bouillotte (obviously, the candles have been replaced by electrical bulbs). The only modern objects are two telephones.[12] The office of Malcolm S. Forbes, owner of *Forbes* magazine, does not make even that compromise with modernity. No telephones disturb the top of his elegant Georgian partner's desk, which is flanked by a pair of Queen Anne corner chairs and a fine Chippendale-style wing chair. A chandelier hangs from the ceiling and illuminates the mahogany-paneled room, originally built in the nineteenth century and free from any reminders of the twentieth. This is as much a place for drinking a glass of vintage port as for transacting business.[13]

This sort of historical verisimilitude is difficult to achieve, and obviously expensive. In any case, outside Mr. Forbes's and Mrs. Lauder's offices are the telex machines, flickering word processors, ergonomically designed stenographer's chairs, steel file cabinets, and fluorescent strip lighting that are necessary for the proper functioning of a modern corporation. One reason that all this equipment is outside is that it is not easy to integrate it into a Louis XVI salon or a Georgian study. Only a few modern devices lend themselves to being camouflaged in period clothing. A Baume & Mercier carriage clock, for instance, has an octagonal case of pearwood with brass fittings, that contains a quartz movement. A strictly modern device like a photocopier, on the other hand, has no precedents, it can only be disguised, and were this ever attempted the result would be about as satisfying as when television sets are made up to look like Colonial credenzas.

So the modern world is kept at bay. These office interiors, like the settings of the Lauren Collection, present the appearance of a way of life that no longer exists. Their reality is no deeper than the flocked covering on the wall; a cynic would point out that the lady in the Louis XVI office was actually born in Queens, and Mr. Forbes in Brooklyn (Lauren, that other anglophile, grew up in the Bronx). But whether the way of life is remembered, or simply imagined, it nevertheless signifies a widely held nostalgia. Is it simply a curious anachronism, this desire for tradition, or is it a reflection of a deeper dissatisfaction with the surroundings that our modern world has created? What are we missing that we look so hard for in the past?

Chapter Two

Albrecht Dürer, *St. Jerome in His Study* (1514)

Intimacy and Privacy

Consider the room which Albrecht Dürer illustrated in his famous engraving *St. Jerome in His Study*. The great Renaissance artist followed the convention of his time and showed the early Christian scholar not in a fifth-century setting—nor in Bethlehem, where he really lived—but in a study whose furnishings were typical of Dürer's Nuremberg at the beginning of the sixteenth century. We see an old man bent over his writing in the corner of a room. Light enters through a large leaded-glass window in an arched opening. A low bench stands against the wall under the window. Some tasseled cushions have been placed on it; upholstered seating, in which the cushion was an integral part of the seat, did not appear until a hundred years later. The wooden table is a medieval design—the top is separate from the underframe, and by removing a couple of pegs the whole thing can be easily disassembled when not in use. A back-stool, the precursor of the side chair, is next to the table.

The tabletop is bare except for a crucifix, an inkpot, and a writing stand, but personal possessions are in evidence elsewhere. A pair of slippers has been pushed under the bench. 15

The haphazard placement of several valuable folios on the bench is not a sign of sloppiness—bookcases have not yet been invented. A holder for paper notes is fixed to the rear wall, which also supports a penknife and a pair of scissors. Above them is a shelf with candlesticks. Some prayer beads and a straw brush hang from hooks; the little cupboard probably contains food. A stoup filled with holy water stands in a niche in the wall. An amazing gourd suspended from the ceiling is the only purely decorative object in the room. Except for the allegorical objects—a pilgrim's hat, a skull, and an hourglass—there is not much here that startles us, except, of course, the saint's tame lion, dozing in the foreground. The rest of the domestic objects are familiar; indeed, we feel that we could easily sit down on the empty back-stool and feel at home in this functional, but not austere, study.

The study in which I am writing is a similar size. Since it is on an upper floor, the roof slopes down sharply to meet the low walls, and if I reach up I can easily touch the angled ceiling, which is wood and resembles the underside of an overturned boat. A window faces west. In the morning, when I usually work, it allows a pale light to reflect off the white walls and the cedar ceiling onto the gray dhurrie that lies on the floor. Although the room resembles a Parisian attic, I do not see any roofs, chimney pots, or television aerials outside; instead I look out on an orchard, a line of poplar trees, and beyond them the beginning of the Adirondack Mountains. This view—it is not grand enough to be called a prospect— is English in its tamed domesticity.

I am sitting in a creaky old swivel-type wooden armchair of the sort that used to be found in newspaper offices; it has a battered foam cushion. When I use the telephone, I tilt back and feel like Pat O'Brien in *The Front Page*. Since the chair is on casters, I can roll around and reach the books, magazines, papers, pencils, and paperclips that surround me. Everything necessary is close to hand, as in any well-organized workplace, whether it is a writer's room or the cockpit of a jumbo jet. Of course, the kind of organization required to write a book is not the same as is needed to fly a plane. Although some writers find comfort in a neatly organized desk, my own is covered three-deep with a jumble of half-opened books, encyclopedias, dictionaries, magazines, sheets of paper, and newspaper clippings. Finding something in this precarious pile is like playing pick-up-sticks. As the work progresses, the pile grows taller and the open space on which I write shrinks further. Even so, there is comfort in this confusion; only when a chapter is finished, and my desk is once again immaculately empty, do I feel a sense of unease. Like a blank page, a neat desk can intimidate.

Hominess is not neatness. Otherwise everyone would live in replicas of the kinds of sterile and impersonal homes that appear in interior-design and architectural magazines. What these spotless rooms lack, or what crafty photographers have carefully removed, is any evidence of human occupation. In spite of the artfully placed vases and casually arranged art books, the imprint of their inhabitants is missing. These pristine interiors fascinate and repel me. Can people really live without clutter? How do they stop the Sunday papers from spreading over the living room? How do they manage without toothpaste tubes and half-used soap bars in their bathrooms? Where do they hide the detritus of their everyday lives?

Many personal mementos, photographs and objects—reliquaries of family, friends, and career—fill my study. A small gouache of a young man—myself—seated in a Formentera doorway. A sepia-colored photograph of a German zeppelin hovering over Boston on the way to Lakehurst. A photograph of my own house under construction. A Gujarati wall hanging. A framed note from a Famous Man. A corkboard, with messages, telephone numbers, visiting cards, yellowing unanswered letters and forgotten bills. A black sweater, some books, and a leather briefcase are lying on the daybed which stands on the other side of the room. My writing desk is an old one. Although it is not a particularly valuable antique, its elegance recalls a time when letter writing was a leisurely art, carefully performed with pen and ink and blotter. I feel a little ashamed as I scrawl untidy notes on legal pads of cheap yellow paper. On the desk, in addition to the mess of books and papers, are a heavy brass padlock used as a paperweight, a tin can full of pencils, a cast-iron Sioux Indian-head bookend, and a silver snuffbox with the likeness of George II on its cover. Did it once belong to my grandfather? I cannot remember. The plastic cigarette box next to it must have—in addition to the prewar Polish marque, it carries his initials.

Personal possessions, a chair, a desk—a place to write. Not much has changed in over four hundred years. Or has it? Dürer's subject was a hermit, so it was natural to show him working alone, but it was unusual for someone in the sixteenth century to have his own room. It was more than a hundred years later that rooms to which the individual could retreat from public view came into being—they were called "privacies." So, although the title of the engraving refers to this as a "study," it was really a room with many uses, all of them public. In spite of the calm that is present in this masterly picture, the type of quiet and seclusion that we normally associate with a writer's workplace would have been impossible. Houses were full of people, much more so than today, and privacy was unknown. Moreover, rooms did not have specialized functions; at noon, the writing stand was put away and the householders sat around the table and had their meal. In the evening the table was taken apart and the long bench became a settee. At night, what now served as a living room was turned into a bedroom. There is no bed visible in this particular engraving, but in other versions Dürer showed the scholar writing on a small lectern, and using his bed as a seat. If we could sit down on one of the back-stools it would not be long before we would begin to fidget. The seat cushion does offer some padding against the hard, flat wood, but this is not a chair to relax in.

Dürer's room contains a few tools—an hourglass, a pair of scissors, and a quill pen—but no machines or mechanical devices. Although glass manufacturing had progressed far enough that the large windows were a useful source of light during the day, after nightfall the candles were brought down from the shelf. Writing became impossible, or at least uncomfortable. Heating was primitive. Houses in the sixteenth century had a fireplace or cookstove only in the main room, and no heating in the rest of the house. In winter, this room with its heavy masonry walls and stone floor was extremely cold. Voluminous clothing, such as Jerome wore, was not a requisite of fashion but a thermal necessity, and the old scholar's hunched posture was an indication not only of piety but also of chilliness.

I too am bent over my writing, not in front of a writing stand but before the amber phosphor screen of a word processor. Instead of the scratching of a quill on parchment, I can hear faint clicks, and occasional purring sounds as words are transferred from my own mind to the machine, and from the machine's memory to the plastic disks on which they are recorded. This machine, which, we are led to believe, will revolutionize the way we live, has already affected literature—it has restored quiet to the act of writing. One thing noticeably missing in old pictures of people writing are wastepaper baskets; paper was much too valuable to be thrown away, and a writer had to edit in his head. In that sense we have come full circle, for the word processor has done away with the crumpling of paper. Instead, I press a button, the screen flickers, and the deed is done; the unwanted words disappear into an electronic shredder. It has a calming effect.

So, in fact, a great deal *has* changed in the home. Some of the changes are obvious—the advances in heating and lighting that are due to new technology. Our sitting furniture has become much more sophisticated, better adapted to relaxation. Other changes are more subtle—the way that rooms are used, or how much privacy is afforded by them. Is my study more comfortable? The obvious answer is yes, but if we were to ask Dürer, we might be surprised by his reply. To begin with, he would not understand the question. "What exactly do you mean by comfortable?" he might respond in puzzled curiosity.

The word "comfortable" did not originally refer to enjoyment or contentment. Its Latin root was *confortare*—to strengthen or console—and this remained its meaning for centuries. We use it this way when we say "He was a comfort to his mother in her old age." It was in this sense that it was used in theology: the "Comforter" was the Holy Spirit. Along the way, "comfort" also acquired a legal meaning: in the sixteenth century a "comforter" was someone who aided or abetted a crime. This idea of support was eventually broadened to include people and things that afforded a measure of satisfaction, and "comfortable" came to mean tolerable or sufficient—one spoke of a bed of comfortable width, although not yet of a comfortable bed. This continues to be the meaning of the expression "a comfortable income"— ample but not luxurious. Succeeding generations expanded this idea of convenience, and eventually "comfortable" acquired its sense of physical well-being and enjoyment, but not until the eighteenth century, long after Dürer's death. Sir Walter Scott was one of the first novelists to use it this new way when he wrote, "Let it freeze without, we are comfortable within." Later meanings of the word were almost exclusively concerned with contentment, often of a thermal variety: "comforter" in secular Victorian England no longer referred to the Redeemer, but to a long woolen scarf; today it describes a quilted bed coverlet.

Words are important. Language is not just a medium, like

a water pipe, it is a reflection of how we think. We use words not only to describe objects but also to express ideas, and the introduction of words into the language marks the simultaneous introduction of ideas into the consciousness. As Jean-Paul Sartre wrote, "Giving names to objects consists in moving immediate, unreflected, perhaps ignored events on to the plane of reflection and of the objective mind."[1] Take a word like "weekend," which originated at the end of the nineteenth century. Unlike the medieval "weekday" that distinguished the days that one worked from the Lord's Day, the profane "weekend"—which originally described the period when shops and businesses were closed—came to reflect a way of life organized around the active pursuit of leisure. The English word, and the English idea, has entered many languages in unchanged form (*le* weekend, *el* weekend, *das* weekend). Another example. Our grandparents inserted paper rolls into their player pianos. As far as they were concerned, the piano and the piano roll formed part of the same machine. We, on the other hand, draw a distinction between the machine and the instructions that we give it. We call the machine hardware, and to describe the instructions we have invented a new word, "software." This is more than jargon; the word represents a different way of thinking about technology. Its addition to the language marks an important moment.*

The appearance of the word "comfort" in the context of domestic well-being is similarly of more than lexicographic interest. There are other words in the English language with this meaning—"cozy," for instance—but they are of later origin. The first use of "comfort" to signify a level of domestic

---

* The first use of the word "software" was in 1963 (according to the *Oxford English Dictionary*), although at that time it was used only by computer engineers. Its entry into the vernacular, and into the public's consciousness, occurred more than a decade later, when inexpensive home computers made their appearance.

amenity is not documented until the eighteenth century. How to explain this tardy arrival? It is said that the Canadian Inuit have many words to describe a wide variety of types of snow. Like sailors, who have an extended vocabulary to describe the weather, they need to differentiate between new snow and old, hard-packed and loose, and so on. We have no such need, and we call it all "snow." On the other hand, cross-country skiers, who do need to distinguish between different snow conditions, do so by referring to the different colors of ski wax: they speak of purple snow or blue snow. These are not exactly new words, but they do represent an attempt to refine the language to meet a special need. In a similar way, people began to use "comfort" in a different way because they needed a special word to articulate an idea which previously had either not existed or had not required expression.

Let us start this examination of comfort by trying to understand what happened in Europe in the eighteenth century, and why people suddenly found that they needed a special word to describe a particular attribute of the interiors of their homes. To do this it is necessary to look first at an earlier period—the Middle Ages.

The Middle Ages are an opaque period of history that is open to many interpretations. As a French scholar has written, "The Renaissance viewed medieval society as scholastic and static, the Reformation saw it as hierarchical and corrupt, and the Age of Enlightenment considered it to have been irrational and superstitious."[2] The nineteenth-century Romantics, who idealized the Middle Ages, described them as the antithesis of the Industrial Revolution. Writers and artists like Thomas Carlyle and John Ruskin popularized the image of the Middle Ages as an unmechanical, rustic arcadia. This latest revision has greatly influenced our own view of the Middle Ages, and has given rise to the idea that medieval society was both untechnological, and uninterested in technology.

This notion is altogether mistaken. The Middle Ages not only produced illuminated books, but also eyeglasses, not only the cathedral, but also the coal mine. Revolutionary changes occurred in both primary industry and manufacturing. The first recorded instance of mass production—of horseshoes—occurred during the Middle Ages. Between the tenth and the thirteenth century, a technological boom produced the mechanical clock, the suction pump, the horizontal loom, the waterwheel, the windmill, and even, on both shores of the English Channel, the tidal mill. Agricultural innovations formed the economic foundation for all this technical activity. The deep plow and the idea of crop rotation increased productivity as much as fourfold, so that agricultural yields in the thirteenth century would not be surpassed for another five hundred years.[3] Far from being a technological Black Hole, the Middle Ages marked the authentic beginning of industrialization in Europe. The period's influence was felt until at least the eighteenth century in all aspects of everyday life, including attitudes toward the home.

Any discussion about domestic life during this period must include an important caveat: it cannot refer to most of the population, who were poor. Writing about the decline of the Middle Ages, the historian J. H. Huizinga described a world of sharp contrasts, where health, wealth, and good fortune (that old toast) were enjoyed as much for their rarity as for their advantages. "We, at the present day, can hardly understand the keenness with which a fur coat, a good fire on the hearth, a soft bed, a glass of wine, were formerly enjoyed."[4] He also made the point that medieval popular art, which we appreciate for its simple beauty, was prized by its makers even more for its splendor and pomp. Its overdecorated sumptuousness, which we often overlook, is evidence of what was needed to make an impression on a public whose sensibilities were dulled by the wretched conditions under which they lived. The extravagant pageants and religious festivals which characterized that time can be understood not only as a celebration, but also as an antidote to the miseries of everyday life.[5]

The poor were extremely badly housed. They were without water or sanitation, with almost no furniture and few possessions, a situation which, in Europe at least, continued until the beginning of the twentieth century.[6] In the towns, their houses were so small that family life was compromised; these tiny one-room hovels were little more than shelters for sleeping. There was room only for the infants—the older children were separated from their parents and sent to work as apprentices or servants. The result of these deprivations, according to some historians, was that concepts such as "home" and "family" did not exist for these miserable souls.[7] To speak of comfort and discomfort under such circumstances is absurd; this was bare existence.

If the poor did not share in medieval prosperity, there was a different class of persons who did: the town-dwellers. The free town was among the most important, and most original, of all the medieval innovations. Windmills and waterwheels could have been invented by other societies, and were, but the free town, which stood apart from the predominantly feudal countryside, was uniquely European. Its inhabitants— the *francs bourgeois*, the *burghers*, the *borghese*, and the burgesses—would create a new urban civilization.[8] The word "bourgeois" first occurred in France in the early eleventh century.[9] It described the merchants and tradesmen who lived in walled towns, governed themselves through elected councils, and in most cases owed allegiance directly to the king (who established the free town) instead of to a lord. These "cityzens" (the idea of national citizenship came much later) were distinct from the rest of society, which was either feudal, ecclesiastical, or agricultural. This meant that at the same time as the vassals were being dragged off to some local war, the bourgeois in the towns had a considerable measure of independence and were able to benefit from the economic prosperity. What places the bourgeois in the center of any discussion of domestic comfort is that unlike the aristocrat, who lived in a fortified castle, or the cleric, who lived in a monastery, or the serf, who lived in a hovel, the bourgeois lived in a house. Our examination of the home begins here.

The typical bourgeois townhouse of the fourteenth century combined living and work. Building plots had restricted street frontages, since the fortified medieval town was by necessity densely constructed. These long narrow buildings usually consisted of two floors over an undercroft, or basement, which was used for storage. The main floor of the house, or at least that part that faced the street, was a shop or—if the owner was an artisan—a work area. The living quarters were not, as we would expect, a series of rooms; instead, they consisted of a single large chamber—the hall—which was open up to the rafters. People cooked, ate, entertained, and slept in this space. Nevertheless, the interiors of restored medieval houses always look empty. The large rooms have only a few pieces of furniture, a tapestry on the wall, a stool beside the large fireplace. This minimalism is not a modern affectation; medieval homes were sparsely furnished. What furniture there was was uncomplicated. Chests served as both storage and seats. The less affluent sometimes used a chest (*truhe*) as a kind of bed—the clothes inside serving as a soft mattress. Benches, stools and demountable trestle tables were common. The beds were also collapsible, although by the end of the Middle Ages more important personages slept in large permanent beds, which usually stood in a corner. Beds also served as seats, for people sat, sprawled, and squatted wherever they could, on chests, stools, cushions, steps, and often the floor. If contemporary paintings are anything to judge by, medieval posture was a casual affair.

One place where people did not often sit was in chairs. The Pharaonic Egyptians had used chairs, and the ancient Greeks refined them to elegant and comfortable perfection in the fifth century B.C. The Romans introduced them to Europe, but after the collapse of their empire—during the so-called Dark Ages—the chair was forgotten. Its reappearance is difficult to pinpoint, but by the fifteenth century, chairs started to be used again. But what a different chair! The Greek *klismos* had had a low, concave backrest that was shaped to the human body, and splayed legs that allowed the sitter to lean back. The comfortable posture of a lounging Greek, with his arm bent casually over the low chair back and his legs crossed, is recognizably modern. No such position was possible in a medieval chair, which had a hard, flat seat and a tall, straight back whose function was more decorative than ergonomic. During the Middle Ages, chairs—even the boxlike armchairs—were not intended to be comfortable; they were symbols of authority. You had to be important to sit down in a chair—unimportant people sat on benches. As one historian put it, if you were entitled to a chair you sat up in it: nobody ever sat *back*.[10]

One reason for the simplicity, and the scarcity, of medieval furniture was the way in which people used their homes. In the Middle Ages people didn't so much live in their houses as camp in them. The nobility owned many residences, and traveled frequently. When they did so, they rolled up the tapestries, packed the chests, took apart the beds, and moved their household with them. This explains why so much medieval furniture is portable or demountable. The French and Italian words for furniture—*mobiliers* and *mobilia*—mean "the movables."[11]

The town bourgeois were less mobile, but they too needed movable furniture, although for a different reason. The medieval home was a public, not a private place. The hall was in constant use, for cooking, for eating, for entertaining guests, for transacting business, as well as nightly for sleeping. These different functions were accommodated by moving the furniture around as required. There was no "dining table," just a table which was used for preparing food, eating, counting money, and, in a pinch, for sleeping. Since the number of diners varied, the number of tables, and chairs, had to increase and decrease to accommodate them. At night, the tables were put away and the beds were brought out. As a result, there was no attempt to form permanent arrangements. Paintings of medieval interiors reflect an improvisation in the haphazard placement of the furniture, which was simply put around the edges of the room when not in use. Except for the armchair, and later the bed, one has the impression that little importance was attached to the individual pieces of furniture; they were treated more as equipment than as prized personal possessions.

Medieval interiors, with their stained-glass windows, pewlike benches, and Gothic tracery, always betray their ecclesiastical origins. The monastic orders were the multinational corporations of that time—they not only were the source of scientific and technological innovation but also influenced other aspects of medieval life, including music, writing, art, and medicine. Similarly, they affected the design of secular furniture, much of which originated in religious surroundings: the chest for storing vestments, the refectory table, the reading lectern, the stall. The first recorded drawers were used for filing church documents.[12] However, since the life-style of the monks was to be ascetic, there was no reason for them to apply their prodigious inventive energy to making life more pleasurable, and most of their furniture was intentionally severe.[13] Straight-backed pews focused the mind on higher matters (and kept the sitter awake), and hard benches (which can still be found in Oxford colleges) discouraged dawdling at the refectory table.

What is unexpected about medieval houses, however, is

not the lack of furniture (the emptiness of modern architecture has accustomed us to that) but the crush and hubbub of life within them. These houses were not necessarily large—except compared to the hovels of the poor—but they were full of people. This was partly because, in the absence of restaurants, bars, and hotels, they served as public meeting places for entertaining and transacting business, but also because the household itself was large. In addition to the immediate family it included employees, servants, apprentices, friends, and protégés—households of up to twenty-five persons were not uncommon. Since all these people lived in one or at most two rooms, privacy was unknown.* Anyone who has been in the military, or in a boarding school, can imagine what it must have been like. Only exceptional people—hermits or scholars (like St. Jerome)—could shut themselves up alone. Even sleeping was a communal business. Not only were there usually many beds in a room—the will of Richard Toky, a London grocer who died in 1391, indicates that he had four beds and a cradle in his hall—there were usually many people in each bed.[14] This explains the size of medieval beds; ten feet square was normal. The Great Bed of Ware was so large that "Four couples might cosily lie side by side, And thus without touching each other abide."[15] How did people achieve intimacy under such conditions? It appears that they did not. Medieval paintings frequently show a couple in bed or bath, and nearby in the same room friends or servants in untroubled, and apparently unembarrassed, conversation.[16]

We should not, however, jump to the conclusion that medieval domestic life was primitive. Bathing, for instance, was fashionable. Here the monasteries also played a role, for not only were they centers of piety, they were also centers of

---

* The concept of privacy is also absent in many non-Western cultures, notably Japan. Lacking an indigenous word to describe this quality, the Japanese have adopted an English one—*praibashii*.

cleanliness. Hygiene was important to the efficiency-minded Cistercian order, for example, St. Bernard, their founder, had spelled it all out in the Rule, an operating manual that dealt not only with religious matters, but also with the mundane. The purpose of the tonsure, for instance, was not symbolic; monks' heads were shaved to control lice. The Rule described work schedules in detail as well as the layout of the buildings, which followed a standardized plan, like businessmen's hotels today. It has been said that a blind monk could enter any of the more than seven hundred Cistercian monasteries and not get lost.[17] Each complex included a *lavatorium*, or bathhouse, fitted with wooden tubs and with facilities for heating the water; small basins with constantly running cold water for hand-washing before and after meals were outside the refectory. The *misericord*, where dying monks were ritually bathed, was situated beside the infirmary, while the *reredorter*, a wing containing latrines, was built next to the dormitory (the *dorter*). The wastewaters from these facilities were carried away in covered-over streams, in effect underground sewers.[18]

Most bourgeois houses in England were provided with household drainage and underground cesspits (although not with sewers). There are many examples of fifteenth-century houses (not only palaces and castles) which had so-called "garderobes" or privies on the upper floor, and chutes leading down to the basement.[19] These were periodically cleaned out, and while the town slept, the "night soil" would be transported to the countryside, to be used as fertilizer. More often, garderobes and privies emptied directly into rivers and streams, which resulted in the contamination of well water and frequent outbreaks of cholera. It was the same type of scientific ignorance, not dirtiness, that accounted for the inability of people in the fourteenth century to resist the Black Death— they did not understand that its principal carriers were rats and fleas.

Lacking the Rule, the laity were not as observant of hygiene as the monks, but there is evidence that they too paid attention to cleanliness. A fourteenth-century manual, *Ménagère de Paris*, counseled the housewife, "The entrance to your home, that is the parlor and the entrances whereby people come in to speak within the house, must be swept early in the morning and kept clean, and the stools, benches and cushions dusted and shaken."[20] The floor of the hall was strewn with straw in winter, and with herbs and flowers in the summer. This charming practice had a practical purpose, both to keep the floor warm and to maintain an appearance, and an odor, of cleanliness. Washstands and tubs were widely used, although there were no bathrooms. Only in the monasteries, or in exceptional buildings such as Westminster Palace, was there a room devoted exclusively to bathing; most tubs, like the rest of the furnishings, were portable.[21] The bathtubs, which were wooden, were often large, and communal bathing was common. Bathing was a social ritual in the Middle Ages, as it is in some oriental cultures today. It was often a part of festivities such as marriages and banquets, and it was accompanied by conversation, music, food, drink, and, inevitably, lovemaking.[22]

Medieval table manners were elaborate. Etiquette was taken seriously, and our custom of giving precedence to guests, or offering them second helpings, originated in the Middle Ages. Washing the hands before eating was another medieval politeness which has survived to the present day. Washing the hands before, after, and during the meal was necessary in the Middle Ages, because although soup spoons were used, forks were not, and people ate largely with their fingers; as in India or Saudi Arabia today, this did not imply indelicacy. Food was served on large platters, cut into smaller portions, and placed on trenchers, large slices of bread that—like Mexican tortillas or Indian chapatis—served as edible plates. The popular image of eating in the Middle Ages is one of homely meals where the food was plentiful but not very sophisticated; quite to the contrary, we would be struck by the diversity of medieval dishes. The growth of cities encouraged the exchange of commodities such as German beer, French and Italian wine, Spanish sugar, Polish salt, Russian honey, and, for the wealthy, spices from the East. Medieval food was far from bland; cinnamon, ginger, nutmeg, and pepper were combined with local herbs such as parsley, mint, garlic, and thyme.[23] There is a good deal of documentation about court banquets, which were extravagant and consisted of many courses served in carefully orchestrated sequence. Much of the variety was the result of eating game as well as domestic animals, and regal menus sometimes sound like lists of an animal protection fund: peacocks, egrets, herons, bitterns, and eagles. Such exotica catch the eye, but even the humbler bourgeois ate well. Here are the ingredients for "farced chycken," a common dish described by Chaucer: a baked chicken stuffed with lentils, cherries, cheese, ale, and oats and garnished with a sauce of "pandemayne" (fine white bread) crumbs, herbs, and salt mixed with "Romeney" (a malmsey wine).[24]

So what are we to make of the home in the Middle Ages? Walter Scott, after describing the interior of a twelfth-century castle in *Ivanhoe*, warned the reader, "Magnificence there was, with some rude attempt at taste; but of comfort there was little, and, being unknown, it was unmissed."[25] According to the twentieth-century architectural historian Siegfried Giedion, "From today's point of view, the Middle Ages had no comfort at all."[26] Even Lewis Mumford, who admired this period, concluded that "the medieval house had scarcely an inkling of . . . comfort."[27] These judgments are true, but should not be misinterpreted. People in the Middle Ages did not altogether lack comfort, as I have tried to show. Their homes were neither rustic nor crude, nor should we imagine that the persons inhabiting them did so without pleasure. But what comfort there was was never explicit. What our medieval ancestors did lack was the awareness of comfort as an objective *idea*.

If we were to sit down at a medieval meal we would complain about the hard bench. But the medieval diner was less concerned with how she or he sat than with *where* he or she sat. To be placed "above the salt" was an honor reserved only for a distinguished few. To sit in the wrong place, or next to the wrong person, was a serious gaffe. Manners dictated not only where and next to whom the members of the five social classes sat, but even what they could eat.[28] We sometimes complain about our own regimented society, but order and ritual governed medieval life to an extent which we would find intolerable. People lived by the bell. The day was divided into eight periods, and the ringing of the matins or nones bells not only signified the time for prayers within the monastery but also regulated work and commerce in the town. There was no all-night shopping; markets opened and closed according to strict times. In the city of London, you could not buy foreign cheese before nones (midafternoon) or meat after vespers (sunset).[29] When mechanical clocks were invented, these rules were refined, and fish could not be sold before ten o'clock in the morning, nor wine or ale before six o'clock. Disobedience was punished by imprisonment.

Rules also governed how people dressed. The prime function of medieval dress was to communicate status, and formal regulations described exactly how the different social classes should dress. An important baron was permitted to buy more new sets of clothes per year than a simple knight; a wealthy merchant was grudgingly allowed the same vanities as a nobleman of the lowest rank, although ermine was always reserved for the aristocracy.[30] Some could wear brocade, others colored silk and embroidered fabrics. Even certain colors were privileged. Headgear was ubiquitous, and hats were rarely removed. Important people wore them while eating, sleeping, and even bathing. This was not necessarily uncomfortable, unless you were a bishop wearing a tall miter all through dinner, but it does indicate the importance that this obsessively ordered society placed on public expression and on formality, and the secondary role that it willingly assigned to personal comfort. This was especially so at the end of the Middle Ages, when conventions of dress became exaggerated to a ridiculous extent.[31] Women wore the *hennin*, a tall conical headpiece with a trailing veil. Men wore *poulaines*—bizarre shoes with extremely long, pointed toes—and tunics with trailing sleeves and doublets resembling miniskirts. All who could afford it ornamented their clothes with tiny bells, colored ribbons, and precious stones. A well-dressed squire resembled Michael Jackson in a rhinestone-covered nightclub costume.

It is possible to describe how medieval people ate, dressed, and lived, but none of it makes much sense if we do not also make an effort to understand how they thought. That is difficult, for if ever the expression "a world of contrasts" applied, it was during the Middle Ages. Religiosity and avarice, delicacy and cruelty, luxury and squalor, asceticism and eroticism existed side by side. Our own more or less consistent world pales by comparison. Imagine a medieval scholar. After a morning of quiet devotion in a cathedral (which itself was a weird combination of sanctum sanctorum and bestiary), he could attend a public execution in which punishments of extreme cruelty would be carried out according to a pedantic etiquette. If he was like most people it would not be an occasion for ribaldry, but for shedding a tear as the condemned man or woman (before being dismembered) delivered a homily to the crowd. Life "bore the mixed smell of blood and of roses."[32] Our idea of the Middle Ages is often based on music and religious art, which give a false impression of medieval sensibilities. Celebrations, for instance, were an astonishing mixture of good and bad taste. The same scholar, invited to a court dinner, would wash his hands in perfumed water and exchange genteel courtesies with his neighbor or take part in a madrigal. At the same time he would guffaw at dwarfs jumping out of a huge baked *entremet* (pie), and have dishes brought to him by servitors mounted on horseback. In trying to explain the apparent incompatibility between the extreme indecency of certain customs and the modesty of behavior imposed by courtesy, Huizinga suggests that the Middle Ages consisted of two superimposed layers of civilization—one, primitive and pre-Christian, the other, more recent, courtly and religious.[33] These two layers were frequently in conflict, and what seem to us to be inconsistent emotions are the not always successful attempts to reconcile a cruel reality with the ideal harmony that both chivalry and religion demanded. The excitable medieval mind was constantly oscillating between these opposite poles.

The combination of the primitive and the refined was reflected in the medieval home. Rooms hung with richly decorated tapestries were poorly heated, luxuriously dressed gentlemen and ladies sat on plain benches and stools, courtiers who might spend fifteen minutes in elaborate greeting slept three to a bed and were unmindful of personal intimacy. Why did they not simply improve their living conditions? Technical skill and ingenuity were not lacking. Part of the explanation is that people in the Middle Ages thought differently about the subject of function, especially when it came to their domestic surroundings. For us, the function of a thing has to do with its utility (the function of a chair is to be sat on, for example), and we separate this from its other attributes, such as beauty, age, or style; in medieval life there were no such distinctions. Every object had a meaning and a place in life that was as much a part of its function as its immediate purpose, and these two were inseparable. Since there was no such thing as "pure function" it was difficult for the medieval mind to consider functional improvements; that would have meant tampering with reality itself. Colors had meanings, events had meanings, names had meanings—nothing was accidental.* Partly this was superstition, and partly a belief in a divinely ordered universe. Utilitarian objects such as benches and stools, since they lacked meanings, were scarcely given any thought.

There was also little differentiation between utility and ceremony. Simple functions, like washing the hands, acquired ceremonial forms, and ceremonies like breaking bread were performed unself-consciously as a natural part of life. The emphasis that the Middle Ages placed on ceremony underlines what John Lukacs has called the external character of medieval civilization.[34] What mattered then was the external world, and one's place in it. Life was a public affair, and just as one did not have a strongly developed self-consciousness, one did not have a room of one's own. It was the medieval mind, not the absence of comfortable chairs or central heating, that explains the austerity of the medieval home. It is not so much that in the Middle Ages comfort was unknown, as Walter Scott would have it, but rather that it was not needed.

John Lukacs points out that words such as "self-confidence," "self-esteem," "melancholy," and "sentimental" appeared in English or French in their modern senses only two or three hundred years ago. Their use marked the emergence of something new in the human consciousness: the appearance of the internal world of the individual, of the self, and of the family. The significance of the evolution of domestic comfort can only be appreciated in this context. It is much

------

* Medieval houses, like church bells, swords, and cannons, were personified by being given proper names. This custom has continued up to the twentieth century—Adolf Hitler called his country house Eagle's Nest, Winston Churchill, with characteristic English self-depreciation, Cosy Pig—but as houses have become invested with economic rather than emotional value, names have given way to numbers.

more than a simple search for physical well-being; it begins in the appreciation of the house as a setting for an emerging interior life. In Lukacs's words, "as the self-consciousness of medieval people was spare, the interiors of their houses were bare, including the halls of nobles and of kings. The interior furniture of houses appeared together with the interior furniture of minds."[35]

After the end of the Middle Ages and until the seventeenth century, the conditions of domestic life changed slowly.[36] Houses were larger and more sturdily built than those of earlier times—stone replaced wood, for instance—but their lack of physical amenities persisted. There were some minor improvements: glass, which had previously been expensive, became less so, and began to be used in windows in place of oiled paper, although openable windows remained a rarity.[37] The manteled fireplace and chimney (which had been invented as early as the eleventh century) gained a wider acceptance, and most habitable rooms were equipped with a fireplace. Unfortunately, fireplaces were not well designed—the flues were too large and the hearths too deep—and for hundreds of years rooms were both smoky and poorly heated, a situation which was remedied only in the eighteenth century. Stoves of glazed earthenware were developed in Germany, but spread slowly to the rest of Europe, and although they were introduced to France in the sixteenth century, they took more than two hundred years to achieve popularity.[38] Lighting also continued to be crude. Until the coming of gaslight in the early 1800s, there was no efficient way of providing illumination at night. Candles and oil lamps were expensive and not widely used; after nightfall most people went to bed.[39]

As far as bathing was concerned, there was a regression from medieval standards. Public baths (which, like hospitals, had been copied from Islamic culture, thanks to returning

Crusaders) had been built in large numbers in most European cities during the Middle Ages. However, after degenerating into brothels in the early 1500s, they were banned, and did not reemerge until the eighteenth century.[40] Since private bathrooms were nonexistent, personal hygiene suffered. Moreover, water supply was becoming a problem. As cities like Paris and London grew larger and denser, the medieval wells became polluted, and people had to rely increasingly on public fountains in the street—there were twenty-three such fountains in Paris in 1643.[41] Water consumption, always a good indicator of hygiene, declined. The effort required to carry water to the home, and especially to the upper floors, severely restricted its use, and bathing, which had been common in the Middle Ages, fell out of fashion.

Sanitation remained primitive, not much better than in the Middle Ages. Some efforts were made to improve the situation, and beginning in the sixteenth century, a Parisian city ordinance required that all houses be equipped with a privy emptying into a cesspool built beneath the courtyard.[42] A common privy was located on the ground floor, and sometimes on an upper level, off the staircase.[43] Considering that thirty or forty persons were living in the building, two or three toilet seats were hardly a luxury. Chamber pots were popular. As there were no sewers and no wastewater pipes, their contents, like all dirty water, were disposed of in a haphazard fashion, which on the upper floors meant directly out of a window and into the street.*

----

* The English slang for toilet—"loo"—is said to have been derived from this practice. An eighteenth-century Edinburgh custom was to shout "Gardyloo" before throwing slops into the street; this was a mispronunciation of the earlier French warning "*Garde à l'eau!*" although why Scotsmen should have chosen to cry this warning in a foreign tongue is unclear. There is another, less convoluted explanation: French eighteenth-century architectural drawings frequently identified the room containing the privy as *petits lieux* or just *lieu*, which in English became "loo."

Physical amenities improved slowly, yet other changes were taking place—not changes in technology but changes in manners and attitudes. The foremost city of Europe was Paris, and we have detailed records of the types of houses that were built there during the seventeenth century.[44] A typical bourgeois house stood on the original medieval plot, but it consisted of four or five floors rather than two—which reflected the price and availability of land in the center of this rapidly growing city. The house was arranged around an internal courtyard. The lowest floors housed a commercial space and stables as well as the living quarters of the proprietor and his family, servants, and employees. This was still a medieval house in the composition of the household and the variety of activities that took place within it. The main room was called the *salle*—a large space similar to the hall and used for dining, entertaining, and receiving visitors. Cooking was no longer done on the central hearth but in a separate room reserved for that purpose. Since cooking smells were considered unpleasant by that otherwise malodorous society, the kitchen was not adjacent to the *salle*, but was usually located some distance away on the other side of the courtyard. Although some people still slept in the salle on collapsible beds, there was a new room, which was often used exclusively for sleeping—the *chambre*. There were also secondary rooms which were connected to the bedchamber: the *garde-robe* (not to be confused with the English privy, this room was a wardrobe or dressing room), and the *cabinet* (storeroom). These names can be misleading, however, for both the *garde-robe* and the *cabinet* were windowed rooms that were large enough to be used for sleeping and often contained a fireplace.

The typical Parisian bourgeois house contained more than one family; it was more like an apartment building. The upper floors consisted of *chambres* with adjoining *garde-robes* and *cabinets* that were rented to tenants. But these quarters were not planned as separate apartments. The tenant rented as many rooms as he needed, or could afford, often on more than one floor. The rooms were large; the bedchamber was at least twenty-five feet square, and the *garde-robe* and the *cabinet* were about the size of a modern bedroom. Since these accommodations were never provided with a *salle* or a kitchen—the fireplace in the bedchamber was large enough to cook in—the life of the family continued to take place in one room. Nevertheless, a desire for a greater measure of privacy was evidenced by the separation of the masters from their servants, who, together with the small children, usually had beds in the smaller adjacent rooms.

The existence of rented accommodations underlines a change that had occurred since the Middle Ages: many people no longer lived and worked in the same building. Although most shopkeepers, merchants, and artisans still lived "over the store," there was a growing number of bourgeois—builders, lawyers, notaries, civil servants—for whom the home was exclusively a residence. The result of this separation was that—as far as the outside world was concerned—the house was becoming a more *private* place. Together with this privatization of the home arose a growing sense of intimacy, of identifying the house exclusively with family life.

Within the home, however, personal privacy remained relatively unimportant. Salomon de Brosse, who was appointed royal architect to Henry IV in 1608 and who designed the Palais de Luxembourg, lived with his wife and seven children, and an unrecorded number of servants, in two adjoining rooms.[45] These rooms were not only crowded with people, they were full of furniture: vertical cupboards, dressers, sideboards, buffets, and commodes. This was the age of literacy, and people also needed writing tables—secretaries and bureaus—as well as bookcases. Four-poster beds became popular—de Brosse owned four of them—and they usually had side curtains, which afforded a greater measure of warmth, as well as some privacy, to their occupants.

The modern fascination with furniture begins in the seventeenth century. Furniture was no longer simply equipment but was thought of as a valuable possession, and began to be a part of the decoration of the room. It was usually made of walnut instead of oak, or (if it was more expensive) of ebony—in French, a cabinetmaker is still called an *ébéniste*. Seating had become more elaborate. The back-stool, which had been invented in the late sixteenth century (to accommodate women's wide skirts), evolved into the side chair, which was usually padded and upholstered. The straight-backed chair, which had survived the Middle Ages, was being replaced by chairs which were angled and shaped to better accommodate the body. There was a greater variety of furniture than in the past, but it was not yet assigned to specialized rooms and it continued to be unimaginatively arranged.

There was something about these seventeenth-century interiors that precluded a true feeling of intimacy, however. Medieval emptiness had been filled with chairs, commodes, and canopied beds, but in an almost thoughtless way. These crowded rooms were not really furnished. It is as if the owners had gone on a shopping spree and the next day discovered that there was not enough space for all their impulsive purchases. This was the result of the sort of bourgeois nervousness that Abraham Bosse satirized in his engravings, which depict people who are always, to some extent, acting, and for whom the house is above all a setting for social theater. Sandwiched as they were between the aristocracy and the lower classes, the French bourgeoisie was always striving to conform, to distance itself from the latter and achieve the standing of the former.

The nobility and the richest bourgeois lived in much larger individual townhouses, called *hôtels*, which were grander and more luxuriously appointed—what we would call mansions. They varied in size from the Hôtel de Liancourt (designed in part by de Brosse), which had five connected pavilions grouped around two large courts, to smaller structures with as few as twelve rooms. They too were beginning to express a growing desire for privacy. They were hidden behind the houses of the commoners and did not present an impressive exterior appearance; their gardens and courts were invisible from the street. Inside, however, everything was planned for show. After crossing an imposing courtyard, a visitor to the Hôtel Lambert, home of Jean-Baptiste Lambert de Thorigny, president of the Cour des Comptes, ascended a grand staircase, passed through an oval vestibule, and reached an antechamber. This was merely a waiting room, that, as in the past, continued to be used as both reception room and the servants' bedroom. The bedchamber of Monsieur le Président was beyond. There were no corridors in these houses—each room was connected directly to its neighbor—and architects prided themselves on aligning all the doors *enfilade*, so that there was an unobstructed view from one end of the house to the other. The priority given to appearances, instead of to privacy, is evident; all traffic, servants as well as guests, passed through every room to get to the next.

Just as privacy was ignored, so also was sanitation. Privies were considered plebian. Eminent personages such as Jean-Baptiste Lambert de Thorigny did not go to the toilet—the toilet came to them. The "close stool" was a box with a padded lid which servants brought into the room as the aristocratic need dictated. The close stools were not left long in the room, however, for as a nineteenth-century historian reminds us, this was a *meuble odorant*.[46] During Louis XIV's reign there were almost three hundred such stools in the palace of Versailles, although this may not have been enough, for, as the Duchess of Orléans noted in her diary, "There is one dirty thing at Court I shall never get used to: the people stationed in the galleries in front of our rooms piss into all the corners."[47] More fastidious Parisians were driven to the public gardens of the Tuileries, where they alighted from their coaches and relieved themselves under the yews.[48]

There were no bathrooms in the Hôtel Lambert. For one thing, frequent bathing was not considered necessary, for another, the idea of a room dedicated exclusively to bathing would have puzzled seventeenth-century Parisians. Not because space was insufficient in these large homes, but because the idea of associating any specialized functions with individual rooms had not yet occurred to them. There were no dining rooms, for instance. Tables were demountable, and people ate in different parts of the house—in the *salle*, in the *antichambre* or in the *chambre*—depending on their mood, or on the number of guests.[49] The *chambre*, which contained a bed (but only one), continued to be the place where people met socially. As in the smaller bourgeois houses, the servants and maids slept in the adjoining *cabinets* and *garde-robes*.

During the seventeenth century there were minor changes in the internal arrangement of the *hôtel* which indicated a growing awareness of intimacy. The *cabinet*, previously used only by the valet, was sometimes converted into a more intimate room for private activities such as writing. In the Hôtel Lambert there was such a room beyond the president's bedroom; it was decorated by the painter Le Sueur according to the theme of Love, and was known as the *cabinet de l'Amour*.* An alcove within which the bed was located was sometimes built within the large, impersonal *chambre*. This was almost a separate bedroom, but not quite. The credit for that discovery belongs to the Marquise de Rambouillet. She had come to Paris from Rome, and after suffering through

---

* Was this room used for seduction, as its name implies? Probably. The forced closeness of the bourgeois family was absent among the nobility; married couples habitually lived, and slept, apart. Madame la Présidente had her own equally extensive apartment, on the floor above her husband's.

the cold winter in her huge and badly heated *chambre*, in 1630 she converted her *garde-robe* into a small private bedroom.[50] The first use of the term *salle à manger* (dining room) occurred in 1634, but the replacement of the multipurpose salle by a series of specialized rooms for dining, entertaining, and conversation had to await the following century.[51]

These *hôtels* were wonderfully ornamented with frescoed ceilings and painted, paneled, and mirrored walls. The ceiling of Lambert's room consisted of three panels by Le Sueur depicting the legend of Jupiter. But there was hardly a sense of hominess in these houses. There was much beautiful furniture, but it appeared uncomfortably forlorn pushed against the walls of huge rooms unrelieved by any nooks or crannies. Although rooms were decorated according to different classical themes—Love, the Muses, Hercules—they lacked the atmosphere of domesticity that is the result of human activity.

What was missing in these interiors was what Mario Praz, in an idiosyncratic essay on the philosophy of interior decoration, called *Stimmung*—the sense of intimacy that is created by a room and its furnishings.[52] *Stimmung* is a characteristic of interiors that has less to do with functionality than with the way that the room conveys the character of its owner— the way that it mirrors his soul, as Praz poetically put it. According to Praz, *Stimmung* occurred first in northern Europe. It was already present in the sixteenth century when Dürer engraved *St. Jerome in His Study*. It is visible in the careful way that he depicted the various objects in the saint's cluttered room, and in the light that simultaneously warms the old man at his desk and introduces the external, natural world into the interior one. Strangely, the domesticated lion only emphasizes the intimacy of the scene. Compare this to a slightly earlier painting of the same subject by an Italian, Antonello da Messina. The elements are similar to those in Dürer's engraving—books, a lectern, a pair of slippers—and there is a lion, although located in the background. These are also painted in a highly detailed way—Antonello had studied in the Netherlands, and introduced the Flemish technique to Italy—but the effect is different. St. Jerome sits, or rather poses, in an improbably theatrical setting, framed by the proscenium of a large vaulted opening. There is no sense of intimacy at all. There is beauty in the elegance of the architectural elements, but their predominance, and the formality of the surroundings, creates an air of artificiality. The interior tells us nothing about this man; indeed, we do not really believe that this awkward little platform of a room even belongs to him, or he to it.

To find interiors that exhibited *Stimmung* in seventeenth-century Europe it is necessary to look northward. We have a well-documented example of a Norwegian family that lived in the town of Kristiania (now Oslo) at the end of the seventeenth century.[53] At that time, Norway was a dependency of Denmark, and Kristiania was a small town with a population of fewer than five thousand souls (it had been destroyed by fire in 1624); it was hardly an important place. Provincial Kristiania was a little "behind the times," and the home of Frederik Jacobsen Brun and his wife Marthe Christiansdatter would have been typical of the way that small-town European bourgeois lived during the early seventeenth century.

Brun was a bookbinder, and he worked at home. A two-story half-timbered building contained the bindery, a stable, a barn, a hayloft, and many storerooms grouped around a courtyard. The dwelling itself faced the street. The Bruns had bought the house as newlyweds and had enlarged it by adding a second floor. The original structure consisted of a large room flanked by a small kitchen and a single adjacent room. The new extension was more ambitious: it included two rooms on either side of a larger *selskapssal* (party room). The house, which was the size of a small modern bungalow (about fifteen hundred square feet) and would have been a tight squeeze for the Bruns and their eight children, actually housed fifteen persons; in addition to the Brun family, there were three employees and two servants.

The Brun home is an example of what Philippe Ariès called a "big house," which was the way that the prosperous bourgeois lived not just in the seventeenth but also in the sixteenth and fifteenth centuries.[54] A chief characteristic of a big house was its public character. Like its medieval antecedent, it was the setting for all aspects of life—business, entertainment, and work. It was always full of relatives, guests, clients, friends, and acquaintances. Although there were many habitable rooms in the Brun home, Frederik and Marthe did not have a "master bedroom"—they slept in the large downstairs room, together with the three youngest children, in one large fourposter bed. The five eldest children—a thirteen-year-old son who worked as an apprentice, a nineteen-year-old son who was sickly and did not work, two young daughters, and a twenty-one-year-old daughter who was engaged to be married—slept in two beds in one room, over the kitchen. The two maidservants slept in the room downstairs, probably so that Marthe could keep an eye on them—they were country girls for whose upbringing, and virtue, the Bruns would have been responsible. Two of the male employees had a bed in the second upstairs room. The third employee, a young apprentice, slept in the workshop, since it was his responsibility to get up early and start the fire.

Following medieval tradition, most daytime activities took place in the large main room. A table with four chairs was in the center of the room; the rest of the furniture was placed around the walls. In addition to the large bed, there were eight chairs, the father's high-backed armchair, a second armchair for visitors, a cupboard, and two chests. When guests came, chairs were placed in the bay window, which became an improvised conversation nook. The kitchen contained a large hearth and a small table with stools. There was no cupboard; the copper and pewter utensils hung on the wall.

The so-called party room was sparsely furnished with a few chairs; like the nineteenth-century parlor, it stood empty most of the time and was used only for special occasions such as holidays and celebrations. The other rooms contained beds, chests for clothes, and little else. There was no bathroom. People washed in the courtyard, or took weekly baths in the kitchen.*

The household awoke at dawn. Breakfast was an improvised affair and taken individually. Brun and his employees went next door to work in the shop. Marthe and the maids fetched water (there was an old well in the courtyard, but most of the water came from a public pump in the street), did minor laundry (major clothes washing occurred twice yearly in the nearby Aker River), and performed other chores. Food preparation occupied much time. Like most town-dwellers, the Bruns owned a small meadow outside the town where they grew hay (for their mare) and vegetables, which explains why a large amount of space in the house was devoted to food storage. Interestingly, they sometimes used a small barn in their meadow for overnight sleeping—an early version of the "summer cottage." Noon lunch at the Bruns was the main meal of the day and was shared by all fifteen persons. In the evening, only the immediate family ate together—the younger children and the apprentices ate in the kitchen. The day finished early, and people went to bed soon after dusk.

How did the Bruns heat their house during the long Norwegian winter? The hearths in the kitchen and in the work-

---

* Throughout Europe the days of the week are named after pre-Christian deities, Wednesday after Wodin, Thursday after Thor, and so on. The unique exception occurs in the Scandinavian languages, in which Saturday, or *Lørdag*, is named after a human activity—it is the "day for bathing"— indicating the importance that was attached to this practice. My colleague Norbert Schoenauer was kind enough to draw this to my attention.

shop would hardly have sufficed; in any case, because of their location they did not contribute much warmth to the other rooms. When the house was extended, stoves were installed in some of the rooms (their exact location is unclear, but there was probably one in the hall, and a second in one of the upstairs rooms). The stoves were an innovation—the Bruns were the "first on their street" to use them—and they would have made a large difference in the thermal comfort of the house, not the least because, unlike the hearths, they did not fill the room with smoke. However, since many of the rooms would have remained unheated, and all rooms had at least two exterior walls, even with stoves the house must have been on the chilly side. Like all houses, this one had no internal corridors; if you wanted to go upstairs or to the workshop, you did so in the fresh air. A winter visit to the privy, which was next to the stable, must have been a rushed affair.

The Bruns lived and worked in the same premises, and most of their activities took place in one or two rooms, but this household was no longer medieval. There was more furniture, although not as much as in a Parisian home. The use of stoves not only provided more convenience and comfort, it also allowed the house to be subdivided into many more rooms than would have been possible earlier. Although the main room resembled the hall, specialized functions were beginning to be assigned to other rooms such as the kitchen and the sleeping rooms.

More important than the technical innovations were the changes in domestic arrangements. The parents still shared their bed with the infants, but the older children no longer slept in the same room. One can imagine Frederik and Marthe, after having sent the children upstairs to bed, sitting in the main room alone. The house is quiet, the day's work is done, and in the light of a candle they talk. A simple scene, and yet a revolution in human relations is taking place. The husband and wife have begun to think of themselves—perhaps for the first time—as a *couple*. Even their wedding night, twenty years before, would have been a public event, celebrated with boisterous, and medieval, informality. The opportunities to experience intimacy were rare and it was in such modest, bourgeois dwellings that family life began to acquire a private dimension. The importance of this event, which is encapsulated in the Brun household but which was taking place all over northern and central Europe, cannot be exaggerated. Before the idea of the home as the seat of family life could enter the human consciousness, it required the experience of both privacy and intimacy, neither of which had been possible in the medieval hall.

The appearance of intimacy in the home was also the result of another important change that was taking place within the family: the presence of children. The medieval idea of the family was different from our own in many ways, especially in its unsentimental attitude toward childhood. Not only did the children of the poor work; in all families, children were sent away from home once they reached the age of seven. Children from bourgeois families were apprenticed to artisans, while those from the higher class served in noble households as pages. In both cases, they were expected to work as well as to learn; the servitors at medieval banquets were the sons of noble families, not paid domestics. (The French word *garçon*, which means both young boy and café waiter, recalls this practice.) The function of this apprenticeship, whether to a trade or at court, fulfilled the role of education. This situation started to change in the sixteenth century when formal schooling, which had previously been exclusively religious, was extended and replaced apprenticeship, at least among the bourgeois.[55] Two of the Brun girls (nine and eleven years old) went to school. Although schooling was not long—the thirteen-year-old boy who worked as an apprentice to his father had already completed his education—it nevertheless meant that children spent much more time at home than in the past. Parents could, for the first time in centuries, watch their children growing up.

The presence of children of many ages also produced a change of manners that is evident in the Bruns's sleeping arrangements. It would have been easy, and desirable, to separate the young people according to sex, but instead it was the servants and employees who had their own rooms. Even the son who was an apprentice slept with his sisters, not with his coworkers. The point was not discrimination— the bedrooms were identical—but the separation of the family members from the others. The isolation of the servants appears almost haphazard—later it would take architectural form, as servants were assigned the basement or the garret— and it was not complete, since the entire household still ate at least one meal together, but it did reinforce the growing self-awareness of the family.

Comfort in the physical sense was still awaiting the eighteenth century and the improvement of such technologies as water supply and heating, as well as refinements to the internal subdivision of the home. But the transition from the public, feudal household to the private, family home was under way. The growing sense of domestic intimacy was a human invention as much as any technical device. Indeed, it may have been more important, for it affected not only our physical surroundings, but our consciousness as well.

Chapter Three

Emanuel de Witte, *Interior with a
Woman Playing the Virginals*
(c. 1660)

Domesticity

> *Domesticity, privacy, comfort, the concept of the home and of the family: these are, literally, principal achievements of the Bourgeois Age.*
>
> —JOHN LUKACS
> *THE BOURGEOIS INTERIOR*

The appearance of intimacy and privacy in homes in Paris and London, and soon after even in such out-of-the-way places as Oslo, was an unwitting, almost unconscious, reaction to the changing conditions of urban life, and it appeared to be more a question of popular attitudes than of anything else. It is difficult to trace the evolution of something so amorphous, and it would be dangerous to claim that there was a single place where the modern idea of the family home first entered the human consciousness. There was, after all, no identifiable moment of discovery, no individual inventor who can be credited with the intuition, no theory or treatise on the subject. There was one place, however, where the seventeenth-century domestic interior evolved in a way that was arguably unique, and that can be described as having been, at the very least, exemplary.

The United Provinces of the Netherlands was a brand-new state, formed in 1609 after thirty years of rebellion against Spain. It was among the smallest countries in Europe, with a population one-quarter that of Spain, one-eighth that of France, and with a landmass smaller than Switzerland's. It had few natural resources—no mines, no forests—and what little land there was needed constant protection from the sea. *51*

But this "low" country surprisingly quickly established itself as a major power. In a short time it became the most advanced shipbuilding nation in the world and developed large naval, fishing, and merchant fleets. Its explorers founded colonies in Africa and Asia, as well as in America. The Netherlands introduced many financial innovations that made it a major economic force—and Amsterdam became the world center for international finance. Its manufacturing towns grew so quickly that by the middle of the century the Netherlands had supplanted France as the leading industrial nation of the world.[1] Its universities were among the best in Europe; its tolerant political and religious climate offered a home for émigré thinkers such as Spinoza, Descartes, and John Locke. This fecund country produced not just venture capitalists and the speculative tulip trade, but also Rembrandt and Vermeer; it devised not only the first recorded war game, but also the first microscope; it invested not only in heavily armed East Indiamen but also in beautiful towns. All this occurred during a brief historical moment—barely a human lifetime—which lasted from 1609 until roughly the 1660s, and which the Dutch call their "golden age."

These unlikely achievements were the result of several different factors, such as the Netherlands' advantageous location in European maritime trade, as well as the defensibility of its national borders, but it was in great measure a result of the peculiar character of the Dutch social fabric, which was different from that of the rest of Europe. The Dutch were primarily merchants and landowners. Unlike England, the Netherlands lacked a landless peasantry (most Dutch farmers owned their land); unlike France, it had no powerful aristocracy (the nobility, decimated by the wars for independence, was small and no longer wealthy); unlike Spain, it had no king (the head of state, or *stadhouder*, was a national symbol, but with limited real power). This republic—the first in Europe—was a loose confederation ruled by a States General, which consisted of representatives of the seven sovereign provinces, chosen from the patrician upper middle class.

The pattern of human settlements was also markedly different than elsewhere. Already in 1500, the Low Countries (which then included Brabant, or Belgium) had numbered more than 200 fortified towns and 150 large villages.[2] By the seventeenth century, most of the population in its three most powerful provinces—Holland, Zeeland, and Utrecht—lived in towns. Amsterdam became a major city of Europe, Rotterdam was a growing port, and Leiden was an important manufacturing and university town. However, it was not its major cities but its many smaller towns that distinguished the Netherlands; there were more medium-sized towns than in much larger countries, such as France, England, or Germany.[3] The eighteen largest towns had one vote each in the assembly of the provincial states, which indicated their importance and their independence. In short, at a time when the other states of Europe remained primarily rural (even in urbanized Italy, most of the people were still peasants), the Netherlands was rapidly becoming a nation of townspeople. Burghers by historical tradition, the Dutch were bourgeois by inclination.[4]

The bourgeois nature of Dutch society in the seventeenth century needs some explanation. To say that it was "bourgeois" does not mean that it consisted exclusively of a middle class. There were farmers (*boers*), seamen, and, in manufacturing towns such as Leiden, factory workers. The last-named, especially, did not share in the prosperity of that time, and their living conditions were as miserable as in other countries. There was also, as in all European cities, an urban rabble (*grauw*), composed of paupers and criminals, the unemployed and the unemployable, itinerant beggars and tramps. However, the middle class predominated, and was broad enough to encompass the international financier as well as the shopkeeper. The former did not, of course, identify, or even associate with the latter, even if, as was often the case, his

economic ascent was recent, for Dutch society was not static,
and social position was defined largely by income. Bourgeois
also was the patrician elite—a ruling class—which provided
the magistrates and burgomasters who governed the towns,
and through them the country. By European standards, this
was a greatly expanded democracy, and this "social dicta-
torship of the merchant class," as one historian called it,
created the first bourgeois state.

Everyday life in the Netherlands in the seventeenth century
reflected the traditional bourgeois virtues—an unruffled moderation, an admiration for hard work, and a financial pru-
dence bordering on parsimony. Thrift evolved naturally in a
society of merchants and traders who, moreover, lived in a
country which required a constant communal investment in
canals, dikes, sluices, and windmills to keep the North Sea
at bay. They were also a simple people, less passionate than
the Latins of southern Europe, less sentimental than their
German neighbors, less intellectual than the French. The Dutch
historian Huizinga claimed that the flat, restful landscape of
polders and canals, which lacked dramatic features such as
mountains or valleys, encouraged the simplicity of the Dutch
character.[5] Equally important was religion. Although only
about a third of the Dutch were Calvinists, this became the
state religion and exercised a major influence on everyday
life, contributing a sense of sobriety and restraint to Dutch
society.

All these circumstances produced a people who admired
saving, frowned on conspicuous spending, and naturally evolved
conservative manners. The simplicity of the Dutch bourgeois
expressed itself in many ways. The dress of a Dutch male,
for instance, was plain. The doublet and trousers were the
seventeenth-century equivalent of the modern businessman's
three-piece suit, and like it they were unaffected by fashion;
the quality of the cloth might vary but the style remained
unchanged for generations. The favorite colors were dark:

black, violet, or brown. The officials of the clothmakers' guild, in Rembrandt's famous group portrait, were prosperous (as their lace collars and amply cut cassocks indicate) but somber to the point of drabness. Their wives dressed with similar moderation, and neither exhibited the nervous flamboyance and constantly changing chic that was so characteristic of the French bourgeoisie. So circumspect were the Dutch that in paintings of the period it is not always easy to distinguish between an official and his clerk, between a mistress and her servant.

The same simplicity and thrift were apparent in Dutch houses, which lacked the architectural pretension of town-houses in London or Paris, and which were built of brick and wood instead of stone. These materials were used for their light weight, since the boggy soil of the Low Countries frequently required pile foundations, the cost of which could be reduced if the foundations carried less weight. Brick does not lend itself to elaborate decoration—unlike stone, it cannot be carved, and unlike cement plaster, it cannot be formed into moldings and reliefs. Consequently, Dutch buildings were plain, only occasionally relieved by stonework at the corners and around the doors and windows. The material was appreciated mainly for its pleasant texture; undoubtedly its economy also appealed to the practical-minded Dutch, who used it even for their public buildings.

The expense of building canals and pilings dictated that street frontages be reduced as much as possible; as a result, the building plots in Dutch towns were extremely narrow, sometimes only one room wide. The houses were built adjacent to each other in a row, usually sharing common walls. The roofs were covered in red clay tiles. Their gable ends, which were often stepped, faced the street and produced the characteristic silhouettes for which Dutch towns became famous. At the top of the gable was a wooden bracket and hook, used for hauling furniture and other goods to the upper floors. The interior of the medieval Dutch house consisted of a "front room" (where commercial activities took place) and a "back room" (where the household cooked, ate, and slept). In front of the house, and slightly raised above the level of the street, was a wide verandah-like *stoep*, or stoop, with benches, sometimes protected with a wooden canopy. Here the family sat in the evenings and socialized with passersby. Below the house was a shallow cellar, its floor never lower than the water level of the adjacent canal. As families became more prosperous, these low houses were extended in the only direction possible—up. Two, and sometimes three, floors were added.

The original ground floors of Dutch houses were often high, so that the first additional space consisted of a gallery or loft, which was reached by a ladderlike stair. As the house grew, this pattern was continued, so that often no two rooms were on the same level, and all were connected by steep, narrow staircases. Initially, these rooms, with the exception of the kitchen, did not have special functions. By midcentury, however, the subdivision of the house into day and night uses, and into formal and informal areas, had begun. The upper floors of the house began to be treated as formal rooms, reserved for special occasions. The second-floor room facing the street was turned into a parlor, the old front room became a kind of living room, and other rooms began to be used exclusively for sleeping. As in the rest of Europe there were no bathrooms, and privies were a rarity.* The Dutch were a seafaring people, and there was something shipshape about

---

* One reason that privies were rare was that most Dutch towns were built on marshy land, and privy pits and cesspools filled with water and ceased to function. The usual alternative was the chamber pot, which was emptied into the canal. Unlike Venice, however, Dutch towns had no sea tide to remove these wastes, with the unfortunate consequence that these pretty towns probably had an unbearable odor. There were occasional efforts to remedy the situation. Canals were periodically dredged, and in some towns

these compact interiors, with the tarred brick walls (to protect them against the humidity) and painted woodwork, the steep, narrow stairs, and the rooms as small as ships' cabins. The atmosphere could best be described as snug—a word which is coincidentally both of nautical and of Dutch origin.

Building on pilings on reclaimed land had its drawbacks, but it also produced an unexpected benefit for the occupants. Since the shared side walls of these houses carried all the weight of the roof and the floors, the external cross-walls served no structural function, and, given the high cost of foundations, there was an advantage to making them as light as possible. To accomplish this, the builders of Dutch houses pierced the façades with many and large windows, whose function may have been to save weight, but which also allowed light to penetrate far into the deep, narrow interiors. In the days before gaslight, this was important. Paintings of Dutch houses in daytime show bright, sunlit rooms whose cheerfulness was in contrast to the dark interiors that were typical in other countries. Before the seventeenth century, the upper parts of Dutch windows had fixed glass, and only the lower portions, which were solid wood, were openable; later these too were glazed. The light coming through these windows was controlled by shutters, and by a new device— window curtains—which also provided privacy from the street. As these openings became larger, they became more awkward to open the windows in the conventional way, and the Dutch invented a new type of window, the sash or double-hung window, which could be conveniently opened without sticking into the room. Like the two-part Dutch door, the sash window was soon copied in England and France.

New inventions such as the sash window were not typical;

---

night soil was collected from the houses in wooden containers and barged out to the countryside for the benefit of the farmers, a practice that was medieval in origin but continued in some towns until the 1950s.[6]

Dutch houses in the seventeenth century were hardly bristling with innovation, and in fact retained many medieval features. This mixing of the old and new was a characteristic feature of Dutch society. At the same time as it pioneered new political forms of organization, it combined these with traditional institutions such as guilds and self-governing towns; these social revolutionaries (although they would have hardly considered themselves that) dressed like their grandfathers, and in many ways lived like them as well. Their houses continued to be built out of wood and brick. In the traditional way, signs indicated the owner's profession—scissors for the tailor, an oven for the baker. The gabled façades of private houses were topped off with a figurative sculpture with literary or biblical connotations. The Dutch loved allegories, and in some houses stone tablets, inscribed with a suitable epigraph, were set into the wall. The small houses with their colorful signs had a medieval, toylike charm. Indeed, they, and their owners, were often described as "old-fashioned."

Unfortunately, the thermal charms of these houses were also medieval. (I once spent a week in January in a seventeenth-century house in Leiden. In this historically protected neighborhood the old house was without insulation, double glazing, or central heating; it was a chillingly authentic experience.) The Dutch climate is not a particularly severe one, but the situation of the country makes for damp winters. In the absence of firewood (Holland has few forests) the main heating fuel in the seventeenth century was peat, which can be burned effectively but requires special stoves. These were unknown at that time and instead, to promote combustion, the peat was piled in tall, open stacks on the fire grate inside the fireplace, or was burned in so-called fire pots; this got rid of the foul-smelling smoke, but unfortunately produced little heat.[7] The only way to achieve some comfort under such circumstances was to wear many clothes, which, as amused visitors noted, is exactly what the Dutch did. Men wore half a dozen waistcoats, several pairs of trousers, and heavy cloaks; their wives wore as many as six petticoats under their skirts. The effect was hardly flattering to the figure and at least partially explains the apparently dumpy physiques of the burghers and their wives in contemporary paintings.

These houses were "small houses," literally as well as figuratively. They did not need to be large, because they contained few people; the average number of people per house in most Dutch towns was not more than four or five, compared to as many as twenty-five in a city such as Paris. Why was this? For one thing, there were no tenants, for the Dutch preferred, and were prosperous enough, to afford the luxury of owning their own homes, however small. The house had ceased to be a place of work, and as many artisans became well-to-do merchants or *rentiers*, they built separate establishments for their businesses, and employees and apprentices had to provide their own lodgings. Nor were there as many servants as in other countries, for Dutch society discouraged the hiring of servants and imposed special taxes on those who employed domestic help.[8] Individual independence was more highly prized than elsewhere, and, equally importantly, it could be afforded. As a result, most homes in the Netherlands housed a single couple and their children. This brought about another change. The publicness that had characterized the "big house" was replaced by a more sedate—and more private—home life.

The emergence of the family home reflected the growing importance of the family in Dutch society. The glue that cemented this unit was the presence of children. The mother raised her own children—there were no nurses. Young children attended infant school at the age of three, and then primary school for four years. The Netherlands had, it is generally agreed, the highest level of literacy in Europe, and even secondary education was not uncommon. Most children lived at home until they were married, and the relations between Dutch parents and their children were characterized by affection, rather than by discipline. Foreign visitors considered this permissiveness to be a dangerous habit. Given the excessive indulgence with which parents treated their children, one observed, "it is surprising that there is not more disorder than there is."[9] For the Frenchman who wrote this, children were small and unruly, but nevertheless adults; the idea of childhood did not yet exist for him. The historian Philippe Ariès has described how the substitution of school for apprenticeship throughout Europe reflected a rapprochement between parents and family, and between the concept of family and the concept of childhood.[10] This is precisely what happened in the Netherlands, where the family centered itself on the child and family life centered itself on the home, only in the Dutch home it occurred about a hundred years earlier than elsewhere.[11]

It was the opinion of more than one contemporary visitor that the Dutch prized three things above all else: first their children, second their homes, and third their gardens.[12] In these narrow houses, built directly on the street and sharing their side walls with their neighbors, the garden was an important space, all the more so because in the mild climate it was used most of the year. Within the restricted area available, there evolved a particularly formal type of landscaping, as artificial, in its own way, as the small urban gardens of the Japanese. The precisely clipped hedges, geometrically shaped box trees, and colored gravel walks echoed the orderliness of the interiors. The Dutch garden was a further indication of the transition from the communal big house to the individual family home. The typical European townhouse of this period, whether in Paris or in Oslo, was built around a courtyard which was essentially public in nature. The secluded back garden of the Dutch house was different—it was private.

While Dutch houses and gardens may have been private, they nevertheless contributed to the overall appearance of the towns. Because of the canals, which were built with tree-lined roadways on both sides, the spaces between the houses were the width of boulevards (this was two hundred years before Baron Haussmann built the Champs-Elysées). Because of the wide use of brick and a building style that was imitative rather than inventive, Dutch towns had a pleasant uniformity. This prompted the Danish historian Steen Eiler Rasmussen to write that whereas the French and the Italians created impressive palaces, the Dutch created incomparable towns.[13]

The rapid, and, as it seemed to many, improbable prosperity of the Netherlands—as that of Japan today—aroused much interest in other countries. Sir William Temple, who was the English ambassador at The Hague from 1668 to 1670 and knew the country well, wrote a widely read book attempting to explain this curious phenomenon to his countrymen. The fourth chapter, entitled "Of Their People and Dispositions," concluded: "Holland is a Countrey where the Earth is better than the Air, and Profit more in request than Honour; Where there is more Sense than Wit; More good Nature than good Humor; And more Wealth than Pleasure; Where a man would chuse rather to travel, than to live. . . ." Harsh words, although intended, perhaps, for a jingoistic audience, since later in life their author gave up the chance to be Secretary of State in favor of returning to his old job in The Hague. Despite what he perceived as penny-pinching cheerlessness in the Dutch character, Temple did point out that in one area, at least, the Dutch did not hold back in their expenditures: they were inclined to invest all their surplus income in "the Fabrick, Adornment, or Furniture of their Houses."[14]

The Dutch loved their homes. They shared this old Anglo-Saxon word—*ham, hejm* in Dutch—with the other peoples of northern Europe.* "Home" brought together the meanings of house and of household, of dwelling and of refuge, of ownership and of affection. "Home" meant the house, but also everything that was in it and around it, as well as the people, and the sense of satisfaction and contentment that all these conveyed. You could walk out of the house, but you always returned home. The Dutch affection for their homes was expressed in a singular practice: they had elaborate scale models built of their houses. These replicas are sometimes—inaccurately—referred to as dollhouses. Their function was more like that of ship models, not playthings but miniature memorials, records of dearly beloved objects. They were built like cupboards which did not represent the exterior appearance of the house. But when the doors were opened the entire interior was magically revealed, not only the rooms—complete with wall coverings and furnishings—but even paintings, utensils, and china figurines.

The furniture and adornment of a seventeenth-century Dutch home were meant, although in a typically restrained way, to convey the wealth of its owner. There were still benches and stools, especially in the homes of the less prosperous, but, as in England and France, the chair had become the most common sitting device. It was almost always without arms, padded, and upholstered in velvet and other rich materials, usually attached to the frame with copper nails. Tables, like chairs, were of oak or walnut and had elegantly turned legs. Curtained four-poster beds were similarly constructed, but less common than in England or France; instead, the Dutch slept in beds that were built into the wall. Such beds, of medieval

---

* This wonderful word, "home," which connotes a physical "place" but also has the more abstract sense of a "state of being," has no equivalent in the Latin or Slavic European languages. German, Danish, Swedish, Icelandic, Dutch, and English all have similar sounding words for "home," all derived from the Old Norse "heima."

origin, were set into an alcove, completely enclosed on three sides, and the opening was screened with a curtain or solid shutters. The most important piece of bourgeois furniture was the cupboard, which the Dutch borrowed from Germany, and which replaced the horizontal chest as the means of storage. There were usually two such cupboards, often ornamented with inlays of precious wood, one for the linens and another for tableware. For storing and displaying the latter there were also glass-fronted credenzas, descendants of the medieval plate cupboards, which held silver and crystal, Delft porcelain and oriental china.*

The type of furniture in a Dutch house was similar to that found in a Parisian bourgeois home; the difference was in the effect. The French interior was crowded and frenetic, the many pieces of furniture jostling each other in rooms whose papered walls were illustrated with scenic landscapes and where all surfaces were embroidered, gilded, or decorated. Dutch decor, by comparison, was sparse. Furniture was to be admired, but it was also meant to be used, and it was never so crowded as to detract from the sense of space that was produced by the room and by the light within it. The walls were rarely papered or covered, although they were adorned with paintings, mirrors, and maps—the last-named a uniquely Dutch practice. The effect was far from severe, and was not intended to be. These rooms, with one or two chairs under a window, or a bench beside the door, were intensely human, and were directed to private use, rather than

---

* Chinese porcelain was evidence of the Netherlands' international trade and its growing colonial empire. It is also a reminder that the Dutch frequently played the role of middlemen of culture, as well as of trade.[15] They were the first Europeans to use Turkish carpets, for instance, occasionally on the floor, but more frequently as a table covering. It was the Dutch, also, through their East India Company, who introduced Europe to japanned and lacquered finishing from the Orient, to the arts of inlaying and veneering furniture from Asia, and, not the least, to tea-drinking.

to entertaining and socializing. They exhibited an intimacy that is inadequately described by words such as "serene" or "peaceful."

As every homemaker knows, the less furniture there is, the easier it is to keep a room clean, and this too may have had something to do with the relative sparseness of the Dutch interior, for these houses were spotlessly, immaculately, unbelievably clean. The well-scrubbed Dutch stoop is famous and has come to serve as an example of public exhibition and bourgeois pretentiousness. Public it certainly was—not only the stoop but the entire road pavement in front of the house was washed and sanded by the householder—but it was no pretense; the interiors of Dutch houses were equally scrubbed and scoured. Sand was scattered on the floor, recalling the medieval practice of covering floors in rushes. Pots were shined, woodwork varnished, brickwork tarred. This was all taken seriously by the Dutch, and produced some curious customs which never failed to elicit comment from foreigners. A German visitor to Delft in 1665 wrote that "in many houses, as in the holy places of the heathens, it is not permissible to ascend the stairs or set foot in a room without first removing one's shoes."[16] Jean-Nicolas de Parival, a French traveler, observed the same thing, adding that frequently straw slippers were put on over one's shoes.[17]

This gives the impression that the streets of Dutch towns were unkempt; instead the opposite was true. Save for those in the oldest neighborhoods, where the poor lived, the streets were paved in brick, and included sidewalks for pedestrians. Whereas in London and Paris the public street was unbearable—a combination of open sewer and garbage dump—in Dutch towns this waste material was disposed of in the canals, leaving the street relatively clean. Moreover, since it was the custom for each household to wash the street in front of its house, these streets were generally as well scrubbed as the stoops. If the streets were so clean, certainly cleaner than elsewhere in Europe, how to explain this collective obsession with cleanliness inside the home? Was it the product of Calvinism (stoops in Calvinist Scotland were equally scoured), or merely of bourgeois decorum? Or was this homely virtue the result of the simplicity of the Dutch spirit, a delight in the neat and the orderly?* Huizinga suggested the latter, adding that it was made possible by the easy availability of water, the dustless marine atmosphere of the Netherlands, and the tradition of cheese-making, an activity requiring special attention to cleanliness.[18] This sounds too deterministic, and in any case, cheese-making was hardly confined to the Netherlands. Another explanation is that the care lavished on their homes by the Dutch was a kind of preventive maintenance. That, at least, was Temple's suggestion: "The same moisture of Air makes all Metals apt to rust, and Wood to mould; which forces them by continual pains of rubbing and scouring, to seek a prevention or cure: This makes the brightness and cleanness that seems affected in their Houses, and is call'd natural to them, by people who think no further."[19]

The importance that the Dutch attached to domestic cleanliness is all the more striking since we know that in their personal habits the Dutch were not especially clean; there is plenty of evidence that they were considered, even by the insalubrious standards of the seventeenth century, to be dirty.[20] "They keep their houses cleaner than their bodies," wrote an English visitor.[21] The Dutch house did not contain a room for bathing, for instance, and public baths were almost unknown. Bathing was further discouraged by the multiple layers of clothing that both men and women wore in the damp winters.

Temple remarked on the unhealthy climate and situation

---

* The Dutch word for clean, *schoon*, also expresses beauty and purity.

of the Netherlands. Although the Dutch originated modern medicine, they were unable to control the many infectious diseases that struck almost every Dutch town during the seventeenth century. The generally low level of public health was indicated by the series of annual epidemics that ravaged Amsterdam for six years during the 1620s, reducing the population by thirty-five thousand. Leiden lost more than a third of its forty thousand citizens in six months of 1635.

It is precisely because Holland's scrubbed floors and polished brasswork did not reflect a profound understanding of health or hygiene that they are significant. The cleanliness of the Dutch interior was not simply a part of the national character, nor a response determined by external causes, but evidence of something much more important. When visitors were required to take off their shoes or put on slippers, it was not immediately on entering the house—the lower floor was still considered to be a part of the public street—but on going upstairs. That was where the public realm stopped and the home began. This boundary was a new idea, and the order and tidiness of the household were evidence neither of fastidiousness nor of a particular cleanliness, but instead of a desire to define the home as a separate, special place.

That we are able to know so much about the appearance of Dutch homes is thanks to two happy accidents: the predominance of painting in seventeenth-century Holland, and the popularity of domestic scenes as a subject of these paintings. The Dutch loved paintings. The richest and the most humble person bought them and hung them in their homes. This was partly as an investment, but also for their own pleasure. Paintings could be found not only in parlors and front rooms but also in taverns, offices, and workplaces and behind shop counters. The bourgeois public supported many painters who, like furniture makers or other craftsmen, were organized in guilds. These Dutch painters diligently worked their way up in their profession, beginning at the age of fourteen as apprentices, then as journeymen assistants, until after six years they could apply for membership in the guild and become independent "masters," at which point they were permitted to sell paintings under their own names.

Although the market for paintings was large, the supply was as well, and few Dutch painters became wealthy. Portraits were painted on commission, but much painting was done on speculation and sold through dealers. The public desired paintings of suitable subjects, whose artistry they could admire and understand. The technically skilled painters, with a direct, uncomplicated approach to painting, and without the self-consciousness of later artists, were happy to oblige. As a result, seventeenth-century Dutch paintings serve not only as art, but also as an unusually accurate representation of the time.

Given the affection of the Dutch for their neat, well-kept houses, it was not surprising that in addition to biblical subjects and family portraits, there developed a genre of painting that dealt with the home itself. To recall the work of an American illustrator such as Norman Rockwell conveys a little of their artistry, but it does give a sense of a type of painting that appealed to a home-loving public. Pieter de Hooch painted wonderful scenes of domestic life, as also did Jan Steen and Gabriel Metsu. Less than forty paintings remain by the great Jan Vermeer, and almost all of them are set within the home. But it was Emanuel de Witte, who specialized in views of church interiors, another popular genre, who painted a domestic scene that has come to epitomize the seventeenth-century Dutch interior. This little masterpiece, painted around 1660, shows a series of rooms opening off each other, bathed in sunlight that falls through the large leaded windows.* Judging from the way that the light passes into all three rooms and the hint of trees visible through the windows, this house is probably on the outskirts of the town. The central figure in the painting, and the one from which it gets its name, is a young woman playing the virginals, a precursor to the spinet, that was popular in Holland at that time.

Like many Dutch painters, de Witte intended his picture to tell a story. On the surface this is an idyllic, peaceful scene. It is early in the day—that is implied by the low angle of the sun, and by the maidservant busy with the morning chores, visible in a distant doorway. The mistress of the house—who else could it be?—sits at the musical instrument. The room in which she is playing, typically, serves many functions. It contains, in addition to the virginals, a table, three chairs, and a curtained bed.

But all is not what it appears to be. Closer inspection of the painting reveals that the woman is not playing for herself alone; on the bed, behind the curtains, someone is listening to the music. It is unquestionably a man—the figure wears a mustache—and, although he is hidden, his clothing is fully visible on the chair in the foreground. The hilt of a sword that is barely within the picture and the casual fashion in which the clothes have been thrown on the chair—instead of being hung neatly on the hooks behind the door—hint, in a delicate way, that this man may not be the woman's husband. Marital infidelity was frowned upon in Calvinist Holland and de Witte fulfilled his social obligations by making it the subject of an allegory, although that tale is hidden in a series of riddles, symbols, and secondary meanings. The jug and towel on the table, the water pump, and the woman sweeping the floor suggest something along the lines of "Cleanliness is next

---

* Genre paintings, since they were to be hung in the home, were usually small; de Witte's was only thirty by forty inches. Many were less than half that size.

to godliness." But part of the delight of this genre is the painter's ambiguity toward his subject. Is the woman properly penitent? If so, why is she playing and not weeping? She has her back turned, as if in shame, but in the mirror hanging on the wall over the virginals, her face is tantalizingly not quite reflected. Maybe she is smiling; we will never know.

One does not need to unravel the turgid story that lies hidden in the shadows and details of de Witte's painting. He was interested not only in narrative but also, like most Dutch painters, in portraying the material world as he saw it. This love of the real world—"realism" is too weak a word—was evident in many details. We can enjoy the way that the shadow of the windows falls on the partly open door, the red taffeta curtains that color the light in the room, the shiny brass of the chandelier, the rich gilt of the mirror frame and the matte texture of the pewter jug. There is a little dog curled up beside the bed; sheet music lies open on top of the virginals. Nothing is too small to escape the painter's attention.

It should be said immediately that it is unlikely that de Witte's was a depiction of an actual house; photographic as his paintings appear, they are imagined, not real. De Witte's churches, for example, were not portraits of existing buildings; although they were based on sketches of identifiable interiors, the finished paintings combine elements from different churches. What we cannot ignore, however, is that while the house may have been imagined, the effect is real, and it is above all one of extreme intimacy.

The furniture is not complicated; the padded chairs look comfortable but lack the fringes and embroidered material that were then popular in France. The rooms are *enfilade*, but the effect is not intimidating. The walls are plain, although they are typically adorned with a mirror, as well as with a map visible through the doorway. The stone floor is a simple pattern of black and white squares of marble. This is a well-to-do household—the musical instrument, the oriental carpet and the gilded mirror attest to that—but the atmosphere is not one of luxury. Objects are not on display; instead, we have the impression of a simple practicality from the way that the furnishings are arranged. The bed is located in a corner, behind the door; the rug is thoughtfully placed beside the bed, to take the morning chill off the cold stone floor. The mirror hangs over the virginals. The table and chairs sit next to the window, near the light. And what light! The rooms are illuminated to emphasize their depth and distance, as well as their physical, material reality. It is above all this sense of interior space, and hence of insideness, that distinguishes this painting. Instead of being a picture of a room, it is a picture of a home.

De Witte's true subject was the domestic atmosphere itself, which is the reason that this genre of painting was for so long dismissed as a minor one, and which is precisely why it is of interest here. De Witte was not, of course, the only practitioner of the domestic genre. Pieter de Hooch, a Delft neighbor, produced an entire oeuvre documenting the everyday life of the ordinary bourgeois. He showed them in their homes, usually at work, engrossed in some commonplace task, and he carefully depicted their houses and gardens with architectural accuracy. Unlike de Witte, he was less concerned with narrative and more interested in portraying an idealized domesticity. Although he subordinated the human figure to its background, his scenes always included one or two persons, usually women with children. During the Renaissance, when women had been solitary figures in a painting, it was as Madonnas, saints or biblical personages, the Dutch painters were the first to choose ordinary women as their subject. It was natural for women to be the focus of de Witte's paintings, because the domestic world that he was depicting had become *their* realm. The world of male work, and male social life, had moved elsewhere. The house had become the place for another kind of work—specialized domestic work—women's work. This work itself was nothing new, but its isolation was. Medieval paintings had always shown women at work, but they were rarely alone, and inevitably their work occurred amid the activities of men—people talking, eating, conducting business, or lounging about. De Hooch's women work alone, quietly.

Jan Vermeer, another Delft painter, was predominantly interested in the female human figure and less in the domestic interior, but since almost all his masterly paintings are set in the home, they also convey something of its character. His subjects act with a concentration that is mirrored in the still atmosphere of the room and its furnishings. Through Vermeer's paintings we can see how the house has changed: it has become a setting for private acts and personal moments. *The Love Letter* shows the mistress of the house being interrupted by her maid bringing her a letter. We can see the corner of an ornate fireplace, as well as a gilt leather wall panel and a seascape hanging on the wall (the last two items actually belonged to Vermeer). Ignoring the narrative clues—the letter, the mandolin, the seascape—what is most striking is the relationship between the two women sharing a private moment, and the way that Vermeer has placed us in another room, emphasizing the intimacy of the event and also achieving a sense of domestic space in a highly original way. The various objects in the home—a laundry basket, a broom, clothing, a pair of shoes—establish the predominance of the women in this space. The man, from whom the letter presumably comes, is far away; even if he were not he would have to tread warily on the freshly cleaned black-and-white-tiled marble floor. When a male is included in a Vermeer, one has the sense that he is a visitor—an intruder—for these women do not simply inhabit these rooms, they occupy them completely. Whether they are sewing, playing the spinet, or reading a letter, the Dutch women are solidly, emphatically, contentedly at home.

• • •

The feminization of the home in seventeenth-century Holland was one of the most important events in the evolution of the domestic interior. It had several causes, chief among them the limited use made of servants. Even the wealthiest household rarely employed more than three servants, while a typical prosperous bourgeois family included, at most, a single maid-servant. Compare this to the Bruns, who had, in addition to their three employees, two servants, or to the typical British bourgeois family of that time which would have had at least half a dozen domestics. Dutch law was explicit on contractual arrangements and on the civil rights of servants, so that the relationship between employer and employee was less ex-ploitive and closer than elsewhere in Europe; servants ate with their masters at the same table, for instance, and house-work was shared instead of delegated. All this produced, for the seventeenth century, a remarkable situation: Dutch mar-ried women, irrespective of their wealth or social position, did most of their own household chores. It has been recorded that when the wife of Admiral de Ruyter was visited on the day after her husband's death by an envoy of the *stadhouder*, the Prince of Orange, she could not receive him, since she had recently sprained her ankle—while hanging out the laun-dry![22] When de Witte was commissioned to paint a wealthy burgher's wife, Adriana van Heusden, he depicted her shop-ping with her little daughter in an Amsterdam fish market. It would be impossible to imagine a wealthy French or English lady performing the same duty, or wishing to be immortalized in such prosaic surroundings.

Dutch married women had "the whole care and absolute management of all their Domestique," according to Temple.[23] This included taking charge of the cooking. Contemporary accounts by foreign visitors were clear on this point, although, particularly in the case of Frenchmen, characteristically disparaging remarks were made about the unsophisticated cuisine of the Dutch. However that might be, this small change had far-reaching consequences. When servants were doing the cooking, the room containing the kitchen was hardly differentiated from the other rooms, and was in any case accorded a secondary position. In Parisian bourgeois houses, for example, the kitchen occupied a room off the courtyard but without direct access to the main rooms. In English terrace houses the kitchen, adjacent to the servant quarters, continued to be located in the basement until the nineteenth century. In most *appartements* the "kitchen" was no more than a pot hanging in the fireplace.

In the Dutch home the kitchen was the most important room; according to one historian, "the kitchen was promoted to a position of fantastic dignity and became something between a temple and a museum."[24] Here were located the cupboards that held the prized table linens, china, and silver. Copper and brass utensils, brightly polished, hung on the walls. The chimney piece was enormous and elaborately decorated—overly so to modern tastes—and contained not only the hearth with the traditional hanging pot, but also a simple kind of stove. The sink was copper, sometimes marble. Some kitchens had interior hand pumps (one is visible in de Witte's painting) and even reservoirs with a continuous supply of hot water. The presence of such amenities signified the growing importance of domestic work and the premium that was beginning to be placed on convenience. This was natural. For the first time, the person who was in intimate contact with housework was also in a position to influence the arrangement and disposition of the home. Servants had to put up with inconvenient and ill-thought-out arrangements because they had no say in the matter. The mistress of the house, particularly when she was as independent-minded as the Dutch woman, did not.

The importance accorded the kitchen reflected the central

position of the woman in the Dutch household. The husband may have been the head of the family and led the mealtime prayers, but in household matters he was no longer "master in his own house." It was the wife, not her husband, who insisted on cleanliness and tidiness, not the least because it was she who had to do the cleaning. This simple self-interest is a much more convincing explanation of the clean Dutch house than either climate or national character.

There are many examples of domestic order in Holland maintained by women. Smoking tobacco was popular among Dutch men, and their wives went to great lengths to keep the odor out of their homes. Some women even had "no smoking" clauses inserted into their marriage contracts; if all else failed they set aside a "smoking room" for their nicotic spouses. In any case, once a year the entire house was emptied for a major cleaning (this was in addition to the regular weekly washings). Men, forbidden access and deprived of hot meals, referred to this period as "hell." Formal parlors were also cleaned regularly, although they were used rarely. One burgher confessed to Temple that there were two rooms in his own house that he was not permitted to enter, and had never done so.[25] Although Dutch men continued to wear their hats at the table (except when saying grace) and rarely washed their hands before eating, the evolution of bourgeois—as opposed to courtly—manners had begun.

The imposition of a special code of behavior within the home was considered odd by foreign visitors, although that opinion may have been biased, since those visitors whose records have survived were exclusively male. Stories of the strictness, if not tyranny, of the Dutch mistress abounded; undoubtedly many were apocryphal. But they all pointed to a change in domestic arrangements. Not only was the house becoming more intimate, it was also, in the process, acquiring a special atmosphere. It was becoming a feminine place, or at least a place under feminine control. This control was tangible and real. It resulted in cleanliness, and in enforced rules, but it also introduced something to the house which had not existed before: domesticity.

To speak of domesticity is to describe a set of felt emotions, not a single attribute. Domesticity has to do with family, intimacy, and a devotion to the home, as well as with a sense of the house as embodying—not only harboring—these sentiments. It was the atmosphere of domesticity that permeated de Witte's and Vermeer's paintings. Not only was the interior a setting for domestic activity—as it had always been—but the rooms, and the objects that they contained, now acquired a life of their own. This life was not, of course, autonomous, but existed in the imagination of their owners, and so, paradoxically, homely domesticity depended on the development of a rich interior awareness, an awareness that was the result of the woman's role in the home. If domesticity was, as John Lukacs suggested, one of the principal achievements of the Bourgeois Age, it was, above all, a feminine achievement.[26]

Chapter Four

François Boucher, *Madame Boucher*
(1743)

Commodity and Delight

> *. . . good taste consists in joining together commodity, firmness and delight.*
>
> —JACQUES-FRANÇOIS BLONDEL
>
> *ARCHITECTURE FRANÇAISE*

Privacy and domesticity, the two great discoveries of the Bourgeois Age, appeared, naturally enough, in the bourgeois Netherlands. By the eighteenth century they had spread to the rest of northern Europe—England, France, and the German states. The household had changed, both physically and emotionally; as it had ceased to be a workplace, it had become smaller and, more important, less public. Since there were fewer occupants, not only its size but also the very atmosphere within the house was affected. It was now a place for personal, intimate behavior. This intimacy was reinforced by a change in the attitude toward children, whose extended presence altered the medieval, public character of the "big house." The house was no longer only a shelter against the elements, a protection against the intruder—although these remained important functions—it had become the setting for a new, compact social unit: the family. With the family came isolation, but also family life and domesticity. The house was becoming a home, and following privacy and domesticity the stage was set for the third discovery: the idea of comfort.

It may seem odd to speak of comfort as an idea. Surely it is merely a physical condition; one sits in a comfortable chair . . . and one feels comfortable. What could be simpler? According to Bernard Rudofsky, an irascible critic of modern civilization, it would be simpler to avoid chairs altogether 77 and sit on the floor. "Sitting on chairs is an acquired habit, like smoking, and about as wholesome," Rudofsky claims.[1] He lists a panoply of alternative—and according to him, superior—devices from other cultures and other periods. He includes daises, divans, platforms, swings, and hammocks, but his favorite alternative is the simplest—the floor.

Differences in posture, like differences in eating utensils (knife and fork, chopsticks or fingers, for example), divide the world as profoundly as political boundaries. Regarding posture there are two camps: the sitters-up (the so-called western world) and the squatters (everyone else).* Although there is no Iron Curtain separating the two sides, neither feels comfortable in the position of the other. When I eat with oriental friends I soon feel awkward sitting on the floor, my back unsupported, my legs numb. But squatters don't like sitting up either. An Indian household may have a dining room with table and chairs, but when the family relaxes during the hot afternoon, parents and children sit together on the floor. The driver of a three-wheeled motor scooter in Delhi has to sit on a seat, but instead of doing so in a western manner he squats cross-legged, his feet on the bench instead of on the floor (precariously to my eyes, comfortably to his). A Canadian carpenter works standing up, at a bench. My Gujarati friend Vikram, given the choice, prefers to work sitting down, on the floor.

Why have certain cultures adopted a sitting-up posture when others did not? There seems to be no satisfactory answer to this apparently simple question. It is tempting to suggest

---

* This bipartite division has been remarkably consistent; there is only one example of a civilization in which both sitting *and* squatting coexisted: ancient China. The chair probably arrived in China from Europe as early as the sixth century. However, although the Chinese used high tables, chairs, and beds, their homes continued to include areas which provided low furnishings for squatting.[2]

that furniture was developed as a functional response to cold floors, and it is true that most of the squatting world is in the tropics. But the originators of sitting furniture—the Mesopotamians, the Egyptians, and the Greeks—all lived in warm climates. And to complicate matters further, the Koreans and the Japanese, who do live in cold regions, never felt the need to develop furniture and managed with heated platforms instead. Fernand Braudel suggests that the development of interior furnishings in different cultures followed two rules. First, poor people could afford few possessions; and second, traditional civilizations remained faithful to their accustomed decor, and altered it slowly.[3] But he is subsequently forced to admit that this deterministic theory does not adequately resolve the question. It explains the scarcity of furniture in Ethiopia or Bangladesh—both poor and traditional cultures—but not in such prosperous and dynamic civilizations as Ottoman Turkey and imperial Persia. Neither does it explain why Moghul India, which was wealthy enough, and skilled enough, to build the Taj Mahal, did not develop sitting furniture. Such exceptions abound. The eighth-century Japanese, who copied much of their technology and culture from China, judiciously ignored Chinese furniture; in the sixteenth century they adopted the European gun but bypassed the chair. Nor has the shunning of furniture been consistent. Like the Japanese, the Indians have long managed without tables and chairs, but unlike them they prefer to sleep in beds, not on the floor.

It is certainly true that people who are used to squatting feel physically at ease, while people who are used to chairs will soon feel tired and uncomfortable in this position, but the cultural choice of one or the other cannot be explained by differences in human biology. The Japanese are generally smaller than the Europeans, but black Africans, who also squat, are not. Sitting on the ground with spine erect may be good for the body, but there is no evidence that sitting cultures such as the ancient (and athletic) Greeks developed chairs because of laziness or physical infirmity.

Perhaps sitting and squatting can be explained only as a matter of taste. In that case, according to Rudofsky, this is yet another example of western wrongheadedness. His criticism of furniture is based on the Rousseauish assumption that since all that is needed for sitting, or lying, is the ground, chairs and beds are unnecessary, unnatural, and hence inferior. The notion that what is artless must be better than what is not requires a precarious leap in reasoning, but for all that it carries great weight with the American public—at least judging from the dozens of advertisements that extol "being natural." It is a shallow conceit. A little reflection shows that *all* human culture is artificial, cooking no less than music, furniture no less than painting. Why prepare time-consuming sauces when a raw fruit would suffice? Why bother with musical instruments when the voice is pleasant enough? Why paint pictures when looking at nature is satisfying? Why sit up when you can squat?

The answer is that it makes life richer, more interesting, and more pleasurable. Of course furniture is unnatural; it is an artifact. Sitting *is* artificial, and like other artificial activities, although less obviously than cooking, instrumental music, or painting, it introduces art into living. We eat pasta or play the piano—or sit upright—out of choice, not out of need. This should be emphasized, for so much has been written about the practicality and functionality of (particularly modern) furniture that it is easy to forget that tables and chairs, unlike, for example, refrigerators and washing machines, are a refinement, not a utility.

When a person sits on the ground, he is neither comfortable nor uncomfortable. Naturally, sharp stones or unpleasant obstructions are avoided, but otherwise one flat surface is pretty much like another. Squatting is natural; that is why a person who squats considers neither how to sit nor where to sit. This is not to say that squatting is crude; as with other human activities it may involve etiquette and decorum. The Japanese, for example, never sit on the ground itself, always on a raised platform. Saudis sit on carpets of stunning beauty. The point is not that this habit is inferior, or less comfortable, but that comfort is not made explicit in either case.

Sitting on a chair is another matter. The chair may be too high or too low. It may cut into the back, or dig into the thighs. It can put the sitter to sleep, or make him fidget, or leave him with back pain. The chair must be designed to accommodate the posture of the body, and hence raises issues unlike any which face the builder of a carpeted dais or platform. Furniture forces the sitting-up civilization, sooner or later, to consider the question of comfort.

The problem of sitting comfort took many hundreds of years to resolve. Although discovered by the ancient Greeks, it remained forgotten, and ignored. Historians of furniture inevitably draw our attention to the changes in chair design and construction and allow us to forget a more important ingredient: the changes that took place in the sitter. For the main constraint on furniture design was not only technical—how the chair was made—but also cultural, how it was used. The easy chair had to be preceded by the desire for an easy posture.

The chair responded to how people wished to sit. As has been pointed out, during the Middle Ages the prime function of the chair was ceremonial. The man who sat down was important—whence the term "chairman"—and his upright, dignified posture reflected his social stature. This association of the seat itself with authority has remained an integral part of European and American culture: we still refer to a judge's bench, or to being in the driver's seat. The movie director continues to have his name on a chair, even if it is printed only on canvas. There are even imaginary seats, like Chairs in Art History, or seats on the boards of corporations. In my own university, a professor who has put in twenty years of service receives not a watch but a wooden armchair with the university's seal.

Although chairs began to service more mundane activities such as eating or writing, the sitting position changed slowly. Throughout the Renaissance and the Baroque period, European sitting furniture, although it increased in quantity, accommodated what was essentially the erect posture encouraged by the earliest chairs. Even the domesticated seventeenth-century Dutch continued to sit stolidly in their straight-backed chairs, both feet planted firmly on the ground.

The chair acquired a different role in the France of Louis XIV, an epoch of prodigious military, political, literary, and architectural accomplishments. It was also the period when furniture was raised to the level of a fine art. It came to be seen as an integral part of interior decoration, and the casual furniture arrangements of the past gave way to a strictly ordered decor. Illustrations of the royal palace at Versailles show a table between each set of windows, a commode on each side of the door, and a stool at the base of each pilaster. Since the function of furniture was to emphasize and enhance the architecture of the room, not to accommodate people, chairs were designed to be admired, but not, strange as it seems, to be sat in. They were lined up in neat rows against the wall, like soldiers. Louis XIV, something of a tyrant, is said to have once scolded his mistress for leaving a chair in the middle of the room instead of returning it to its proper place against the wall.

Although the chair's function was secondary, it did play an important role in court etiquette. In a modern office the size of an executive's chair is an indication of status and influence; similarly, at Versailles, the kind of chair one was occasionally permitted to sit in denoted rank and social position. In some rooms, nobody but the king was allowed to sit—the state bedroom contained no visitor's chairs at all. In the rest of the palace a strict hierarchy prevailed. Armchairs were reserved for the Sun King, and no one else was permitted to sit in them. Chairs without arms were reserved for members of the immediate royal entourage. Backless stools could be used by certain members of the nobility, and unpadded folding stools by lesser notables. Since the number of such stools was strictly controlled—an inventory taken when Louis XIV died showed that there were only 1,325 at a time when the daily population of Versailles numbered many thousands—a game of musical chairs generally resulted, with most of the courtiers left standing.[4] One can imagine that when they did sit they did not relax; perched on stools, they assumed a posture of upright attention. Although this curious chair etiquette prevailed mainly at Versailles and not in bourgeois homes, one would hardly expect an evolution in the direction of comfort under such circumstances. Ebénistes such as Golle, Cucci, and Boule created pieces of extraordinary beauty—especially cabinets, armoires, and commodes—but sitting furniture stagnated in gilded discomfort.

This was soon to change: with Louis XIV's death in 1715 and the accession of his young great-grandson Louis XV to the throne, formality was replaced by vivacity, grandiosity by intimacy, and magnificence by delicacy. "Versailles in the eighteenth century," wrote Nancy Mitford, "presented the unedifying but cheerful spectacle of several thousand people living for pleasure and very much enjoying themselves."[5] Our image of this period has been colored by the disapproving attitude of the Victorian historian—and of the twentieth-century prude—for whom the pursuit of pleasure was profligate extravagance, and a sophisticated living style base corruption. However, it was precisely during this period, and mainly because of its hedonistic interests, that comfortable furniture first appeared.

Sitting was no longer only ritualistic or functional, but

became a form of relaxation. People sat together to listen to music, to have conversations, to play cards. A new sense of leisure was reflected in their sitting positions: gentlemen leaned back and sat with their legs crossed—a new posture—and ladies reclined. A casual stance became fashionable. Chairs were adapted to these new positions, which is to say, they were adapted, for the first time since the ancient Greeks, to the human body. Their backs were slanted instead of vertical, their arms curved instead of straight. They were broader and lower, and allowed more flexibility in arranging the body. The most common form of seating was the upholstered armchair which had a shaped, padded back and which was much wider than chairs in the past. The sitter could turn this way or that, lean on the padded arms, and converse comfortably with his or her neighbor. Stools were not just for sitting on but for putting up one's feet, another typical posture. There were seats for two, and a variety of couches whose names—*ottomane*, *sultane*, *turquoise*—recalled, like the word "sofa" itself, the Arabic inspiration for these low, padded, divan-type seats. Women reclined on the chaise longue, which could also be used as a couch.

The French solved the problem of comfort in furniture in a characteristically rational way. They did not abandon the traditional, formal type of furniture which had characterized Louis XIV interiors, but created a new category of additional seating that was not constrained by rigid aesthetic needs and that could respond to their desire for a more relaxed sitting posture. The two types of seating were known as *sièges meublants* and *sièges courants*.[6] The former referred to the type of seating that continued to be considered as a part of the decor. It was also called "architectural furniture," and was chosen and located by the architect; like paintings, which were not hung at random but made expressly for a particular wall, it was integrated permanently into the decoration of the room. The heavy *fauteuil à la reine*, which had a vertical back and stood against the wall, was named in honor of the king's wife. *Sièges meublants* were rarely moved from their preordained locations, so rarely, in fact, that the chairbacks, because never seen, were frequently left unfinished.

Sièges courants, on the other hand, were both movable and everyday (*courant* means both in French). They did not have a fixed position and were light enough to be moved easily around the room. They could be placed in informal groupings, around a tea table or in groups for conversations. Such light armchairs were called *fauteuils en cabriolet*—literally, cavorting chairs. While the *sièges meublants* were used in the salons, the *sièges courants* were designed for informal use and were the furniture of the boudoir and the intimate sitting room. They were not constrained by the formal requirements of architectural decoration, which tended to be rectilinear, but could assume new fluid shapes which were based on sitting comfort instead of on formal aesthetics.

The distinction between fixed and movable furniture also existed among different sorts of tables. In addition to large bureaus and marble-topped tables, which were situated decoratively but impractically against the wall, there were smaller pieces, intended for more intimate or personal use. There were reading tables, game tables, and night tables. These were often ingeniously constructed with different-sized drawers and sliding or folding tops. There was a great variety of dressing tables—for both sexes—as well as washstands. Women were great letter and diary writers, and had special writing tables and desks made for this activity. A lady's apartment also included small tables for needlework, for breakfast, and for serving that fashionable new import, coffee.

The variety of types of furniture in eighteenth-century France reflected the specialization that was taking place in the arrangement of the house; different rooms were acquiring different functions. People no longer ate in anterooms but in a suitably furnished dining room. They no longer entertained visitors in their bedchambers but in a salon; gentlemen had their studies, ladies had boudoirs—part dressing room, part sitting room—where special intimates could be received. All of these rooms were smaller, less grand, and more intimate than in the past. They were no longer arranged *enfilade* in long rows, but in a more casual way, so that one room could be reached without crossing another. This separation of the house into public and private areas was reflected by a change in the language. The place where one slept was no longer called simply a "room"—it was now referred to as a "chamber." The public rooms continued to be called *salles* (hence *salle à manger*—dining room—and *salon*), but the bedchamber was a *chambre à coucher*.*

Today, when servants have become a luxury (at least in North America), they are ostentatiously displayed. This was not the case in the eighteenth century, when inquisitive, gossiping servants began to be considered an intrusion on the privacy of their masters. Louis XV's hunting lodge at Choisy contained a mechanism that enabled a fully set table to be elevated into the dining room from the kitchen below, eliminating the need for servants and permitting the king and his friends to enjoy complete intimacy. It was the custom in Versailles for the servants to be dismissed and for the king himself to serve his guests after supper-parties when the company retreated into the salon for coffee.

A desire for greater privacy characterized the eighteenth century; it was found in the bourgeois home no less than in the palace. Since the Middle Ages, servants had either slept in the same rooms as their masters or in an adjoining room. They were summoned by clapping the hands, or ringing a

---

* This same distinction exists in Italian (*sala* and *camera*); in English, the old word "bedchamber" is no longer used, although in the legal profession a judge's private room continues to be his or her "chambers," and confidential hearings are called "in camera."

small hand bell. In the eighteenth century the hand bell was replaced by the bell cord.[7] This device operated a complex system of wires and pulleys and rang a bell in another part of the house. It was invented because the new sense of family privacy demanded that servants be kept at a distance. They were housed either in separate wings or in a small room between floors, the result of lowering the ceiling of the bed-chamber. Other efforts were made to limit the intrusion of servants. The growing popularity of stoves during the eigh-teenth century, for example, was due in no small measure to the way in which they could be tended, through the wall from an adjacent room. Another aptly named device that was in-vented at this time—also meant to keep the servants at bay—was the dumbwaiter.*

The Versailles of Louis XIV had been a "big house," the biggest in France. It was a public place, with few restrictions on where courtiers could go, and consequently little privacy. This began to change. The first thing that Louis XV did when he moved to Versailles was to rearrange his living quarters. The enormous state bedroom remained, as did the ceremonies of the *lever* and the *coucher*—those odd public spectacles of royal awakening and repose—but they were now formalities; the king slept elsewhere, and did so in seclusion. His private suite, to which access was restricted, was called the Petits Appartements, not because there were few rooms (there were fifty of them), but because the rooms themselves were small, at least by the standards of the time. The royal chambers, which a wag had christened "the rats' nests," included secret passages, concealed staircases, and many alcoves and intimate rooms, all exquisitely decorated and furnished.

---

* The same technology was used to operate "chair hoists," which were common in wealthy homes. Madame de Pompadour had a private chair hoist which carried her up to her second-floor apartment at Versailles; at the Hotel Luxembourg the hoist served all the floors.[8]

That the king, previously a public figure, should feel the need for privacy illustrates the extent of the influence of bourgeois values on court life, and, in this case, the influence of that great bourgeoise Jeanne-Antoinette Poisson, or as she is better known, Madame de Pompadour. She was briefly Louis XV's mistress, then his confidante, friend, and adviser for almost twenty years. A formidable dabbler in politics, she was also the mediator of court fashion, and hence of style in general. She not only encouraged Louis's interest in domestic architecture, but also directed it toward the small, the precious, and the intimate. In a letter to a friend she described the Hermitage, her residence at Versailles: "It is sixteen yards by ten, nothing above, so you see how grand it must be; but I can be alone there, or with the King and a few others, so I am happy."[9] The Hermitage was the smallest of her houses —she built or renovated half a dozen. Having aroused the king's interest in decoration, she kept him enthralled by one project after another. This promoted a general fashion for interior decoration that facilitated and accelerated the introduction of "modern" ideas such as privacy, intimacy, and comfort.

The fashionable interest in the domestic interior was reflected throughout French society. Bourgeois Parisian houses were more subdivided than in the past. Apartments no longer consisted of two or three rooms—there were at least five or six major rooms, whose arrangement was recognizably modern. The entrance door, off a common staircase, led into an antechamber which functioned as a large vestibule, and from which every other room could be reached. In addition to the kitchen, there were a dining room and a salon. The other rooms included private bedchambers, often a boudoir, and several smaller rooms which were used for storage and for servants.

It would be a mistake not to mention the appearance of these rooms, decorated in a style which originated in France

and which came to be known as Rococo.* Rococo architects
were fond of decoration in the form of shells, foliage, and
extravagant scrollwork, all of it usually finished in gilt. Everything that could be decorated was. Although it was executed
with extreme skill and delicacy, the overall effect of that much
ornamentation could be overwhelming. Architectural style is
not the subject of this book, but it was often an indication
of public attitudes for style and often imposed limits on how
houses could be arranged. In this case what is interesting is
the way Rococo ornament was applied. The architectural
historian Peter Collins has pointed out that Jean-François
Blondel, the designer of many famous Rococo interiors, never
used such ornament on the façades of his buildings, which
were always severely classical.[10] Indeed, Rococo features were
almost never found on the exteriors of French buildings (although they did appear, later, in Italy and Spain). Rococo
was the first style to be developed exclusively for the *interior*,
as opposed to the exterior. This underlined not only that the
insides of houses were being thought of as very different from
the outsides, but also that an important distinction was being
made between interior decoration and architecture. This distinction was not as obvious then as it now seems; previously,
the architecture of rooms had been the architecture of façades,
turned inside out. It was not until the Rococo that architects
such as Blondel could specialize in "interior decoration." This
accelerated the improvement of domestic comfort and, in the
long run, made possible the changes that would follow. In
the future, Rococo would be replaced by other styles, but the
conviction that the inside of a building should be considered
separately from its exterior would remain.

* The word was a pun on *barocco*; "roc-" came from *rocaille*, which meant
shellwork or pebblework, a characteristic motif. Like all art-history ap-
pellations, it was created after the fact, around 1836. Nor was it a com-
plimentary term; it was coined by disapproving critics who also referred
to this type of decoration as "chicory."

• • •

The principles that governed the design of buildings during this period were elucidated by the great French architect and educator Jacques-François Blondel, in his monumental four-volume *Architecture française*, which was first published in 1752. Blondel, the nephew of Jean-François, was Louis XV's architect and founded the first full-time school of architecture in Europe. He repeatedly emphasized that the basis for successful architecture should be the doctrine which had been first suggested by the Roman Vitruvius—"commodity, firmness, and delight." In this context it is the first concept—commodity—which bears closer examination.

Like his contemporaries, Blondel used the word "commodity" to imply convenience and suitability to human use, and he differentiated it from the purely aesthetic ("delight"), or that which was required by structural necessity ("firmness"). It also meant "comfort," but it did so in a very particular way. According to Blondel, the correct way to plan a house was to divide the rooms into three categories: ceremonial rooms (*appartements de parade*), formal reception rooms (*appartements de société*) and a third category that he called *appartements de commodité*. "In a large building. the *appartements de commodités* consist of rooms which, unlike the others, are rarely open to strangers, and are intended for the private use of the master or mistress of the house. It is in these rooms that they sleep during the winter, they rest in case of illness, and they conduct personal matters and receive their friends and family."[11] Just as light, movable furniture did not displace formal, Baroque furnishings, so convenience did not replace ceremony and formality; the *appartements de commodités* were a kind of backstage, a place to let one's hair down (that is, to take one's wig off) and relax in cozy comfort.

It is significant that Blondel mentioned the use of these

rooms as bedrooms during the winter; not only were they smaller, they were also better heated. During the seventeenth century, when rooms had been huge, they had been impossible to heat, even if fireplaces had been effective, which they were not. Louis XIV's Versailles contained many magnificent fireplaces, but these were more ornamental than practical. In bourgeois houses fireplaces had been primarily places to cook in, and only secondarily, and not very effectively, sources of warmth. Around 1720, builders discovered how to build fireplaces and chimneys in such a way as to induce a draft. This not only eliminated the smoke, it also improved combustion, throwing more heat into the room. Whether or not the combination of smaller rooms and better fireplaces should be called a "revolution in heating," as Braudel claims, it was at least a major improvement in what had previously been a neglected field.[12] New houses were built with the smaller, more efficient fireplaces; old fireplaces in existing houses were cut down in size and converted. The effectiveness of these new fireplaces was enhanced by the use of folding screens, which could be set up behind the sitter to contain the warmth and reduce drafts. Comfort was greatly improved.

Porcelain stoves of the kind used in Germany now also became fashionable. They were usually placed in a niche, so that they could be fed through the wall from an adjacent anteroom. Because they were considered aesthetically inferior to fireplaces—even though they were more efficient as heating devices—stoves were at first installed only in dining rooms and antechambers. After the 1750s, however, their clean, smokeless, radiating heat won out and they began to be used in more important rooms as well.[13] Even so, good taste required that stoves in fashionable houses be disguised, usually as a kind of credenza or decorative urn.

Another aspect of commodity was the increased presence of the bathroom—or rather the "bathsroom," as it was called in French, for often these rooms contained two bathtubs, one for washing and one for rinsing. The palace of Versailles included at least one hundred bathrooms; there were seven in the royal apartment alone. Bathrooms frequently contained bidets—a useful device in this ardent period—but no toilets. An early type of water closet was housed in the "English place" (oddly named, since water closets were then unknown in England).[14] More common than the toilet was the traditional closed stool that stood in its own room, or, more casually, in an antechamber near the bedroom.

It is not clear what priority cleanliness was accorded during the eighteenth century. Our nineteenth-century forebears were convinced that Louis XV's France was a licentious, and hence an unhygienic, place. Siegfried Giedion, a fastidious Swiss it should be said, maintained that "the most elementary sense for cleanliness was lacking."[15] Other historians are less categorical.[16] On the one hand, evidence suggests that bathing was considered to be a pleasurable pastime, rather than a necessity, and bathrooms were thought of as a fashionable accessory—rather like a hot tub—and not as a required amenity. How else to explain the frequent records of bathrooms being installed and then capriciously being removed? On the other hand, the attention paid to the provision of heated water, and the elaborate decoration of these rooms, indicated that cleanliness, or at least bathing, was assuming increased importance. The plan of a grand house by Blondel shows three bathtubs in a large room, although it is somewhat impractically situated at the end of an *enfilade*, next to a library, and at some distance from the bedchambers.[17] Bathrooms were confined to the houses of the wealthy, however, and portable full-length baths did not become popular until the turn of the century, until which time most people washed in copper or porcelain basins. But even bourgeois homes were not without their refinements. An inventory (1771) of the home of Jacques Verberckt, a court carpenter who was responsible for some of the beautiful wood paneling at Ver-

sailles, included a wall-mounted tap and copper basin specifically designed for hand-washing. It was located in the
vestibule adjacent to the dining room.[18]

Was the search for commodity a pagan escape from the
medieval religiosity that had for so long dominated domestic
furnishings? J. H. B. Peel suggested that the eighteenth century's preoccupation with physical comfort was a result of
the decline in religious faith, or at any rate of the abatement
in religious fervor.[19] It is certainly hard to imagine a society
more materialistic than that of Louis XV, but it was a complex
society, full of contradictions (like all societies) and difficult
for us to understand. It was a society that prayed *and* played.
Its pursuit of pleasure impelled it toward the sometimes out-
rageous luxury of the Rococo, but it also, at the same time,
led it to discover comfort. Our modern concern for consistency is confounded by the eighteenth century. We find it
difficult to reconcile Louis XV's taste for opulence and his
appreciation for a painter of domestic vignettes like Chardin,
two of whose scenes of bourgeois home life the king owned.
Or to understand the values of a monarch who adored hunting (he is said to have killed over two hundred stags every
year of his adult life) and also personally raised pigeons and
rabbits on the roof of his palace. It is also not easy to distinguish between what was done for pleasure and what was
merely ostentation. When Louis and his mistress hid out in
the Hermitage and she cooked boiled eggs for him, were they
seeking comfort, or the vicarious thrill of playing house? Were
the ladies in François Boucher's paintings as casually relaxed
as they appeared, or were they as affected in their posture as
they were in their speech, or in their manner of walking?*

Women, in any case, had an enormous influence on the

---

* The "Versailles shuffle" consisted of small, hurried, sliding steps. Women
wore extremely long skirts suspended over wire panniers, and this gave
the effect of gliding.

manners of the time. The delicate refinement of French Rococo has often been called feminine. It was that, and not only in a metaphorical sense. If the interiors and furnishings of houses reflected a different sensibility, it was not just because Louis XV—and hence his court—was dominated by Madame de Pompadour, but because all social life during the *ancien régime* was dominated by women.

The preeminence of women in French social and cultural life did not begin in the eighteenth century. Such patronesses as Madame de Sévigné, Madame de Maintenon, Madame Geoffrin, and the Marquise du Deffand were preceded by that famous seventeenth-century *grande dame*, the Marquise de Rambouillet, whose introduction of the private sleeping room has already been noted. Her home (said to have been designed by her) outshone even the royal court as a center for the arts, letters, and fashion. The Duchess of Burgundy, who was Louis XIV's granddaughter, is supposed to have been responsible for the informality of the Regency style that characterized the final years of his reign. But it was during the eighteenth century that aristocratic and bourgeois women fully established themselves as the arbiters of manners. Their influence manifested itself in many ways, but especially in a softening effect on decorum and domestic behavior, which became more intimate and relaxed. Just as the Dutch woman introduced domesticity into the home, the French woman demanded, and got, furnishings which were more informal and more convenient. The feminine touch produced different results in France, certainly, than the homely domesticity of the Dutch, but it was an equally important step in the evolution of the home.

Nowhere was the influence of women on fashion more evident than in the great number of new types of sitting and reclining furniture which were designed especially for them. We can be confident that upper-class women influenced the development of furniture, since it was then customary for aristocrats to play an active role in the furnishing and even in the design of their homes.[20] There were a variety of chaises longues and easy chairs created exclusively for women's use. The *marquise* and the *duchesse*, two types of reclining chairs, are a reminder of their original patronesses. Even the ubiquitous upholstered armchair owed its shape to women's fashions: the set-back armrests accommodated their broad skirts, and the low backs gave room for their extravagant coiffures.

The production of this furniture was in the hands of cabinetmakers, who, with time, became more and more skillful in understanding the ergonomic, as well as the decorative, aspects of their craft. Today we admire the latter, but it was their knowledge of the former that was their greatest accomplishment, for these beautiful Rococo chairs were, above all, extremely comfortable. This was largely the result of the proper use of padding. Medieval chairs, which had flat wooden seats, had almost never been padded; instead a loose cushion was placed on them. Later, various materials such as leather, cane, and rushes were used to make seats which were slightly more accommodating. Inevitably, attempts were made to attach the cushion to the chair to keep it from sliding around, which led, at about the end of the seventeenth century, to upholstered seats. This development reached its full apogee in French Rococo furniture when seats, seat backs, and even armrests were padded.

Sitting comfort is achieved when the body is properly supported; this is not as easy as it sounds. Indeed, it is such a complicated business that what is surprising is not that the Middle Ages forgot how to make comfortable chairs, but rather that the Greeks ever discovered how in the first place. To ensure comfort—that is, a lack of discomfort—the chair must simultaneously provide for a number of conditions. There must be sufficient padding to prevent pressure on the bones, but not so much that the thighs and buttocks will themselves press up painfully against the pinbones at the base of the pelvis. The front rail of the chair, which is required for structural reasons, must be located lower than the cushion, or it will dig into the thigh. A back support is necessary—the sitter should be held more or less erect. A perfectly vertical back, however, is uncomfortable; the ideal is a slight backward angle, preferably with a curve to accommodate the spine, which is not straight. The angle must not be too great, however, or the sitter will slide forward. If the body does slump forward its weight will cease to be carried to the lumbar region, and the chest will be folded against the stomach. This will cause a slight collapse of the lungs, a consequent reduction in oxygen intake, and fatigue.[21]

Here is an explanation of why the world came to be divided into sitters and squatters. The coincidence of all the factors necessary to comfortable sitting is so unlikely, the probability of awkwardness and discomfort is so great, that it is not hard to imagine that many cultures, having had a try at it, would abandon the effort and wisely resort to sitting on the ground. This choice, in turn, would have affected the development of furniture in general, for without chairs, there would be no need for tables and desks, and little likelihood that a floor-sitting society would want to surround itself with other upright furniture such as cupboards, commodes, and bookcases.

Rococo cabinetmakers resolved all of the problems of comfortable sitting. There is evidence that they had access to studies of the relationship between poor seating and postural defects, which had been published in France by Nicholas Andry de Boisregard as early as 1741.[22] Andry not only pointed out how badly designed seating affected the body, he even suggested appropriate dimensions for different sorts of chairs. Partly as the result of such analyses, and partly by trial and error, the French cabinetmakers developed solutions to seating which subsequent designers have been unable to improve on.

Chair seats were padded with horsehair, which gave firm

support; women's chairs, which had to carry less weight, were often stuffed with down (springs were unknown and did not come into common use until the 1820s). Padding was not flat but given a dome shape (bombé), which took the larger weight at the center of the seat and also kept the front rail from cutting into the thighs. Angled chairbacks had been discovered in the previous century; when they were padded, as they almost invariably were, they assumed a gently curving shape. The padding was covered with silk brocades, velvets, and embroidered tapestry, all of which were rough (unlike wood or leather) and kept the sitter from sliding forward.

This explanation of the achievement of comfort may sound too clinical. Chairs were comfortable because they accommodated biology, but also because they accommodated the postures of the time. The languorous chaise longue encouraged an easy intimacy, not to mention lovemaking. Sofas were broad not to provide for many sitters, but to allow space for the grand gesture, the leg drawn up, the arm thrown out over the back, and for the capacious clothing of that time. The broad armchair allowed a variety of positions. Eighteenth-century society was characterized by animation and movement; paintings often show men and women sitting sideways or leaning across the chairback. While in the nineteenth century people would sit alone, or primly separated in stuffed chairs, in the eighteenth they often brought their light chairs together in easy intimacy and chatty conversation.

French chairs were identified by a variety of names. These were not technical labels (like the English "shield-back" or "ladder-back") but affectionate and charming names, which were always given the feminine gender. The "shepherdess" (bergère) was a small easy chair with a solid curved and padded back and a deep down cushion; the "looking chair" (voyeuse) was a chair with a padded rail across the tall back, which allowed a second person to lean on it from behind and watch a card game or take part in a conversation. The "vigil chair" (*veilleuse*) was a low divan for reclining. The "warming chair" (*chauffeuse*) was a small armless chair on short legs that could be drawn up to the fire while dressing; its low height made it easier to draw on one's stockings—whence its modern name, the slipper chair.

Furniture has always had a symbolic as well as a utilitarian function. Today, eighteenth-century Rococo furniture, especially if it is authentic, conveys the wealth, and hence power, of its owner. It carries many associations—with monarchy, with past gentility, and with the prestige of antique-collecting. At least that is what we are supposed to think of when we see it in Mrs. Lauder's office, or in the Yellow Oval Room of the Reagan White House. Most of these associations are recent. The figurative decoration, which to us is only ornamental, generally referred to classical antiquity, whose literature was well known to the French, and much admired. They called a cheval glass, a full-length mirror suspended between upright supports, a *psyché*, after the nymph whose beauty attracted the attention of Cupid. A tripod, supporting a small table or a washbasin, was an *athénienne*.

Rococo furniture had other meanings. Different pieces were located in different rooms, indicating different degrees of formality, and hence different modes of behavior. Since decor was altered according to the seasons, furniture could even denote different times of year, just as for us a canvas deck chair signals the summer holidays, and a padded wing chair recalls winter fireside reading.

This short examination of French Rococo furniture underlines the complexity, and the richness, of the idea of comfort in the eighteenth century. It had a physical component—the sitter was relaxed—but there was more to it than that. A Louis XV armchair was comfortable, but it also had the *appearance* of ease. The latter was at least as important to its owner as the former. The bombé shape was useful, but it also complimented the curves of the chair frame, which itself reflected the voluptuous visual taste of the time. The fanciful floral needlework on the chair seat kept the sitter erect, but it also echoed the ormolu scrolls on the wall paneling. The charming idea of masculine and feminine furniture—previously unknown—underscored a social reality which was likewise evident in dress and manners. The chair was a decorative object that invited sitting, but gave as much pleasure to the eye as to the arse. The eighteenth century discovered physical comfort, there is no doubt of that, but convenience never dominated its thinking, as it sometimes seems to do our own. Perhaps that is why the word "commodity" is not the first that springs to mind when describing a Louis XV chair—elegance, delight, yes, certainly beauty, but not prosaic comfort. Yet comfortable is precisely what it was.

Chapter Five

Georg Friedrich Kersting, *Girl Embroidering* (c. 1814)

Ease

Period styles come and go, and sometimes come again. They enjoy a time of favor—fifty years or so is typical—then become "old-fashioned," and eventually slip back into obscurity, or into history books, which, at least as far as the public is concerned, is much the same thing. Occasionally, they reemerge for an Indian summer of acclaim. Of course, until the eighteenth century it is not strictly accurate to speak of "period styles" at all. Even though architects since the Renaissance had looked to the past for inspiration, it would not have occurred to them to imitate it. Although classically inspired decoration reflected an appreciation of Greek and Roman culture, there was no historical precedent for the Baroque, and still less for Rococo interiors.

Rococo was out of fashion by 1770, replaced by the Classical Revival, the first conscious attempt to recreate whole the style of the past, in this case that of ancient Rome. The nineteenth century went on to resuscitate many old styles; most, like Elizabethan and Egyptian, did little to advance domestic comfort. Neo-Gothic was adequate for parliament buildings, but it produced interiors with a funereal, churchlike atmosphere. Moorish and Chinese rooms were exotic but wearying; William Morris's tendentious medievalism was too fussy. They all sank in the confusion of the Victorian style wars.

101

Although wholesale historical revivalism burned itself out by the beginning of the twentieth century, we continue to be fascinated by the idea of recreating the past. The "Louis styles," which made a comeback in the 1860s, resurfaced again in the early 1900s, thanks largely to the influence of Elsie de Wolfe, America's first woman interior decorator. De Wolfe was eclectic in her taste (although she despised Victorian plush and bric-a-brac), and when she refurbished her Villa Trianon at Versailles, it was in an amalgam of Louis XV and XVI. The antique furniture was all authentic, but it included other period pieces (Art Deco, for example), and it was combined with large comfortable cushioned sofas of no particular style. The overall effect was vaguely historical, but not pedantic. De Wolfe's intention was to adapt history to contemporary life, not vice versa.

The current interest in architectural history also stops short of being a revival. Much so-called postmodern architecture incorporates Classical elements—moldings, pediments and arches—but rarely does so in a historically accurate way. The Chippendale top of the American Telephone and Telegraph Building in New York, for example, is a sly allusion to history, but certainly not an attempt to recreate it. The Neue Staatsgalerie in Stuttgart is covered in marble like its neo-Classical neighbors, but the exterior handrails are enormous shocking-pink sausages made out of fiberglass. The effect is histrionic rather than historical. The idea is to play with history, but to do so in such a way that the building will never be mistaken for anything but what it is—a contemporary design.

The impulse to rehabilitate old buildings rather than to build new ones reflects the same sort of insecurity in contemporary ideas that produced the nineteenth-century revivals. But preserving the past is not quite the same thing as recreating it. If actor George Hamilton, a southerner, buys a plantation mansion in Mississippi, it is natural that, with the aid of Hollywood set designers, he should restore it to its antebellum splendor.[1] Such full-blown restoration is expensive, but even a more modest renovation—of a nineteenth-century townhouse, for example—will often be furnished in a more or less traditional way, to complement the architectural character of the rooms. When a house contains a collection of antique furniture it is also reasonable to create an appropriate setting, as in the case of Mrs. Lauder's Louis XVI office. The fact that the room is located in a conventional high-rise office building is of little consequence. Such settings are rarely meant to be historically accurate; they are intended primarily to create an appropriate mood, and they freely mix objects from different periods.

We are becoming used to seeing historical allusions in modern buildings, and we expect historical houses to be furnished in period styles. The practice of decorating a room in a home or in an office in a particular historical style is more likely to bring a reaction of respect than of surprise. But the historically accurate reconstruction of an *entire* house, both inside and out—and not meant as a museum exhibit but for daily living—is less common. Such a house has recently been designed by David Anthony Easton for a family in Illinois.[2] Although it is made of modern materials (sometimes doctored to give an appearance of age, or at least to reduce their newness), and it accommodates air conditioning, central heating, and electricity, its appearance, plan, and room arrangement are those of two hundred years ago. The details are also historically correct—everything from the door handles to the crown moldings. The furniture consists solely of either authentic antiques or reproductions of eighteenth-century period designs. It is neither a copy of a specific house nor a modern "version" of a historical style. Nor is it an interpretation of the past. Rather, it is the work of an architect from the eighteenth century who, somehow, has found himself in the American Midwest in the twentieth. It is, as much as such a thing is possible, the real thing.

The style of the house is Georgian, a period roughly corresponding to the reigns of Georges I–IV (1714–1830). Is Easton's handsome replica the harbinger of yet another revival? It would be incorrect to speak of "reviving" the Georgian style, however, for it has never really gone out of fashion. Except for a brief hiatus, when public taste favored a more opulent and densely decorated interior, houses have continued to be built in the Georgian style, at least in the English-speaking world, without a break for the last hundred years. The author of a book on recent English "country houses," that is, palatial homes built on large country estates, has compiled a gazetteer that lists all such houses built since the 1950s.[3] As one would expect, the houses, although conceived in the grand manner, are slightly smaller than those built in the eighteenth century, and the patrons are not only dukes and earls but include a real-estate promoter and a race-car driver. Nevertheless there are more than two hundred of them. That statistic in itself is unexpected, but what is more surprising is that all but a handful of the houses have one thing in common: they are neo-Georgian.

The continued attractiveness of the Georgian interior is no accident of fashion. It typified a period that combined domesticity, elegance, and comfort more successfully than ever before, or, many have argued, since. The idea of comfort did not enter the European consciousness fully formed; it developed over a long period of time, and although it made great progress in Rococo France its evolution did not end there. From about the middle of the eighteenth century, or slightly earlier, it came increasingly under the influence of Georgian England. Here, thanks to a happy confluence of economic and social conditions and national character, it flowered.

French social life was focused on Versailles and adjacent Paris. In France, the court, and court personages like the Pompadour, played a major role in introducing new fashions such as light, movable furniture. Some of these fashions may have been based on bourgeois notions of intimacy and informality, but they were always filtered through court society. It was above all an urban society. The aristocrats owned estates on which they built beautiful châteaux, but a French château, splendid as it was, was not a permanent place to live—it was more like a weekend cottage, albeit on a grand scale. The only French nobility who lived in the country were those who were in disgrace or could not afford to live in Paris.

England was different. For one thing, the Court of St. James's had little influence over society's behavior. The Hanoverian George II (who could at least speak English, unlike his father, George I, who spoke only German) was an unimaginative monarch who never acquired the prestige of Louis XV. Although he did manage to entice Handel to London from Hanover, his court, unlike Versailles, was a lackluster place. The English aristocracy, moreover, were much more powerful, and independent, than their French counterparts. They were landed gentry whose wealth, and whose pride, were their rural properties. There was, then, no equivalent in England to the French courtly style; instead the countryside was held in high regard, and it was not considered provincial to live there. Out of this state of affairs emerged a singular phenomenon, the English country house, which supplemented, if it did not replace, the city as the locus for social life. This prompted the American ambassador to remark: "Scarcely any persons who hold a leading place in the circles of their society live in London. They have *houses* in London, in which they stay while Parliament sits, and occasionally visit at other seasons; but their *homes* are in the country."[4] This preference for the country home had architectural repercussions. The plan and arrangement of the English townhouse, which was usually part of a row (unlike the Parisian *hôtel*, which was freestanding), had been standardized before the end of the seventeenth century, and it changed little for the next 150 years. Country houses, on the other hand, exhibited much variety, and it was to their planning and design that owners and their architects gave the most attention.

The preference for country homes had an enormous effect on English society in general, but especially on the bourgeoisie, which, as in France, imitated the upper class. This resulted in a style of living that was much more relaxed than its French counterpart, and that eventually produced a different domestic ideal. The first appearance of comfort in France had been in an aristocratic setting, and to that extent it was always constrained by its surroundings. If it is true that Rococo furniture introduced informality to the palace, it nevertheless never shed its courtly origins; even today, a room full of Louis XV furniture cannot, for better or worse, avoid looking regal. But when the idea of comfort was transplanted to England it assumed a different demeanor. It is revealing that after the seventeenth century, the English less and less referred to their homes, however grand, as anything but "houses"—there was no special word such as "château," "palazzo," or even "villa" to distinguish the large from the small, the grand from the merely mundane. To the English they were all houses.

This domestication of comfort was facilitated by the structure of English society, in which wealth was slightly more equally distributed than in France. The difference between the nobility and the wealthy middle class was less strictly observed; a "gentleman" could belong to either group; the important thing was how he behaved. While this did not quite make for a situation akin to that of the seventeenth-century Dutch republic, it was one in which bourgeois practicality exerted a major influence on domestic comfort.

The prosperity of Georgian England allowed a great deal more leisure than before, and the English bourgeois, unlike the Dutch, took advantage of the opportunity. How did they use this free time? The British eighteenth century was almost

completely uninterested in strenuous athletics. Except for riding and cricket, physical sports were rare. Sometimes, in the
winter, young people went skating, a pastime that had been
introduced from Holland in the previous century. The benefits
of "sea air" were starting to be appreciated, but people went
to the beach to walk, not to bathe, and swimming did not
become popular in England until the late 1800s. Indeed, none
of the traditional bourgeois sports appeared until the nineteenth century. Croquet came to England from France in the
1850s, at about the same time as golf and bowling were
introduced from Scotland; lawn tennis began to be played,
at Wimbledon, around 1874. Even the bicycle, which did so
much to transform the leisure of the middle class—especially
of women—did not achieve commercial success until the 1880s.

Consequently, the sedentary eighteenth-century English
bourgeois spent most of their time at home. Those who lived
in the country—without the theaters, concerts, and balls of
the city—visited each other. It was the age of conversation—
and of gossip. The novel became popular. So did indoor
games; men played billiards, women embroidered, and together they played cards. They organized dances, dinner par-
ties, and amateur theatricals. They turned *tee* from a Dutch
word (and a foreign beverage; it was also known as China
drink), into a national ritual. They went on placid walks and
admired one of their great accomplishments, the English garden. Since all these activities took place in and around the
house, the result was that the home acquired a position of
social importance that it had never had before, or since. No
longer a place of work as it had been in the Middle Ages, the
home became a place of leisure.

The home was a social place, but it was so in a curiously
private way. This was no medieval "big house" where people
came and went with easy familiarity. Quite the opposite, the
English bourgeois house was an isolated world into which
only the well-screened visitor was permitted; the world was

kept at bay, and the privacy of the family, and of the individual, was disturbed as little as possible. There were "at home days" and "morning calls" (which were in the afternoon). Domestic etiquette was based, above all, on reticence; next-door neighbors exchanged notes—which were delivered by a servant—in order to avoid an unannounced visit. It was impolite to drop in uninvited, even on your close friends. If a visit was planned, it was necessary to leave one's "visiting card" and await a reply.

An invitation having been received and properly accepted, the first room which greeted a visitor to the house was the hall. Although aristocratic homes were often organized around a medieval-style centrally located hall, the hall in a middle-class house was a room adjacent to the entrance, located so that doors led from it to the main common rooms.* Since it contained the main staircase, it was a large room, and, in keeping with its medieval ancestry, one that often contained coats of arms and suits of armor. Although it was no longer the main gathering room, it did serve an important function as a setting for the ceremonial arrival and departure of guests on formal occasions. Here visitors waited, under the frosty gaze of a family retainer, to gain admittance to the house. This was the room where carolers were invited in to sing at Christmas, and where the servants gathered to be addressed by the master on important occasions.

The lower floors contained most of the rooms devoted to common activities. The French tradition of locating public rooms on the first floor was continued in some houses, but more often the main rooms were situated at ground level, which gave direct access to the garden. The most spacious of

---

* With time, the once-grand hall became little more than a large vestibule. In modern homes, although the medieval term remains, the space it refers to—the hallway—has been reduced to a utilitarian corridor.

these common rooms was the drawing room; wealthy families often had two—one for special occasions, and one for daily use. The drawing room usually contained a musical instrument—a pianoforte, an organ, or a harp—and was large enough to be used for musical events, especially dances. It was in this room, also, that folding tables were set up for a favorite pastime of that period—card games. To accommodate these various activities, drawing rooms became larger and larger, to the point where they sometimes occupied the entire floor.

The arrangement of public rooms in the Georgian house represented an intermediate stage in the evolution of house planning. The simplified modern combination of living-dining or living-dining-family room was to come. Instead, having abandoned the medieval hall, the eighteenth century created a variety of common rooms. There was no fixed rule concerning exactly how many and what kind were needed; this depended on the imagination of the architect and the wealth of the owner. The minimum requirement was for at least one public reception room and a formal dining room; the French habit of eating in antechambers was never adopted by the English. The dining room was used only in the evenings and smaller rooms—called breakfast rooms—for the other meals. There were, in addition, any number of other common rooms, and a good-sized house might also contain a library, a study, a gallery, a billiard room, and a conservatory.

The large number and variety of public rooms in the Georgian house are sometimes explained on functional grounds, but the names of these rooms do not necessarily give a precise description of their actual, or intended, use. The gallery, which was originally a long room for displaying paintings, might be used as a drawing room; the library, which did always contain books, might also be the main family room. The breakfast room was also used for informal visits. There was a certain amount of experimentation in all this, which is reflected in the imprecision of room names. The public reception room was sometimes called a parlor or a front room. A smaller room for more intimate conversations might be called a sitting room. People who followed the French fashion had antechambers, which were small spaces located between larger rooms, and they called their drawing rooms salons, or saloons. Although the term "living room" did not come into common use until the nineteenth century, the provision of two drawing rooms, or the use of the library as what we would call a family room, reflected a need to have a place in the house which was more relaxed, where behavior could be less formal, and where social conventions could be set aside or at least loosened. This idea of providing two types of common rooms, one less formal than the other, was absent in French planning and was probably inherited from the Dutch.

The house was not only subdivided into common rooms for dining, entertaining, and leisure, but also included private rooms for the members of the family. Now that children were spending most of their time in the home, they had not only their own bedrooms—separated according to gender—but also accompanying nurseries and schoolrooms. The multiplication of bedrooms indicated not only new sleeping arrangements, but a novel distinction between the family and the individual. Activities in the home were separated vertically; public below, private above. "Going upstairs" or "coming downstairs" meant not just changing floors but leaving, or joining, the company of others. Everyone had his own bedroom. These bedrooms were not simply rooms for sleeping, however; children used their rooms for play, wives and daughters used their bedrooms for quiet work (sewing or writing) or for intimate *tête-à-têtes* with friends. The desire for a room of one's own was not simply a matter of personal privacy. It demonstrated the growing awareness of individuality—of a growing personal inner life—and the need to express this individuality in physical ways.

Much had changed since the seventeenth century. The room in which de Witte portrayed a woman playing the virginals had no clearly defined function—was it a bedroom containing a musical instrument, or a music room containing a bed? Nor did the room have a clearly indicated owner; the woman was in *a* room, but we do not feel that it was especially *her* room. On the other hand, when we look at Georg Friedrich Kersting's painting of a girl embroidering—painted 140 years later— we know immediately that the room is hers. Those are her plants on the windowsill; it is her guitar and sheet music on the settee; it is she who has hung the picture of the young man on the wall and draped it with flowers. The sense of intimacy evident in this scene was not improvised; it was not, as in Vermeer's paintings, something that was the result of a passing moment. This was a room consciously arranged as a personal retreat and a quiet place of seclusion.

Fanny Price, the heroine of Jane Austen's novel *Mansfield Park* (written the year before Kersting painted this picture), had a room where she could go "after anything unpleasant below, and find immediate consolation in some pursuit, or some train of thought at hand. Her plants, her books—of which she had been a collector from the first hour of her commanding a shilling—her writing desk, and her works of charity and ingenuity, were all within her reach; or if indisposed for employment, if nothing but musing would do, she could scarcely see an object in that room which had not an interesting remembrance connected with it." Like the settee and chair in Kersting's painting, the furniture in Fanny's room was simple and worn. There were mementoes (a drawing of a ship by her absent sailor brother) instead of finery. Like Kersting's subject—the painter Louise Siedler—Fanny had flowers on the windowsill and embroidery paraphernalia.

Kersting was a German, Austen an Englishwoman, but their descriptions of these rooms exhibit the same sense of intimacy and character.

Jane Austen was born in 1775, eleven years after Madame de Pompadour's death. In two brief creative bursts, the first during her early twenties and the second just before her death at forty-one, she wrote six brilliant novels. Her life was unremarkable; the spinster daughter of a country clergyman, she lived with her sister and their widowed mother in Hampshire. She did not, as far as is known, have any great romances; her life was circumscribed by her letter writing, her sewing, and her domestic duties. She was not a traveler and never visited the Continent, indeed, she rarely left the rural county of southern England where she was born. She had some acquaintance with town life; although she visited London rarely, she knew Bath, then considered to be the most beautiful city in England. None of this was an impediment to her being a novelist, however, for her subjects were neither wealthy aristocrats nor swashbuckling adventurers, and she did not write historical potboilers like Walter Scott, or dark urban dramas like Balzac. What she did write about was a world that she knew well, which she observed with precocious irony and not a little humor—the homelife of the English provincial middle class.

An Austen novel is a *tour de force*, at least by modern standards. Nothing extraordinary happens—no murders, escapades, or disasters. Instead of adventure or melodrama we read about the prosaic daily comedy of family life. There is little complexity to the plots (compared to Dickens, say), and the suspense, such as it is, arises chiefly out of questions of love and marriage. Jane Austen single-handedly invented, and brought to perfection, what could be called the domestic genre of novel-writing, the literary equivalent to the seventeenth-century Dutch school of interior painting. Her books are, of course, much more than a faithful representation of the period, just as Vermeer's paintings were more than illustrations of young Dutch women at home. Like Vermeer, de Witte, and the other Dutch domestic painters, Austen chose to stay strictly within the limits of the everyday, not because her talent was small, but because her imagination did not require a broader canvas.

On the whole, Jane Austen did not devote much space to describing the appearance of the homes in which her novels were set. Hers were stories that focused primarily on character and behavior, and she probably took the appearance of her characters' surroundings for granted anyway. Obvious though those interiors may have seemed to her, however, the arrangement of the late-eighteenth-century English home had taken a course which, in the context of continental Europe, was uncommon. This was partly the result of temperament, and partly a matter of historical tradition.

The prosperous Dutch were a dominant influence throughout Europe, and especially in England, where they had affected public taste during most of the seventeenth century. It was to be expected that the two small, northern, coastal countries, sharing a maritime tradition and a Protestant belief, would establish strong trade and cultural links. Not only were tea-drinking and ice-skating imported, but also Dutch building techniques, such as the use of unadorned brick construction and the sash window. Perhaps more important, a general appreciation of the unglamorous practicality of Dutch domestic architecture and of its small scale and intimacy made its way across the North Sea. The result was that although English public buildings tended toward the Parisian, domestic architecture tended toward the Dutch.[5] The small brick English country house, with its unpretentious charm, was in many ways a rural version of the Dutch row house.

There were other influences on the design of English houses.

While most of Europe followed the French lead and adopted the Rococo style of decoration, the English pursued a different course. Uneasy with what they considered, and still consider, to be a frivolous style, they adopted instead a more sedate architectural vocabulary based primarily on the work of the great sixteenth-century Venetian architect Andrea Palladio, whose influential book *I quattro libri di architettura*, had been published in England by Inigo Jones as early as 1620. Not only did the classical serenity of Palladio's late-Renaissance designs appeal to the English gentry, but since Palladio had specialized in country villas, it was especially easy to adapt his ideas to the country house. At first, Palladianism affected only the planning of houses, but after 1700 it developed into a uniquely English architectural style and exercised considerable influence on English taste throughout the eighteenth century, even after the formality of these interiors was replaced by more casual arrangements.

Georgian furniture reflected this Palladian tradition; it has often been called "architectural," and was more simply structural than decorative. It was more rectangular than curved. Although "French" or "cabriole" chairs with arms and padded backs were popular, the typical English chair lacked arms and usually had a wooden, not an upholstered, back. Its splats were decoratively shaped and produced many different models: bended-back, ladder-back, and shield-back. To preserve the squareness of their designs, English cabinetmakers developed various techniques for stitching and securing the stuffing in the seat so that it would stay flat and not take on the puffed-out look of French upholstery.[6] This also tended to produce a more comfortable chair. Because they used less padding, English cabinetmakers had to pay close attention to the dimensioning of the chair, and cabinetmakers such as Thomas Chippendale and George Hepplewhite included exact sizes of chair heights, widths, and depths in their pattern books. These pattern books, which included illustrations of every sort of domestic furniture, from chairs to door handles and picture frames, were the precursor of the modern do-it-yourself manuals and were extremely popular. With their aid, a skilled craftsman was able to reproduce the latest ideas of the most fashionable cabinetmakers. This not only helped to demystify furniture design, but also promoted, and accelerated, the spread of furniture "in the English taste," as it was coming to be known.

A German magazine instructed its readers, in 1786, that "English furniture is almost without exception solid and practical; French furniture is less solid, more contrived and more ostentatious."[7] English cabinetmakers used mahogany, an extremely hard wood, imported to Europe from Santo Domingo and the Bahamas. This material, which could be worked only with high-quality steel tools, produced chairs and tables that combined strength with extreme lightness and delicacy. The use of mahogany also affected the appearance of English furniture, for although it lent itself to carving, its darkly lustrous, grained surface required less decoration—it was best varnished, rather than gilded or painted, as was the French custom.

One design not found in the gentlemen's pattern books was the Windsor chair, which had been developed in the late seventeenth century by rural craftsmen, not by urban cabinetmakers. Like the rocking chair in America, this rustic design evolved and achieved a rare refinement. Along the way it made the transition from country to town, and could be found alongside classically inspired chairs. The Windsor chair was an unpadded all-wood chair, usually of beech, which is a light but strong wood, and ideal for making its delicately curving backs and arms supported by slender sticks. The solid seat was carved to support the sitter and to prevent him from sliding forward. Inexpensive and practical, well proportioned and gracious, it was the epitome of English comfort and common sense.*

The Dutch had introduced oriental carpets to Europe, but they either hung them on the wall or draped them over tables; their patterned stone floors were usually left bare. French homes and palaces had beautiful floors of wood parquetry in elaborate designs, and were also left uncovered. It was the English who popularized the use of carpets as floor coverings, which of course was the way that they were used by their oriental makers. Large carpets were placed in dining rooms and drawing rooms. They were located beneath tables and chairs, which eventually led to a new idea: fitted carpets that covered the entire floor. The less wealthy used "floor-cloths"—canvas painted to resemble carpeting. In both cases, color was concentrated on the floor instead of on the walls, which were less decorated; English wallpapers were often plain. Thermally, the benefits of a carpeted floor would have been considerable, especially as heating was still primitive. Carpeted rooms were also quieter.

There was another crucial difference between English and French interiors. When Chippendale published his guide to furniture design he named it *The Gentleman and Cabinet-Maker's Director*, and in the introduction to his pattern book Hepplewhite hoped that his book of designs would be "useful to the mechanic, and serviceable to the gentleman." Both cabinetmakers took it for granted that women would have little interest in furniture. This indeed was the case; it was not until later that women in English-speaking countries began to participate in interior decoration. Until then it was considered to be a man's business. It is difficult to say how much

---

* Although replicas of many eighteenth-century chairs continue to be manufactured today, their hand-carved shapes are difficult to reproduce by machine. The Windsor chair, on the other hand, with its standardized, lathe-turned spindles, has survived industrialization intact and continues to be made, and used, in England and America.

this influenced the character of Georgian houses. Was it simply a case of "masculine" Georgian versus "feminine" Rococo?[8] The interiors of Robert Adam were just as delicate in their way as any Rococo room, as were English garden structures. Nevertheless, a British historian has described English furniture as "masculine and functional, designed for its usefulness rather than for a luxurious indolence," contrasting it with what he considers to be female-inspired French furniture.[9] This sounds like chauvinism, both national and male. So also does another claim that the arrangement of the house "was a subject beyond the mental capacity of a woman," and the suggestion that good taste was a masculine preserve.[10] It is true that English decor was usually plainer than French, but this was much more likely the result of a certain kind of bourgeois practicality which the English shared with the Dutch, and of the inherited Palladian tradition, than of gender differences.

In any case, by the last quarter of the eighteenth century, the gentlemen's influence over the arrangement of the Georgian house was being eroded. This is particularly evident in the development of the drawing room. During the seventeenth century it had been customary for the women to go to a "withdrawing room" after dinner while the men stayed in the dining room to drink brandy, smoke cigars, and indulge in boisterous conversation. Although the post-dinner separation continued over the century, the now-renamed drawing room became a larger, more important space, usually located next to the dining room, although sometimes separated from it, for acoustical reasons, by an antechamber. The decor of the two rooms acquired two specifically different characters, the dining room being more masculine, the drawing room less so.[11] It was then in response to the growing influence of women that, as Peter Thornton has observed, important changes to comfort first made their appearance in the drawing room, the one public room that was under women's direct control.[12]

Furniture, now more comfortable, began to invade, and gradually to displace, the purely architectural character of the drawing room. Tables and chairs were permanently located within the center of the room, no longer against the wall. Sofas were pulled away from the sides of the rooms—a landmark moment in the evolution of domestic comfort—and placed at right angles to the walls. Eventually low tables—the first coffee tables—were arranged in front of the sofas. This typical furniture grouping, which also included several easy chairs, was usually set in front of the fireplace to create a cozy corner. By the end of the century, as manners became even less formal, many of these changes began to appear in other rooms, especially in the library, which had originally been a male preserve but was now the favorite room for family get-togethers. Cut flowers and potted plants became a part of the decor. The casual arrangement of the rooms was accompanied by a growing informality in dress. The short coat and leather boots worn for riding began to replace the long frock coats previously worn by gentlemen. Beau Brummell popularized the monochrome, three-piece suit. Wigs were abandoned; women's hairstyles became less contrived and more natural. Ease and relaxation characterized life in the Georgian house.

Many of these changes were due to the English enthusiasm for nature—and naturalness—which produced the first original English contribution to European culture: the Romantic Movement. An interest in the irregular and the picturesque began to dominate the design of houses, and, of course, of gardens. The strict geometry of the neo-Palladian plan, in which each room on the left side of the house required an identical, corresponding room on the right, did not always accord to functional requirements, and never achieved the sophisticated subdivision of a Parisian *hôtel*. This rigidity was now replaced by less formal and more rambling layouts. This change in visual perception echoed a broader change in public taste; irregularity replaced symmetry just as the romanticism of Lord Byron replaced the dry wit of Samuel Pepys.

The interior of the house was also affected. No longer a compact mass, the house was developing long wings. These required corridors for movement and inevitably produced a greater measure of privacy for the individual rooms. At the same time the hall—no longer required to give access to the rooms—grew smaller. Since the arrangement of the rooms was no longer constrained by geometry, it became easier to combine rooms of different sizes and to dimension and proportion them according to need. Whereas previously the drawing room had been identical to the dining room, it now began to occupy a larger area. The freer planning made it easier to incorporate new types of rooms. Windows could be located and proportioned according to the function of the room, instead of according to the requirements of façade composition. As a result, the room, which up until the Rococo period had been considered as an artifact, if not as a work of art, began to be seen as a locus for human activity; it was no longer only a beautiful *space*, but was becoming a *place*.

"The English taste" in domestic furnishings would be worthy of note in any case, but it is important because it was not confined to its native country. Just as the French idea of the home led European thought during the Rococo period, the English interior came to be much admired throughout the Continent. Of course, part of its success was the result of the Napoleonic Wars—from the beginning of the nineteenth century, it was England, and no longer France, that dominated European politics. The spread of English ideas was also facilitated by the ascendancy of England as a trading nation, especially in America. The American middle class, which was, if anything, growing more quickly than in England, responded to the practical comfort of Georgian furniture. Thanks to the cabinetmakers' guides, which were widely read, "American Chippendale" became extremely popular, and lasted longer than the style did in England. American furniture, although locally made, was indistinguishable from Georgian, and American craftsmen such as Benjamin Randolph became famous in their own right. More important than the adoption of a specific style, however, was the assimilation of a way of thinking about the home, which was to have a decisive influence on future American developments.

There is something extremely appealing about the Georgian interior. It reflected a sensibility which, as Praz put it, reconciled bourgeois practicality with fantasy, and common sense with refinement.[13] This is the judgment of posterity, but it was also the stated intention of the English themselves. "To unite elegance and utility, and blend the useful with the agreeable, has ever been considered a difficult, but an honourable task," begins the preface to Hepplewhite's pattern book.[14] "Elegant and useful" was how Thomas Chippendale characterized his furniture. It is this potent combination, perhaps, that accounts for the continued attraction of the Georgian interior: the idea that comfort should include not only visual delight and physical well-being, but also usefulness. This was the French idea of commodity carried one step further; the down-to-earth notion of comfort was no longer a simple idea, it had become an ideal.

It is surprising how often one comes across the words "comfort" and "comfortable" in Jane Austen's novels. She used them in the old sense of support or assistance, but more frequently she intended them to convey a new kind of experience—the sense of contentment brought about by the enjoyment of one's physical surroundings. She described Fanny's room as a "nest of comforts." There were not only comfortable rooms and comfortable carriages, but comfortable meals, comfortable views, and comfortable situations. It was as if she couldn't get enough of it—this new, undramatic word which was so well-suited to the bourgeois coziness of the world she described.* In one of her last novels, *Emma*, she used the expression "English comfort" and did not elaborate on this curious phrase, which makes one think its meaning must have been evident to her readers. She used it to describe not a house, but a country view: a short avenue of limes leading to the end of the garden and a stone wall; beyond the stone wall a steep slope of meadows and some farm buildings, enclosed by the bend of a river. "It was a sweet view—sweet to the eye and the mind. English verdure, English culture, English comfort, seen under a bright sun, without being oppressive." Comfort was meant to be undramatic and calming. It was to appear "natural" but, like the English garden, or the English home, it was carefully contrived.

---

* "Comfort" is a word of Old French origin (*confort*), but it acquired its modern, domestic meaning in England. From there, at the end of the eighteenth century, it was imported back to France.[15]

Chapter Six

GLEDHOW HALL. LEEDS.
J. Kitson Jun.r Esq.r
BATH-ROOM in BURMANTOFT FAIENCE.
Mess.rs Chorley and Connon.
Architects.

Victorian Bathroom (c. 1885)

Light and Air

We have now to consider all the arrangements of a house whose working depends on motive power of any kind—such as heating and flues, ventilation, lighting, hot and cold water supply, drains, bells, speaking-tubes and lifts. On the proper arrangement of these things, the comfort of a house in a great measure depends.

—JOHN J. STEVENSON
HOUSE ARCHITECTURE

What a change has taken place between the modest workplace depicted by Albrecht Dürer and the eighteenth-century gentleman's study! The bare ceiling, stone walls, and planked floor have been replaced by delicate plasterwork, wallpaper, and a fitted carpet. Instead of small, blurred panes the windows contain large pieces of clear glass, and their frames slide conveniently up and down for ventilation. There is much more furniture, and a larger variety of it: special chairs for writing at the desk, easy chairs with padded arms for reading, a sofa for conversation, low convenient tables. What is more, this is furniture designed for relaxing in, quite unlike the hard back-stools and plain benches of two centuries before. Even the table for writing is made especially for that purpose. No longer improvised out of planks laid on a de-mountable trestle, the desk is a delicately carved mahogany 123 box with a curved front that slides smoothly back to reveal useful-looking drawers and pigeonholes. Upright commodes with drawers have replaced chests; books are kept in tall cupboards with glazed doors. The overall effect, seen through Dürer's eyes, is one of an increased density of objects and decoration and also a pronounced softening effect, due not only to the upholstered furniture, but also to the patterned paper that covers the walls, the heavy cloth that is draped over the library table, the curtains drawn apart on each side of the window, and the soft carpeting on the floor.

The end of the eighteenth century marks a point roughly halfway between Dürer's time, where we began, and the present day. Histories of furniture tend to focus our attention on the evolution of design and ignore the more fundamental issue of ownership. The achievement of the eighteenth century was not just the production of comfortable and elegant furnishings, but their availability to a broad clientele. This fact would have impressed Dürer the most; this level of comfort was present not in a royal palace, but in the home of a moderately well-off family. That a private individual might personally own dozens, if not hundreds, of books would have astounded Dürer, as would the idea of devoting a special room in the home exclusively to writing and reading.

Yet from *our* vantage point, a surprising number of things had not changed at all. The Georgian study was still heated—and not very effectively—by an open fireplace, or, if it was on the Continent, by a porcelain stove not much different from what Dürer had been accustomed to. The writing desk was elegant, no doubt, but people still wrote with a quill pen dipped in ink. At night, they read uncomfortably by candle-light, just as Dürer had done two hundred years before. If a letter writer wished to wash his ink-stained hands, he was obliged to call a servant for a bowl of water—there were no sinks or plumbing. Nor were there bathrooms—a small cupboard in the corner contained a chamber pot.

The truth was that although people in the eighteenth century frequently referred to "utility" and "convenience" in speaking about their homes these terms had as much to do with good taste and fashion, as with functional efficiency. That is they could speak of a "comfortable view" as easily as of a "comfortable chair." Comfort was a generalized feeling of well-being, not something that could be studied or quantified. So ingrained was this attitude that fifty years after Jane Austen's death the idea of "English comfort" still held sway. "What we would call in England a comfortable house is a thing so intimately identified with English customs as to make us apt to say that in no other country but our own is this element of comfort fully understood."[1] Americans would have hardly been expected to agree with this claim, but until at least the 1850s comfort was seen by most people as something first of all cultural (and arguably English), and only secondarily something physical.

Furniture design, which did go to some considerable pains to achieve physical comfort, was an exception. This was because of the special circumstances under which the eighteenth-century cabinetmakers worked. The mystique that has grown up around eighteenth-century furniture and the men who produced it has made us forget that the craftsmen who designed and built comfortable chairs and ingenious writing desks were not only artists but businessmen. Although Thomas Sheraton was a draftsman who hired others to manufacture his designs, most cabinetmakers, like Hepplewhite, owned their own factories; Chippendale not only ran a factory but also had his own shop. They not only made pieces to order, but developed standard designs for serial production; in that sense the cabinetmakers' books were not scholarly works, or even, really, pattern books—they were intended as catalogs for prospective customers. Because their furniture was produced for a large market and because it was a competitive field—there were over two hundred cabinetmakers in London alone—furniture makers were pressed to innovate. This innovation was all the more effective because it was not the result of individual effort. Chippendale's pattern book contained 160 plates, Hepplewhite's over 300. It would have been impossible to produce such a quantity of work without the collaboration of many assistants, and it is generally agreed that most of the designs that are attributed to the famous cabinetmakers were the work of their employees. This was especially true of Hepplewhite, who died two years before "his" book was published, and whose factory ran on for many years after his death, as did Chippendale's business after his.

The forces that encouraged innovation in furniture design were absent in house construction. The eighteenth-century home incorporated no major innovations in domestic technology. It has been suggested that as long as large numbers of servants were available to light the candles, tend to the fireplaces, heat up and carry water, and empty the chamber pots, there was not much incentive to improve lighting, heating, water supply, and sanitation.[2] If this were the only reason, however, one would expect the number of servants to have decreased immediately before any technological improvements took place, and there is no evidence that this was the case. Moreover, not all domestic improvements were concerned with saving labor, some, like better heating and ventilation, or brighter illumination, were qualitative meliorations that had nothing to do with servants. The reasons for their slow appearance must be sought elsewhere.

Architecture was not practiced as a business but was considered an art, and it was carried out by gentlemen, not by journeymen, and more often than not by skilled but untrained

amateurs—dilettantes.* Houses were built one at a time, and
since the architect was not a contractor, he was not in a
position to introduce substantive innovation to the building
process. Unlike the cabinetmaker, who controlled all aspects
of production, from manufacturing to marketing, the architect was primarily a draftsman who prepared drawings for
work carried out by others. As a result he developed theo-
retical knowledge that was based not on construction, but
on a study of history and historical precedents. In any case,
architects were then, as they are now, interested more in the
appearance of buildings than in their functioning. They were
not prepared, by either training or inclination, to involve
themselves in such mechanical matters as plumbing and heating. They also paid more attention to the exterior rather than
to the interior.† Once the size and shape of the rooms were
determined, the detailed arrangement of the interior was usually left up to the owner. Faced with the bewildering array
of objects that were now required to furnish a room properly,
owners relied increasingly on outside help. This came to be
provided by the so-called upholsterer.

Originally, the upholsterer had been concerned solely with
textiles and upholstery coverings, but, being a tradesman and

---

* Architectural education was not formalized in England until 1850. This
was much later than in France, where the Académie Royale d'Architecture
had been founded by Louis XIV in 1671, and where Jacques-François
Blondel established the first school of architecture in the 1730s. The availability of formal education may account for the greater sophistication of
French house planning, which early incorporated such mechanical devices
as baths and toilets.

† Palladianism can be at least partly blamed for this. Palladio's books
contained no information about interiors, and his rooms are basically
abstract volumes, manipulated more for external effect than for internal
convenience. The French were much more conscious of the interior, both
its planning and decoration, although less so after the demise of the Rococo
style.

recognizing a business opportunity, he had enlarged his service to include coordination of all interior furnishings and set himself up, according to a 1747 British trade paper, "as a connoisseur in every article that belongs to a house. He employs journeymen in his own proper calling, cabinet-makers, glass grinders, looking-glass framers, carvers for chairs, Testers and Posts for Beds, the Woolen Draper, the mercer, the Linen draper and several species of smiths and a vast army of tradesmen of the other mechanic branches."[3] Neither an artist nor a craftsman, the upholsterer was a businessman who organized himself to respond to the houseowners' need for expert advice. By the time that architects realized that they had lost control of the interior arrangement of the house, it was too late. Upholsterers, or interior decorators as they were later called, came increasingly to dominate domestic comfort.

Domestic technology fell into the gap between the architect and the upholsterer. The upholsterer could determine how rooms looked, and even, to some extent, how they could be used, but his concern for convenience and comfort could not, and did not, extend to any of the mechanical systems that were part of the fabric of the house itself. The architect, on the other hand, who was in a position to introduce innovations to the arrangement of the house, still considered himself to be an artist, not a technician, and was content to follow conventional wisdom when it came to domestic conveniences. This division of labor retarded the introduction of technology into the home.

It was not until the end of the eighteenth century that domestic technology began to develop, although it was a slow and uncoordinated evolution. Joseph Bramah, a cabinetmaker with a mechanical bent, produced many inventions unrelated to furniture. The first, patented in 1778, was the Bramah Valve Closet, a toilet bowl that maintained a water seal to prevent cesspool smells from entering the room. Although this was not the first water closet—the honor for that invention belongs to Sir John Harington (1596)—it was the first to be commercialized. But it was only a modest success; it would take a long time for water closets to become popular—as long as forty years later they were still considered to be "newfangled."[4] Although Bramah claimed to have sold over six thousand valve closets in the first ten years, this was hardly enough to support a business, and he turned his attention elsewhere, going on to invent a startling number of other devices, including a bank-note machine that printed serial numbers, a suction apparatus for drawing beer, a hydraulic press, and improvements to paper-making machinery. During his lifetime, he was best known not for the valve closet but for the impregnable Bramah Lock, which remained unpicked for over fifty years.

The limited use of the water closet was not due to any ignorance about plumbing. Mark Girouard observes that "By 1730 . . . any country house could in theory have running water on all floors, and as many baths and water-closets as its owner wanted or could afford. But comparatively little use was made of this technology in the next fifty years."[5] A few country houses did have piped water—usually fed by a rainwater cistern under the roof—but this did not necessarily mean that bathrooms were provided. According to Girouard, it was the natural conservatism (and snobbery) of the wealthy that kept them from adopting new technologies such as plumbing. Even as late as the early 1900s, there were still English aristocrats who preferred to have their portable tubs brought to their bedrooms and placed in front of the fireplace, and to whom the practice of sharing a bathroom with others seemed crude and unacceptable.[6]

As for the bourgeoisie, the explanation for the lack of indoor plumbing is simpler: until the middle of the nineteenth century most people had no access to centrally supplied water; water had to be brought by hand from a well, or from a pump in the kitchen. Lacking pressurized water, and hence plumbing, homes could not be fitted with a bathroom, let alone with a "Bramah." For sanitation they relied on an older technology—the chamber pot. The 1794 edition of Hepplewhite's guide illustrated several "pot cupboards" as well as "night tables," the latter being a small cabinet which opened to reveal a seat with a built-in receptacle.[7] He also described a pedestal and vase which he suggested using in the dining room in pairs, one on each side of the sideboard.[8] The vases were fitted with spigots and contained iced water but the pedestals below were actually chamber-pot cupboards. After the ladies had withdrawn, it was opened and the vessel was brought out for the convenience of the gentlemen. This practice became so common that when water closets were first introduced, there was inevitably a toilet for the men's use adjacent to the dining room.

Another reason for the slow introduction of technology into the home was the lack of effective demand. Upholsterers were interested in fashion and architects in aesthetics, and their ideas of comfort and convenience were accordingly circumscribed by these preoccupations; as for the homeowner, he accepted their advice. This did not mean that technology stood still, however. The first large-scale installation of gaslight, in 1806, was in a cotton mill, and initially this form of lighting was used only in factories and public buildings. One of the earliest recorded attempts at artificial ventilation was a study of the British Houses of Parliament, done in 1811 by Sir Humphry Davy, a chemist, not an architect. Many of these environmental improvements were the work of enlightened entrepreneurs or of socially minded reformers, and, until the 1820s, one was more likely to encounter central heating in a poorhouse or in a prison than in a wealthy family's home.

Following this pattern, a major improvement to the fireplace and stove first occurred not in a home but in an almshouse kitchen, and typically it was the work of neither an

architect nor a builder. The American-born Count Rumford
(Sir Benjamin Thompson) was a soldier, a diplomat, a gar-
dener (he laid out Munich's famous Englischer Garten), and,
in the pattern of Franklin and Jefferson, a self-educated inventor. This peripatetic man of the world—the knighthood
was acquired after service to George III of England, the title
was from the Holy Roman Emperor—was also a scientist.
Among his many interests was the physics of heat, and because he was a practical man he devised improved methods
for cooking and heating. In Bavaria, where he spent eleven
years as, among other things, minister of war, he built several
military hospitals in which he incorporated cooking ovens
and stoves of his own design. He was, in the unspecialized
manner of his time, a social reformer and the inventor of the
soup kitchen, in which he also included indirectly heated
baking ovens.

During a visit to London, Rumford proposed a series of
changes to fireplaces to reduce their tendency to smoke. These
involved narrowing the throat of the chimney, making the
fireplace opening much smaller, and angling the side walls to
radiate more heat into the room. The result was not only less
smoke, but an improvement in heating. By this time—it was
1795—the public seems to have become more receptive to
innovative technology, and, since the modifications were neither complex nor expensive and could be carried out by homeowners themselves (without the assistance of architects or
upholsterers), improved fireplaces achieved some popularity.
(Jane Austen described a "Rumford" in *Northanger Abbey*,
which was written only three years after the Count presented
his ideas to the Royal Society.) Rumford's importance to the
history of technology is due largely to his pioneering attemps
to apply scientific reasoning to an aspect of home life. His
proposal did not completely solve the problem of smoking
fireplaces, however, as is suggested by the continued concern
for proper chimney design throughout the nineteenth century.

Out of the 169 British patents taken out between 1815 and 1852 relating to stoves and fireplaces, almost a third were designed to prevent or reduce smoking. In 1860, C. J. Richardson devoted one entire chapter of his book on house design to "Flue Construction and Smoke Prevention," and wrote that "it still remains to find such a construction as will remedy its serious defects."[9] He also produced a pamphlet entitled *The Smoke Nuisance and Its Remedy*. Even twenty years later books on house construction were suggesting various ways to reduce "the annoyance of a smoky chimney."[10]

No nineteenth-century book on house planning was complete unless it included at least one chapter on the subject of ventilation and "the evils of bad air." At first glance this seems to have been mainly a question of keeping the smog and smoke of industrialization out of the house. On closer examination it turns out to have been a more complicated issue, for the Victorians were not just concerned with ventilation, they were obsessed by the subject of fresh air.

To begin with, there is no doubt that these interiors with their smoky fireplaces, open cooking fires, and ill-washed inhabitants contained a great deal of what we would now call indoor pollution. We do not know whether houses were necessarily stuffier than they had been in the previous century (there is no reason to think they were) but there is plenty of evidence that people's sensitivity to smell was more highly developed in the Victorian period. They had a horror of cooking smells, for example, and so they located the kitchen as far as possible from the main parts of the house; there are large Victorian country houses in which the kitchen is more than 150 feet from the dining room! The smell of tobacco was similarly affronting. During the first part of the eighteenth century, people stopped smoking almost entirely, and when, later, cigars started to come back into fashion, they were still forbidden indoors. Queen Victoria banned smoking in her homes, and many followed her example. In some country houses visitors who insisted on smoking were archly directed to the kitchen, and then only after the servants had left.[11] When guests at Cragside, the Northumberland estate of Lord Armstrong, craved a cigar they had to go outside to smoke, not because their host was a nonsmoker—he often joined them—but because the smell of tobacco was considered offensive.[12] When smoking became more common, a special room—the smoking room—was added to contain this activity.

Ventilation involved more than getting rid of unpleasant odors, however. Characteristically, the nineteenth century had approached the problem of air in a scientific way. Since the eighteenth century, it was known that air consisted of oxygen, nitrogen, and carbon dioxide, or carbonic acid as it was called. Practical experience showed that a crowded room eventually became stuffy and unpleasant. Experimentation established that as people breathed air they produced carbon dioxide, and scientists reasoned that it was the increased level of carbon dioxide in a room which affected the comfort of its inhabitants. The solution, or so it seemed at the time, was simple: reduce carbon dioxide levels by evacuating the stale air and introducing fresh air in its place. We now know that this theory was wrong, although the philosophy wasn't. Human comfort is not simply a function of the carbon dioxide level. Temperature, water vapor content, air movement, ionization, dust, and odors are equal, if not more important, factors. If the air in a room is too hot or cold, or too humid or dry, or too still, and if it contains dust or smells, discomfort will occur long before unhealthy carbon dioxide levels are reached.

The complexity of the factors influencing atmospheric comfort did not become apparent until the early 1900s; before then ventilation was seen only in terms of diluting carbon dioxide. For that reason its effect was exaggerated. We consider that the carbon dioxide level in a room may safely be about two and a half times as high as it is outdoors. Throughout the nineteenth century it was firmly believed that the carbon dioxide level in a room should not exceed *one and a half* times that found outdoors. Partly because of this excessive requirement, partly because scientists and engineers underestimated the amount of air that entered a house through cracks, leaky windows, and open doors, and partly because cooking, heating, and lighting did produce smoke and odors, the engineers and scientists concluded that extremely large amounts of fresh air should be introduced into the home. In a book on "healthy dwellings" that was first published in 1880, Douglas Galton, a British engineer, recommended that fifty cubic feet of fresh air per minute per person was needed to properly ventilate a room.[13] W. H. Corfield, an English physician, cited the same figure.[14] Dr. John S. Billings, an army doctor, mentions sixty cubic feet per minute per occupant in a contemporaneous American publication.[15] These figures should be compared to current ventilation standards, which consider that between five and fifteen cubic feet per minute per person is adequate, and may even be excessive, depending on how well humidity, heat, and the other factors are controlled.

There was another scientific theory that contributed to the alarm with which people viewed "foul air." The urbanization and overcrowding of the nineteenth century caused many epidemics. This coincided with the growth of science and rudimentary medical research, which attempted to find explanations—and cures. It was erroneously believed that many diseases—malaria, cholera, dysentery, diarrhea, and typhoid fever—were caused by substances and impurities in the air. The so-called miasmatic theory made fresh air an issue not only of comfort but of life and death, and since the proponents of ventilation made their case with the same zeal that distinguishes current opponents of food additives, or advocates of fluoridation, public awareness grew accordingly.

"When people are well clothed and well fed, the more fresh air, however cold, the better," counseled a book on house planning.[16] It comes as something of a surprise to recall that the stodgy Victorian figures in early photographs, stiff and unrelaxed in their wing collars and corseted dresses, buried in rooms overladen with dark draperies and filled with overstuffed furniture, were also addicted to the outdoors. After all, they popularized bicycle riding, sports, and gymnastics, as well as seaside holidays. Theirs was not the Georgian sybaritic enjoyment of nature; the Victorians exercised for health—moral as well as physical. They seem to have authentically enjoyed the bracing feeling of the outdoors, even inside their homes. It is a habit that the British have persisted in following, much to the dismay of American visitors. But perhaps "enjoyed" is not the right word, for there was an element of cheerless endurance in this love of the outdoors. It was also present in another nineteenth-century custom. During the second half of the century the bath underwent a revival, and various models of hip baths, sitting baths, and sponge baths became popular. Victorian bathing should not be confused with comfort, however. The recommended water temperature was tepid (for those with fragile physiques), and preferably cold. The purchaser of a new shower bath was warned that "nearly freezing water from a Shower Bath produces a feeling somewhat akin to what might be imagined to result from a shower of red-hot lead; the shock is tremendous, and the shower, if continiued for any length of time, would assuredly cause asphyxia."[17]

Science and medicine apart, there was also an element of fashion in the proliferation of air ducts. It is easy to understand the need for ventilation in public buildings, such as the Capitol in Washington, or the Houses of Parliament in London, both of which were supplied with mechanically driven fresh air, or in a crowded factory where workers sweated beside hot machines. It is much less obvious why large, high-ceilinged middle-class houses, which were occupied by small numbers of people, required such extensive ventilation. It is true that overcrowding and pollution characterized the nineteenth-century city, but neither of these conditions affected the country houses of the wealthy, many of which were nevertheless fitted with elaborate systems of artificial air supply and evacuation. What was their function? Could it be that like the "energy-conserving" solar panel on an Aspen ski chalet, or the "economical" diesel engine in an expensive German station-wagon, the ventilating systems were not utilitarian, but instead intended to suggest that their owners were forward-looking and up-to-date?

Fashion, science, and medicine were all ingredients in the ventilation mania. Houses, which in any case were not particularly airtight, were equipped with air ducts and ventilating flues. It was not easy to introduce the massive amounts of fresh air that scientific theory required without at the same time cooling the badly heated room. There are documented examples of enthusiastic engineers installing ventilating grates throughout the house, only to find that these were later blocked up by owners seeking relief from cold drafts.[18] An inventor named Tobin proposed a system of five-foot-high tubes that supplied fresh air at the level of the ceiling. This seemed to have worked well, except when houseowners used the tubes as pedestals and placed potted plants or decorative urns over the openings.[19]

The concern for ventilation had another negative effect. It prolonged the use of fireplaces and generally retarded the introduction of more efficient devices such as stoves and central furnaces. The architect John James Stevenson, a commonsense Scot, admitted that the fireplace was unscientific, wasteful, dirty, and ineffective, but he still claimed that it was "the best system" since it was "a tolerable efficient mode of ventilation."[20] He criticized radiating stoves and central heating on the grounds that rooms warmed this way became stifling and uncomfortable, and in a strained passage he likened hot-air heating to the oppressive atmosphere of the Sahara. This sounds like an attempt to rationalize the British public's affection for the cozy hearth and its resistance to any other type of heating device. In America, where cast-iron stoves and hot-air central heating were more widespread, there were also many critics who considered these types of heating unhealthy. Andrew Jackson Downing's influential 1850 book *The Architecture of Country Houses* sternly admonished, "We know that there are few 'notions' of which our people are fonder than *stoves*—of all descriptions—but we protest against them boldly and unceasingly. Closed stoves are not agreeable, for they imprison all the cheerfulness of the fireside; and they are not economical, for though they save fuel, they make large doctor's bills."[21] In *A Treatise on Domestic Economy*, Catherine Beecher was less categorical, and merely suggested good ventilation (as well as methods for humidification) when stoves were used.[22]

The emphasis on ventilation had an important influence on domestic comfort. Although Galton and Billings were mistaken about the actual amount of air required—an error that would be realized soon enough—they did identify a real problem. Their research introduced people to the idea that domestic comfort was something that could be studied, measured, and explained. It also had another effect. It was impossible to achieve such massive air changes by simply opening windows—especially in the winter. All sorts of ingeniously designed ducts and pipes were required to circulate the air, as were various filters to clean it. Not only was much of this early technology to be useful later for ventilating and air-conditioning large buildings, it also underlined the fact that comfort in the home was something that could be achieved with the help of machinery. In a curious way, Victorian engineers had the right answer to the wrong question.

Another reason for the slow development of environmental technology during the eighteenth century was the generally slow growth in technical and scientific knowledge in general. Nowhere was this more evident than in domestic illumination. Wax candles had been invented by the Phoenicians before A.D. 400, and although torches and crude oil lamps were used during the Middle Ages, no better device than the candle was discovered (not even by Leonardo da Vinci, who tried, unsuccessfully, to improve the oil lamp). Candles remained the only source of artificial light. We enjoy candlelight for romantic dinners, but as an everyday form of illumination it had many disadvantages. Candles produced a flickering, uncontrollable light that was a poor aid to reading or writing. One hundred candles provide less light than an ordinary electric light bulb; the dim illumination of a large drawing room required dozens of candles, as well as considerable labor to light, snuff, and replace them. In the eighteenth century, candles were made out of tallow (beeswax was reserved for the wealthy), and the burning animal fat not only irritated the eyes but was also uncomfortably smelly.

As candles had been the only form of illumination for over fourteen hundred years, it was no wonder that weak artificial light was taken for granted. All this changed in 1783, when Ami Argand, a Geneva physicist, invented a new type of oil lamp. The so-called Argand lamp consisted of a meshed wick contained in a cylindrical glass funnel which controlled the flow of air to the flame, thus reducing flickering and improving the quality as well as the intensity of the light. A lamp placed in the center of a small table allowed social activities such as card playing to be carried on in comfort during the evening, and lamps in studies and drawing rooms permitted reading, writing, and sewing. The public was quick to appreciate these advantages, and the market for the inexpensive, mass-produced lamps expanded. Once the marvel of strong, steady lighting became known, improvements to the Argand lamp followed quickly. There were many variations on the basic design. The French Astral lamp incorporated a ringlike reservoir beneath the lampshade, making it especially useful for lighting circular tables; in 1800, Bernard Carcel added a clockwork pump to feed oil from a reservoir in the base to the wick, which also produced a steadier light.

What limited the effectiveness of the Argand-type lamps was the poor quality of the oil that they burned, and as the demand for better lamps increased, so did the efforts of entrepreneurs to develop cleaner and brighter-burning fuels. In America, whale oil was popular; in Europe, colza oil, which was extracted from the seeds of a kind of turnip, was used, as well as camphine, a distillate of oil of turpentine. In 1858, Abraham Gesner, a Canadian doctor and amateur geologist, developed and patented a method of extracting from asphalt rock a fuel that was clean, and cheaper than whale oil: he named it kerosene.

Gesner's invention was superseded by a much more important discovery, that of petroleum in 1859. Petroleum could also be distilled and cracked to produce kerosene, an extremely high-grade lighting fuel that accelerated the development of artificial lighting. Conversely, the demand for kerosene for lamps was the mainstay of the new petroleum industry.* Although the kerosene lamp was brighter than other types of oil lamps, it still required constant trimming and frequent cleaning and refilling. Since light was produced by simple combustion, kerosene lamps produced much heat

---

* It is interesting to note that gasoline was a by-product of kerosene production from crude oil, and not an immediately useful one; there was no significant demand for gasoline until the early 1900s.

and soot, and in return for a small amount of light they burned a lot of fuel. Since lamp oil was produced by many small manufacturers, and standards and quality control were lacking, the volatility of kerosene varied enormously. One never knew if a lamp would produce a blaze of light or simply a blaze; in 1880 in New York, over one hundred house fires were attributed specifically to kerosene lamps.[23]

The main alternative to kerosene lamps was gaslight. Gas street lamps appeared early in London (1807), Baltimore (1816), Paris (1819), and Berlin (1826), but gas was not used to light homes until the 1840s in Europe, and not until after the Civil War in America. There was, at first, considerable public resistance to using gas in the home—it was considered dangerous—and the coal gas itself was impure and did not produce a bright light. Moreover, there were problems with the early gasoliers. The imperfectly burning gas produced an unpleasant smell which induced drowziness; gaslit rooms had to be specially ventilated or they soon became uncomfortable. Walter Scott installed gaslight in his own newly built country house in 1823, but it was apparently not a complete success; his biographer, writing about this experiment fourteen years later, still considered that "The blaze and glow and occasional odour of gas, when spread over every part of a private house, will ever constitute an annoyance for the majority of men."[24] The "noxious vapors" were said to tarnish metal, kill plants, and destroy coloring.[25] One wag suggested that the best way to light a room with gas was to place the burner outside the window.[26] In fact, this was how the House of Commons was illuminated; the gasoliers were installed behind a suspended glass ceiling, so that the fumes could be vented directly to the exterior.

The first wide use of indoor gaslighting was in public buildings, factories, and shops, as has already been mentioned, at least partly because the smell and heat could be more easily dissipated in larger spaces. The factory and shop owners also had an economic incentive—because of the American and Napoleonic Wars, whale oil and Russian tallow became expensive, and coal gas was available and cheap. Eventually, as gas became more commonplace, it began to be used in houses, although for a long time gasoliers were used only in passageways and service rooms, never in public rooms, which were lit by lamps or candles. In wealthier homes, candles often prevailed, since there were plenty of servants available, and beeswax candles produced a pleasant light and no smell. In the 1850s, Buckingham Palace was still lighted by hundreds of candles, a great expense which the thrifty Prince Albert did his best to reduce.[27]

The invention of the atmospheric burner allowed more complete combustion of the gas, and together with the technique of purifying coal gas, resulted in brighter illumination while overcoming—or at least reducing—the unpleasant side effects. Soot was still produced by the burning gas and blackened the ceiling, as well as the draperies and furniture upholstery. This gave rise to the practice of spring cleaning, when all the dirty fabrics and furniture were taken outdoors to be aired and the ceiling washed or given a fresh coat of paint.[28] Nevertheless, so strong was the extent of the public's demand for better lighting that after 1840 gaslight rapidly became popular, soot, fumes, and all.*

Gaslight produced what one historian has called "a major revolution in human life."[29] This is an accurate description. Changes in domestic privacy, or seating comfort, had taken place gradually, over a long period of time, and the changes themselves had been small, sometimes barely perceptible except with hindsight. The improvement in domestic lighting was, by contrast, rapid. Candles had produced a light too

---

* The incandescent Welsbach mantle, introduced in 1887, solved the problem of soot in gas lamps, and also produced a brighter, more pleasant light. By the time it appeared, however, gaslight was already being replaced by electricity.

weak for most household tasks; oil lamps had been able to throw a pool of light onto a table or a writing desk; but gaslight was strong enough to illuminate the entire room. The quantitative change in lighting levels was huge. A single gasolier was the equivalent of a dozen candles. It has been estimated that between 1855 and 1895 the actual amount of illumination (expressed in candlepower) in an average Philadelphia household increased *twentyfold*.[30] The effect of brighter interiors was not simply increased comfort. Better light made reading at night possible and encouraged an increase in general literacy. Brighter rooms also coincided with a heightened awareness of cleanliness, both personal and domestic.

The gasolier was the product of scientific and technological development that was financed by entrepreneurs with the main goal of selling it to the largest number of people possible. It was, in other words, the first successful domestic consumer device. Precisely because gaslight required large investments in gasworks and networks of gaslines under city streets, it also required many users; by its nature it was a mass commodity. This was one reason for its slow spread—until most people were willing to use gas, it was prohibitively expensive. Once most people did, it became dramatically cheaper: by 1870, English gas cost one-fifth of what it had forty years earlier, and only about one-fourth what lamp oil cost.

Although gas was cheap enough to be afforded by the middle class, it was still too expensive for the rest of the population. At the beginning of the nineteenth century, even tallow candles were considered to be beyond the reach of most laborer families, whose houses remained dark, as they had been since the Middle Ages. But even here the democratizing character of mass technology began slowly to make itself felt, and by the 1880s most families had at least one oil or kerosene lamp, which, being portable, could serve the whole house.[31] In 1890, the English gas companies, seeking to expand their clientele (and seeing the threat of competition from a new technology, electricity), offered coin-operated gas meters to working-class households, which finally brought the new domestic technology within the means of most of the urban population.[32]

The public's appreciation of the convenience, and comfort, of artificial illumination was evident in its eventual acceptance of gas for lighting even as it rejected it for other uses. The advantages of cooking with gas were less compelling, and although gas ranges and ovens were made available to the public in the 1820s, they were not popular. For the next sixty years, despite the best efforts of the gas companies, most households continued to cook with coal or wood. When gas stoves did come into broad use, they were designed like free-standing coal-burning stoves (often they combined gas and coal), which had the important effect, as Giedion noted, of delaying the development of the integrated kitchen work counter.[33]

Gas was an urban technology, and since most people who used gas were middle-class, it could be described as the first specifically *bourgeois* technology. This caused a curious situation: at least in England, modern conveniences, such as gaslight (or bathrooms), came to be seen by upper-class homeowners as vulgar, and the comfort associated with these mechanical devices as nouveau-riche.* In this context one comes across derogatory references to "luxury." In America there was no such opposition, and photographs of interiors show gasoliers in the palatial drawing rooms of the wealthy, as well as in the modest parlors and kitchens of the middle class.

---

* Thoresby Hall was an enormous country estate finished in 1875, which was entirely lit by oil lamps, not gas, and which, according to at least one historian, seems to have had no bathrooms at all.[34]

Chapter Seven

Electric Appliances (c. 1900)

Efficiency

*Comfort in living is far more in the brains
than in the back.*

—ELLEN H. RICHARDS

THE COST OF SHELTER

The arrival of gaslight and ventilation, flawed as these technologies were, signified the beginning of the rationalization, and moreover the mechanization, of the home. Domestic technology such as the gasolier and the ventilation duct represented an invasion of the home, not only by new devices, but by a different sensibility—that of the engineer and of the businessman. This was an invasion that most architects (though not their clients) chose to ignore. In the 1871 edition of his influential book *The Gentleman's House*, the architect Robert Kerr did not feel it necessary to discuss gaslight, except to laconically instruct the reader that "the architect's province need go no further than to accommodate the gas-engineer according to his demands."[1] A similar book published three years later in the United States by Calvert Vaux, *Villas and Cottages*, makes no mention of artificial illumination at all, even though by that time gaslight was a common technology.

Ventilation affected the fabric of the house even more than gaslight. Modern buildings circulate air with electric fans. Although there are examples of public buildings that used steam-driven fans, this was too expensive and complicated for houses, which instead had to rely on gravity for the movement of the air. This required very large air ducts and meant that the house had to be designed specifically to accommodate 145 the pipes and other ventilating spaces; if architects were not prepared to deal with this, others would. In 1872, a Liverpool doctor, John Hayward, built his own house to demonstrate his ideas of proper ventilation.[2] It was a remarkable and uncommon example of how the new environmental technology had to be integrated with architecture if it was to work well. All the gaslights were so-called Ricket's globes, in which the flame was enclosed in a glass ball and the fumes were never allowed to enter the room. The windows were not openable. Fresh air was fed in from the basement, warmed in a furnace, and distributed via a central lobby on each floor and through a perforated cornice into the room. Over each gasolier was an outlet grille that led to a duct. The exhausted air was collected in a "foul air chamber" in the attic; from here a shaft led to the kitchen fireplace, which pulled the air down and evacuated it through the chimney. Not only the main rooms but also the kitchen, dressing rooms, bathrooms, and water closets were ventilated in this way.

Henry Rutton was a Canadian engineer who had designed ventilating systems for railroad cars in Canada and the United States. In 1860 he published a book detailing how many of his ideas (double glazing, for example) could be applied to house construction. Rutton was critical of architects: "Amid the blaze of light which in this nineteenth century has so illumined the world, architecture alone lies motionless, covered with the dust of ages. Not a single new idea, so far as I know, has been suggested by the profession within the memory of man."[3]

The lack of interest of most architects in new technologies marks a watershed in the evolution of domestic comfort. No architects were as successful as Hayward in integrating environmental systems into their designs. Even Stevenson, who was more aware than most of the need to deal with the new technologies, and who devoted a quarter of the second volume of *House Architecture* to a discussion of domestic environmental systems, was uneasy about the increased mechanization of his art and concluded with the warning that "machinery in a house may be overdone."[4] Architecture and the new domestic technologies drifted apart. When technological advances were introduced, they seem to have been due to the interest of the client rather than of the architect. When Lord Armstrong, an industrialist and arms manufacturer, built his estate, Cragside, in 1880 he included not only the first recorded installation of electric lighting (Armstrong was a friend and neighbor of Joseph Swan, inventor of the carbon-filament lamp), but also room-to-room telephones, central heating, and two hydraulic elevators. His architect, the famous Norman Shaw, did not repeat such experiments in his later houses.

Until the eighteenth century the interior had been conceived as all of a piece. Blondel had designed Rococo rooms as single entities—walls, furniture, and furnishings together. So did Georgian architects such as Robert Adam and John Nash. Later, interiors were the result of architects working with upholsterers and cabinetmakers (not always in easy harmony). By the mid-nineteenth century, however, upholsterers, who were now referred to as interior decorators, were taking sole responsibility for everything connected with the inside of the house.

Interior decorators, even more than architects, were ill equipped to deal with the new technologies, and fashion and physics often found themselves in opposition. In 1898, when central heating and ventilation were already advanced, an American book on interior decoration still maintained that open fireplaces were the only acceptable form of heating and concluded with the warning "It might be said that the good taste and *savoir-vivre* of the inmates of a house may be guessed from the means used for heating it."[5] With the introduction of devices such as the gasolier and the vent duct a rift appeared between the mainly visual approach of decorators and the primarily mechanical approach of the engineers. As we shall see, with time this rift widened and contributed to a schizophrenic attitude toward domestic comfort that still troubles us.

The Victorian effort to improve domestic comfort through the use of technology faced a serious stumbling block. It was as if people were trying to complete a jigsaw puzzle with some of the pieces missing. Stevenson had characterized environmental devices as depending on "motive power of any kind," but the speaking tubes, ventilation pipes, and dumb waiters that he described all used human energy—mechanical motive power was absent.[6] Steam was the prime mover of the nineteenth century, but although you could take a train from San Francisco to New York and a steamship from Montreal to London, steam engines themselves were too big, and too expensive, to have any domestic application. There were a few examples of extremely large Victorian country houses with their own steam plants, but these were exceptional.* Gas was the only artificial energy source in the home, and, as we know, it had many drawbacks, whether it was used for lighting or, less commonly, for cooking.

The absence of power severely limited domestic technology. Ventilation and heating were crude and ineffective because they depended on gravity and natural convection. Air circulated lazily from room to room; kitchen smells lingered. Rooms with fireplaces were heated without mechanical help, by radiation; those sitting next to the fire roasted (or hid behind a so-called fire screen); while those sitting away from the fireplace were cold.

There were many attempts to solve the problem of mechanization with the means available. An American invented a gas-heated iron—a rubber tube connected it to the gasolier.

---

* At the end of the nineteenth century, tiny steam engines were produced for domestic use, but they were soon supplanted by more effective motors.

In the 1870s, when pressurized water came into the home, it seemed to some that hydropower might be the answer. Several companies manufactured "water engines," small turbines that were attached to the faucet, and to which appliances were connected by pulleys. Where water rates were low enough, water engines seem to have been popular, and clothes washers and wringers, sewing machines, fans, and ice-cream machines were powered this way. One company manufactured the "Water Witch," a water engine that developed air suction and was used to power a vacuum cleaner, a massager, and a hair dryer.

The main motive power, however, remained what it had always been—human effort. There was a variety of nineteenth-century domestic appliances that were manually operated, not only sewing machines, apple corers, and eggbeaters, but also clothes washers and dishwashers.[7] These last two bore a startling resemblance to their modern counterparts, except that they were powered by a crank or lever; hand-powered washing machines were used in rural Canada as late as the 1950s. The much-needed carpet sweeper made its appearance in the 1860s. Victorian interiors were full of drapes and carpets, and brighter gaslight showed the chimney soot that had accumulated both from inside and outside the home.* In addition to the now-classic rotating-brush design, suction devices powered by various types of bellows were developed. One model required the user to push the handle up and down like a pogo stick, another had long handles which were pumped sideways, like an enormous pair of shears. The most bizarre vacuum cleaner consisted of two bellows which the hapless maid was to wear as shoes, and which caused the nozzle to suck air as she walked around the room.

---

* Ventilating engineers like Douglas Galton were vehemently opposed to carpets, which they denounced as unhealthy dust catchers. Their warnings seem to have been heeded, for by the end of the nineteenth century, wall-to-wall carpeting had been replaced by smaller rugs on varnished wood floors.

What was needed to make these devices practical was a small, effective powering device; this was one of the missing pieces to the home-technology puzzle. Actually there were two others as well: a more efficient source of heat, and a brighter and cleaner source of light. All three were provided by the discovery of electricity, or more specifically, by the invention of the small electric motor, the resistance heater, and the incandescent light bulb.

The first use for electricity was for lighting. In 1877, eighty arc lamps were installed in a Parisian department store; that same year a building in London was similarly lighted. Arc lamps were extremely bright, but for technical reasons were more suitable for large installations—they were also used in lighthouses, for example. They were also popular as street-lights (for the first time in Cleveland), and Parisian boulevards continued to be lit this way for several years. The real break-through, as far as domestic lighting was concerned, occurred when Thomas Edison and Joseph Swan, working independently in America and England, produced the first inexpensive carbon-filament light bulbs. In 1882, Edison built a generating station in the Wall Street area of New York City, and through a distribution network of buried cables he provided power to a square-mile area. Five thousand Edison lamps burned brightly in the homes of more than two hundred wealthy businessmen, including the financier J. Pierpont Morgan.

Gaslight had taken more than fifty years to achieve public acceptance; electricity proceeded at a faster rate. Within two years, Edison's power station was serving five hundred subscribers, including the New York Stock Exchange, which had been converted from gaslight. More American installations followed, and Edison also supplied the dynamos for the first European generating station, in Milan. After some legal bickering, he and Swan formed a partnership and proceeded to build electric plants all over England. Only a few years after

Lord Armstrong's pioneering effort at Cragside, several public buildings, including the House of Commons and the British Museum, were lit by electricity, and soon houses—and not only rich men's mansions—were using electric light. Electric companies sprang up in New York, London, and all the major cities of Europe.

By 1900, electric lighting was an accepted fact of urban life. The first large-scale use, indeed the only use, for electricity was for illumination. Edison's generating plants were referred to as "electric light stations," and just as gas technology was built on the gasolier, so the proliferation of electric technology was based on the incandescent light bulb. The superiority of electricity over gas was obvious. It was brighter, safer, more reliable, and clean; it meant the end of noxious fumes, soot on the ceiling, scrubbing of globes, and the need for special vents over each light fixture. In just over a hundred years, the evolution of domestic lighting—from Argand's oil lamp to the incandescent electric bulb—was complete.

Once electricity had entered the home, it was available for other uses. The first recorded application of electricity to run a machine occurred in 1883, in a grocery store in New York, when an electric motor was used to run a coffee grinder. Isaac Singer saw the possibilities of electricity and introduced an electrically powered model of his sewing machine as early as 1889. That year, Nikola Tesla, a Croatian immigrant, patented the efficient multiple-phase electric motor, and two years later, in association with George Westinghouse, he produced a small portable fan. The first electric vacuum cleaner was patented in 1901, and by 1917 vacuum cleaners had achieved such popularity that they could be ordered from the ubiquitous Montgomery Ward catalog. That same year, electric refrigerators began to be manufactured on a large scale in France and America. The Thor electric washing machine was first produced in 1909, and the Walker electric dishwasher began to be sold in 1918; by the 1920s both were being marketed on a large scale. The first small electric motors were inexpensive to build and to operate—in 1910 Westinghouse advertised its fan as costing one quarter of a cent an hour. Another reason for their rapid application was that most electric appliances, including fans, were simply motor-driven versions of earlier, hand-powered devices; since vacuum cleaners, dishwashers, and washing machines were all available in hand-driven versions long before they were fitted with electric motors, it was a simple matter to convert them into powered devices. All that was needed was that missing piece of the puzzle.

A less visible but equally important benefit of the discovery of the electric motor was the availability of electrically driven fans for heating and ventilation. The portable electric fan had a major effect on comfort in America, where summers were hot and humid. Although fans were not cheap—in 1919 they cost five dollars, more than a day's wages—they were widely used.[8] Overhead ceiling fans made their appearance in the southern states in the 1890s. By breaking up the still air in a room, overhead fans reduced the feeling of stuffiness that the early proponents of ventilation were trying to overcome. They were frequently combined with electric lamps, solving, at a stroke, the problem of both light *and* air. Electric duct fans did much to popularize inexpensive central heating. Hot-air heating had always been cheaper than hot-water systems, which required expensive plumbing and radiators, but it was unpopular with many people because, without fans, air would rise through delivery ducts only if it were heated to extremely high temperatures, as high as 180 degrees. It is no wonder that doctors complained about the health effects of over-heated homes. Now, with electric fans to help air circulation, heated air could be mixed with fresh air, artificially moved all over the house, and delivered to the room at a comfortable temperature.

The ability of electricity to provide direct heat was quickly appreciated, and the Chicago World's Fair of 1893 exhibited a "Model Electric Kitchen" that included a kitchen range, broiler, and a water heater—all electrically heated. After 1907, when long-life nickel-chrome alloy resistors were perfected, efficient and durable electric appliances proliferated. In 1909, Westinghouse introduced an electric iron, and within a few years toasters, coffee percolators, hot plates, and cookers became common, at least in America.

The popularity of electric appliances in the home was a function of the low cost of electricity. Edison's first customers were obliged to pay as much as twenty-eight cents per kilowatt-hour, which was a great deal, and at first electricity, and electrical appliances, were considered a luxury. This situation did not last long, and rates quickly began to fall. By 1915, electrical rates had dropped to ten cents per kilowatt-hour, and in 1926 stood at seven cents, which in 1915 dollars was about four cents a kilowatt-hour.[9] In 1885, when gas was in its heyday, it had been available to only about two million British households—less than a quarter of the population; in 1927, over seventeen million American homes—over 60 percent—had electricity. The number of American homes that were electrified (mainly in the towns and cities; rural electrification would follow) was equal to the rest of the world combined. This represented a consumer market of unprecedented scale.

The most widely used electrical appliance (apart from lighting) was the electric iron; by 1927, over three-quarters of the American homes that were electrified had one. An electric iron weighed less than three pounds, while the traditional, massive flat-irons, which were heated in series on top of the cookstove, had weighed from three to twelve pounds, depending on what was to be pressed.[10] Flat-irons were known as "sad irons" (an archaic meaning of "sad" is heavy or dense) which was coincidentally an appropriate description of the arduous activity of using them. The first electric irons were expensive—about six dollars—but they were cheaper to operate than heating the entire stove. Another major advantage of the electric iron, which it shared with the portable gas and alcohol models that were also available, was that ironing did not have to be done immediately next to the hot stove, but could be performed coolly—and comfortably—elsewhere.

More than half the electrified homes in 1927 contained a vacuum cleaner. Considering that this device had been widely available for less than a decade, this is an astonishing figure. In 1915 a small suction sweeper with external dustbags could be had for thirty dollars, although larger vacuum cleaners with attachments were more expensive (about seventy-five dollars).[11] As they became more popular, prices dropped. A Swedish company which had developed an inexpensive cylinder-type vacuum cleaner began to sell its product in the United States, and the Electrolux design became the prototype for cleaners for the next fifty years. Like the electric iron, the vacuum cleaner reduced labor; carpets could be cleaned in place instead of having to be removed once a week and beaten outside.

Mechanization in the home is sometimes described as if all it achieved was a saving in time. If that had been its only advantage, it is unlikely that the vacuum cleaner and the electric iron would have become so popular so quickly. Nor was their rapid proliferation the result only of marketing, although this was a factor, especially in the case of the vacuum cleaner, which was one of the first products to be sold by traveling door-to-door salesmen. The greatest saving produced by the new electrical devices was not time but effort; they allowed household tasks to be performed in much greater comfort. Although frivolous gadgets would follow—electric carving knives and toothbrushes, for example—the earliest electrical appliances were distinguished by the authentic improvement that they achieved in easing the labor of domestic work. A new expression was coined to describe them: labor-saving appliances.

The American interest in reducing housework was at least partly the result of the generally small use that was made of domestic help. Not that servants were entirely absent; despite a self-proclaimed republicanism, the United States was not a modern version of the seventeenth-century Netherlands, where the president's wife hung out her own laundry. In 1870, fully 60 percent of all the gainfully employed women in the United States worked as servants. Andrew Jackson Downing differentiated between houses and cottages according to the number of servants that they contained—anything with less than *three* servants was a cottage. Nevertheless, as early as 1841, Catherine Beecher was arguing that more compact houses were necessary since "as the prosperity of this Nation increases, good domestics will decrease."[12] Indeed, this is what happened, and by 1900, there were less than half as many servants in the United States as in England; more than 90 percent of American families employed no domestics.[13]

The lesser number of servants in the United States was not a question of demand—there were always people who were looking for domestics—but of supply. Domestic employment—that is, female domestic employment, for the great majority of servants were women—was not pleasurable, and before the advent of electrical appliances it was especially onerous. If their husbands earned more or if there were other jobs available, poor women preferred almost anything, including factory work, to domestic service. This continues to be the case. It is in the poorest and least industrial countries that the middle class employs many servants. In countries such as Mexico, where a growing economy has recently offered alternative employment to women, one is more likely to hear complaints about the difficulty of finding, and keeping, domestic help.

Wartime encouraged the entry of women into the labor force and also slowed down immigration, so that after World War I the number of servants in America declined markedly.* This also had the effect of raising servants' wages, by a half to a third.[14] In 1923, an American housekeeper earned about three hundred dollars a year; her British counterpart was paid less than half that amount.[15] The effect of higher wages and a shrinking supply of women willing to work as domestics meant that American homes, if they had servants, had few of them. More than two servants in a household was unusual; a single maidservant was typical. More common was part-time help. During the 1920s, it was generally considered that an income of at least three thousand dollars a year was required to afford domestic help. Since the *average* income at that time was about one thousand dollars, few people could afford full-time domestic help.

The American housewife's reliance on fewer servants was not only the result of economic factors but was encouraged by the many books on housekeeping that made their appearance after 1900. In *The Cost of Shelter*, Ellen H. Richards considered domestic service to be an expensive and unnecessary social convention, an "adjunct to luxurious living," which most young families could ill afford.[16] Mary Pattison was opposed to the use of servants on social grounds and in *Principles of Domestic Engineering* described domestic service as a "barbarous state of vassalage."[17] Christine Freder-

---

* Immigrant women were, and continue to be, the main source for domestic employment. In the early 1900s they came from Ireland and eastern Europe; in the 1980s they come from Central America and the Caribbean. Nevertheless, the total number of domestics continues to fall; between 1972 and 1980, the number of cleaners and maids employed in American homes dropped by one-third.

ick, a proponent of the "servantless household," argued that the chief impediments to the efficient management of the home were servants, who were usually poorly educated immigrant or rural girls, and who were often resistant to new ideas and new devices. Frederick recounted that in her own home a gas iron and a rocking-type washing machine stood unused—save by herself—because she had been unable to persuade her servants to operate them.* [18]

For a variety of reasons—some social, some economic—the American woman (like her seventeenth-century Dutch counterpart) did all or at least a good part of her own housework. This meant that at the same time as electricity and mechanization were entering the home, many middle-class women were in a position to appreciate, at first hand, the benefits of labor-saving devices and improvements to domestic work, and had the disposable income to buy them. The coincidence of these factors explains the rapidity with which the American home altered in the early 1900s.

A greater interest in domestic efficiency was not uniquely the result of a lack of servants, nor was it caused by the mechanization of housework. The author of an early handbook on housekeeping, *Housewifery*, made this distinction when she cautioned, "Labor-saving tools are not necessarily tools with much mechanism, or a motor to do the work, while the housekeeper reads or visits; they are often hand tools which are fitted to the task they are to perform." And, she continued, innovation was not to be followed blindly. "Let the housewife read, investigate, and be willing to try a new method until she proves that it is better or worse than her own." [19] Such

---

* The 1984 film *El Norte* humorously depicted a similar incident in which an American housewife tries unsuccessfully to persuade her Mexican maid to use a clothes washer and dryer; instead the maid does the wash by hand, and spreads it out over the suburban lawn to dry in the sun.

warnings were typical. There was no mad dash toward mechanization. Electrical appliances were welcomed as an aid in
the process of domestic reorganization, but they were not its
cause. What was changing radically in the American home
was not the result of whirring electric motors or glowing
resistance heaters. These were almost incidental to the greater
change that was taking place in how domestic comfort was
defined.

The great American innovation in the home was to demand
comfort not only in domestic leisure, but also in domestic
work. Giedion makes the point that the organization of work
in the home was well under way before mechanized tools
became available.[20] He should have added "in America," for
the introduction of efficiency and comfort into housework
occurred first in that country. The earliest exponent of what
would come to be called home economics was Catherine E.
Beecher, who wrote *A Treatise on Domestic Economy for
the Use of Young Ladies at Home and at School* in 1841.
Although it was concerned primarily with managing the
household, this textbook also included a chapter "On the
Construction of Houses." Like her English contemporary
Robert Kerr in *The Gentleman's House*, Beecher emphasized
the importance of health, convenience, and comfort in house
planning, although she placed a good deal less emphasis on
"good taste," holding it to be "a desirable, though less important, item."* But there were other differences. Like all
books on house planning written by men, Kerr's made no
reference to women's activities in the home, or to the relationship between convenience and domestic work, except in
the vaguest possible way. Beecher, although writing twenty
years earlier, was explicit about this matter: "There is no

---

* Unlike Kerr, Beecher was not a trained architect—she was a school-
teacher—although most of the designs of the houses in this and later books
were her own.

point of domestic economy, which more seriously involves the health and daily comfort of American women, than the proper construction of houses."[21] Unlike *The Englishman's House*, or any of the many books on domestic architecture, Beecher's *Treatise* was addressed to women, not to men, and because she was dealing with the principal user of the house she addressed a different set of issues. She dealt not with "finical ornaments" and fashion, but with adequate closet space and comfortable kitchens; not with how the house looked, but with how it functioned.

In the *Treatise* and in later books she elaborated her ideas in architectural and technical detail. Her different point of view was evident throughout. Other architectural books depicted the kitchen as simply a large room labeled "Kitchen." She indicated not only the location of the major components such as the sink and the stove, but also a variety of other practical innovations: drawers for towels and scouring powder beneath the sink, a continuous work surface with storage below and shelves above, the cookstove separated from the other work area by sliding glazed doors. Nor did she confine herself to the kitchen. To save space, she placed the beds in little alcoves (these were called "bedpresses" and resembled the Dutch sleeping cupboards of the seventeenth century) which were distributed throughout the house, even in the parlor and dining room. Although architectural books of that time generally omitted showing the direction of door swings, she carefully included them because "the comfort of a fireside very much depends on the way in which the doors are hung."[22]

Catherine Beecher has been described as a precursor of modern architecture by historians such as James Marston Fitch and Siegfried Giedion, but, as Douglas Handlin has suggested, to call Beecher a revolutionary is to ignore the fundamentally conservative message of her books.[23] Although she was an abolitionist like all her family (her sister was Harriet Beecher Stowe), she was neither a radical nor a feminist and was in fact opposed to women's suffrage. Beecher did not dispute that the woman's place was in the home; what she did assert was that the home was not a particularly well-thought-out place for her to be.

What she was reacting against was the current male conception of the home, which was primarily visual. This idea was typified in Downing's *The Architecture of Country Houses*. Downing paid lip service to the idea that houses should combine both utility and beauty, but there was no question which he considered to be more important. He devoted four pages to "the useful in architecture," but the following section, "the beautiful in architecture," was twenty-two pages long. Like most architectural writers, when he did refer to convenience it was in a highly generalized way. A dining room was judged to be "convenient" because it was near the kitchen; a bedroom was "useful" because it was large. When Robert Kerr wrote about house planning, he also distinguished between comfort and convenience: comfort had to do with the passive enjoyment of the home by its owners, convenience had to do with the proper functioning of the house, which, Kerr assumed, was the business of the servants and needed little elaboration. Since Beecher, on the other hand, felt that some, if not all, of the domestic work would be done by the woman of the household, she singled out "the economy of labor" as the *first* consideration in planning a home.

Beecher was expressing a point of view that had not been heard since the seventeenth century in Holland—that of the user. This was the prime characteristic of American domesticity—it was seen through the eyes of the persons who worked in the home, that is, through the eyes of women. Beecher, and many women writers after her, altered the European image of the home as a male preserve—the gentleman's house— and in doing so enriched the definition of home.[24] The masculine idea of the home was primarily sedentary—the home as a retreat from the cares of the world, a place to be at ease.

The feminine idea of the home was dynamic; it had to do with ease, but also with work. It could be said to have shifted the focus from the drawing room to the kitchen, which was why, when electricity entered the home, it was by the kitchen door.

Much has been written about the environmental technology that was incorporated into the model house described in Beecher's *The American Woman's Home*, which she wrote together with her sister Harriet in 1869. It included a ducted system of heating and ventilation which supplied hot air from a basement furnace to every room and did away with fireplaces altogether.[25] Pressurized water was fed by a cistern under the roof; there were two water closets, one in the basement and one on the bedroom floor. What was equally remarkable about the house was the way that it made use of space. What would normally have been a dining room contained a large movable closet on rollers. At night, the closet was moved to one side and the room served as a bedroom. In the morning, the room could be divided in two and used as a sitting room and a breakfast room, while during the day the closet was used to create a small sewing area and a larger parlor. In this way, "small and economical houses can be made to secure most of the comforts and many of the refinements of large and expensive ones," wrote the Beecher sisters.[26] The house plans Catherine Beecher included in her *Treatise*, which were intended for "young housekeepers" in "moderate circumstances," were indeed small. In one example, by resorting to bedpresses and small bedrooms, she managed to provide space for eight persons in less than twelve hundred square feet, not ignoring generous closets and storage space. "Every room in a house adds to the expense involved in finishing and furnishing it, and to the amount of labor spent in sweeping, dusting, cleaning floors, paint, and windows, and taking care of, and repairing its furniture. Double the size of a house, and you double the labor of taking care of it, and so, vice versa."[27]

Beecher's obsession with reducing the size of the house was not simply a question of saving money—though a small house always costs less to build than a large one. She was suggesting something different: that a small house, because it was easier to take care of and use, could be *more comfortable* than a larger one. The disadvantage of a large house, she wrote, was that "the table furniture, the cooking materials and utensils, the sink, and the eating-room, are at such distances apart, that half the time and strength is employed in walking back and forth to collect and return the articles used."[28] This appreciation for smallness was something that had disappeared from the domestic scene since the snug Dutch home. Its reappearance marked an important moment in the evolution of domestic comfort. In this, as in so many things, Beecher was ahead of her time, for the nineteenth century still associated comfort with spaciousness, and the idea of living in a reduced area would have been difficult for most people to accept. But it was only a question of time.

One of the designs in C. J. Richardson's *The Englishman's House* was entitled "A Suburban Villa."* This was, by Victorian standards, a small house—it had only three bedrooms—and accommodated a young, well-off family with two or three children. In addition to an attic (for the servants) there were three floors, over six thousand square feet of area in all. This area was not, Richardson felt, an extravagance. He specifically singled out the "compactness of arrangement" and the "economy of space" of this "small suburban villa,"

---

* Richardson was not an important architect; he lacked the authority of Kerr and the talent and expertise of Stevenson. But precisely because he was less innovative and his ideas more conventional, his book was popular; it went through several editions and remained in print until the turn of the century.

which, he claimed, was based on contemporary American ideas.[29] Indeed, the rooms are arranged in a compact square, and relatively little space was devoted to hallways.

Compare this house with one that Christine Frederick chose to illustrate the chapter "Planning the Efficient Home" in *Household Engineering*. This house had been built in Tracy, Illinois, a suburb of Chicago, in 1912, only forty years after Richardson published his book. It too was designed for a middle-class family, but in size it was much closer to Beecher's model. Although it had four bedrooms, its entire area (not including the basement) was only one-fourth that of the English house. One-fourth! It was not that the American home had many fewer rooms. It contained both a living room and a dining room, although instead of a library it had a playroom. It also incorporated a sleeping porch (common in American houses since 1900) and a glazed and screened living porch. What accounted for the difference in sizes was that every room in the English house was considerably larger; the dressing rooms, which were among the smallest rooms in the nineteenth-century house, were bigger than most of the bedrooms in the Chicago house, and as for the bedrooms, they were, by modern standards, palatial, exceeding in area even the living room of the American home.

It would have taken the continuous labor of at least two persons to dust, sweep, and clean the seventeen large rooms of Richardson's "small" suburban villa. By contrast, the American home was designed to be taken care of easily by a single housewife, with perhaps part-time help. This consideration resulted not only in rooms of reduced size, but also in the extensive use of "built-in" furniture—shelves, kitchen cabinets, bookcases, fireside seats, a sideboard—which was absent in the Victorian home. The main advantage of built-in furniture, according to Frederick, was that it never had to be moved, and it therefore simplified cleaning. The kitchen contained many useful features that would become common:

high windows over the counter, drainboards on either side of the sink, cupboards of various sizes, and a closely related sink, refrigerator, and work area. Another American invention, dating from the early nineteenth century (it was present in Beecher's plans), was the built-in closet that replaced wardrobes, cupboards, and chests, not only in the bedrooms, but also in the kitchen. The shape and location of the closets is fully resolved and has not been improved on since: a coat closet next to the front door, a broom closet near the kitchen, a linen closet in the upstairs hall, a medicine cabinet in the bathroom.

The idea of locating the water closet and bathtub together in a single room, for the common use of all the family, was an American one. Many of Downing's house plans (1850) showed a "bathroom" that included a water closet and a tub adjacent to each other, and Downing does not seem to have regarded this as unusual. By the turn of the century the compact three-fixture bathroom, with the tub placed across the end of the room and the water closet and sink side by side, was commonplace. This was not the case in Europe. It is evident from Richardson's description that centrally heated water was piped to each dressing room, but since people continued to use portable baths which stood in the dressing rooms, there was no bathroom as such. That the tradition of the portable bath was coming to an end was hinted at by Richardson's suggestion that the small dressing room on the ground floor could be fitted with a bathtub, although this would hardly have been a convenient location. The "American" bathroom was an important device in planning a small house, since it meant that the dressing rooms could be dispensed with altogether, and the bedrooms (in which the bathtub had sometimes been placed) could be made smaller. Comfort was also affected; not for the bather (what could be more pleasant than lounging in a bath in front of a cheery fire?) but for the person who had previously to fill and empty the tub, not just for one, but for each of the bedrooms. The modern bathroom with its engineered plumbing fixtures and tiled walls looked efficient and functional, but it evolved as a result of the servantless household, not of any major technical advance.

Technology helped, elsewhere. In the nineteenth-century home it would have taken a servant a good part of each day simply to stoke and empty the fourteen fireplaces and to trim and tend the many gaslights. The more modern house was heated by a furnace in the basement which circulated hot water to radiators located below the windows in each room. The furnace was coal-fired and had to be manually loaded, but only once a day. Lighting was electrical, of course.

The strict zoning of the Victorian household was absent in the American house. The playroom was intended not only for the children, but, according to Frederick, for the parents when the "young people" were using the living room. She stressed that it should always be possible for children to reach their rooms without disturbing adult activities. In this house they could enter by the back door (and use the conveniently placed lavatory) and go either upstairs or to the playroom, without crossing either the living room or the kitchen (and without tracking dirt into these rooms). This separation of movement and activities was difficult to achieve in a small house, so that whereas in the large Victorian home quiet and privacy had been taken for granted, these now became important considerations in domestic comfort. The closets, the bathroom, the stairs, and the sewing room were placed so as to separate and provide greater privacy among the bedrooms. The parents' bedroom was located over the living room, the children's rooms above the quieter kitchen and playroom.

The rooms in a French eighteenth-century *hôtel* were carefully located to separate the movement of servants from their masters; in the modern American home the same degree of effort went into separating the noisy activities of children from those of their parents. This separation differed from the strict zoning of the *hôtel*, however, for parents and children shared certain activities, and this communality had to be integrated with privacy. Nevertheless, the same sense of *commodité* that informed Rococo planning was present in the architectural planning of this modest family home.

This design was the work of a competent but not particularly fashionable architect—H. V. van Holst.* Christine Frederick might have chosen a house by a better-known architect such as Frank Lloyd Wright; after all, she must have been familiar with Wright's work. Frederick was friends with Edward Bok, the publisher of *The Ladies' Home Journal*, who had commissioned Wright to design "A Small House with Lots of Room in It" for the July 1901 issue of his magazine. Wright's architecture did incorporate many of the space-saving features that Frederick advocated; in his Cheney House, designed as early as 1893, he included a combined dining room, living room, and library, a well-organized kitchen, compact bathrooms, central heating, and an efficient floor plan. But Wright, like most architects, had other fish to fry. The exterior appearance of the house always predominated in his work, and practical as many of his ideas about internal planning were, they inevitably took second place to architectural and aesthetic considerations.

One senses a suspicion of architects in general, not only in Frederick, but also among other proponents of domestic management, who were, without exception, women. Years before, Beecher had criticized "the ignorance of architects, house-builders, and men in general" for their failure to find effective and economical methods for ventilating homes.[31] Frederick advised that detailed plans of what was required

---

* Van Holst published *Modern American Homes*, a collection of modest and inexpensive house plans, in 1914.[30] He was the only architect mentioned by name in Frederick's book, and by Lydia Ray Balderston in *Housewifery*.

should be furnished by the housewife to the architect, whose role she limited to suggesting improvements to the external appearance of the house and preparing the technical drawings for the builder.[32] Another woman author warned that the housewife should expect to encounter opposition from the architect, since "certain things have been done for so long—almost centuries—that the new ideas, so-called, of the house-wife are often considered non workable."[33] To counter this, she provided her reader with a compressed course in architectural drafting so that she could make plans and "check" the architect's drawings. Ellen Richards also seemed skeptical of architects' ability, or at least of their interest, in the area of domestic planning. Writing in 1905, she saw the need for a concerted effort to educate "house-experts," but pointedly did not include architects in this category.[34] Such statements indicated that the rift between the visual approach of the architect and the practical approach of the nineteenth-century engineer—after all, these women called themselves "domestic engineers," not "domestic architects"—had grown wider than before.

The idea of the efficient home that was being put forward by these "domestic engineers" arose out of an unlikely marriage between women's efforts to rationalize and organize house-work and theories that had been developed to improve industrial production in factories. While working in a steelworks, from 1898 to 1901, a Philadelphia engineer named Frederick Winslow Taylor evolved the notion of improving the work process by looking in detail at how workmen performed specific tasks, and what changes could be introduced to reduce time, increase efficiency, and hence increase productivity. Taylor's method involved direct observation (usually with a stopwatch) and often the simplest of improvements—a modified tool, a rescheduling of rest breaks, physical relocation of equipment. The results, in terms of increased productivity, were dramatic. More to the point, it quickly became clear that Taylor's method could be applied, with equal success, by others, and to various activities. A short time later, Frank Gilbreth, another efficiency engineer, studied bricklaying. Traditionally, bricks had been delivered to the mason in random piles. Gilbreth devised a brick pallet which could be placed on an adjustable scaffold that was always waist-high and permitted the worker to reach a brick easily without stooping. The work output of the bricklayer tripled as a result of such simple changes.

The application of what was coming to be known as "scientific management" to housework was due as much as anything else to a series of remarkable coincidences. Christine Frederick's interest in the subject was stimulated by the fact that her husband George, a businessman and market researcher, happened to be working on a project with some efficiency engineers. One day she asked him: "If this new efficiency idea is all you claim, and can be followed in work as widely different as iron foundries and shoe factories, I don't see why it can't be applied to housework as well."[35] He introduced her to his colleagues, and Frederick visited factories and offices where the new science was being put into practice. Much of what she saw struck her as applicable to the home. The proper height of work surfaces to eliminate stooping, the location of tools and machines to reduce fatigue, the organization of work according to a definite plan were recognizably domestic problems. She began to study her own work habits and those of her friends. She timed herself, she made notes, she photographed women at work. As a result, she remodeled her kitchen and found that she could do her housework more quickly and with less effort.

It might have ended there, as a hobby, except that, like Beecher and Richards, Frederick was trained as a teacher, and she was not satisfied with keeping her newfound knowledge to herself. In 1912 she wrote a series of four articles for *The Ladies' Home Journal* entitled "The New Housekeeping," later published as a book.[36] In her Long Island home she established the "Applecroft Efficiency Experiment Kitchen" where she tested and evaluated tools and appliances. Three years later, she wrote *Household Engineering*, which was organized as a correspondence course for women. With the aid of diagrams and many photographs she suggested how every aspect of housework—cooking, laundering, cleaning, shopping, and budgeting—could be made more efficient. It was a combination of textbook, tract, consumer guide, and do-it-yourself handbook.

The same year that *Household Engineering* appeared, Mary Pattison published *The Principles of Domestic Engineering*. Although there does not seem to have been direct contact between the two women they both arrived at the same conclusion, and in much the same fashion. Under the direct influence of Frederick Winslow Taylor (who wrote the introduction to her book and went so far as to compare Pattison to da Vinci and Newton), Pattison spent several years in applying Taylor's method of direct observation, measurement, and analysis to home activities. She established the "Housekeeping Experiment Station" in Colonia, New Jersey.

The foreword to Frederick's *Household Engineering* had also been written by one of the efficiency engineers—Frank Gilbreth. Gilbreth had more than a passing interest in domestic management. Much of his industrial research was done in collaboration with his wife, Lillian, who was a psychologist, and it was natural, as she rather lyrically put it, that "when he came to organize his own family he tried to apply the principles and practices he had used in making his own life an adventure and a quest."[37] Since the Gilbreths had a large family, this was not simply an academic venture; as a result of this personal experimentation, Lillian Gilbreth wrote several books on domestic management—*The Home Maker and Her Job*, and *Management in the Home*.

Some of the suggestions of the domestic engineers now appear pedantic and forced. One wonders, for example, how many housewives really compiled exhaustive minute-by-minute records of their daily activities, or prepared written cleaning schedules for themselves. Or kept an elaborate inventory of every household article on card files (think what the domestic engineers could have done had the home computer been available). Or completed the recommended cost-benefit studies before purchasing even the cheapest domestic tool.

The answer is, probably very few. But that does not gainsay the success of what was primarily an exercise in mass education. It is remarkable how quickly comfort-as-efficiency established itself in the home. While the Victorian engineers had had to struggle to convince the public of their ideas about ventilation and sanitation, the proponents of domestic management met with little opposition. Frederick's books were popular and her articles in *The Ladies' Home Journal* were widely read; eventually she became a "consulting household editor." Lillian Gilbreth was hired to conduct studies of more efficient kitchen planning by appliance manufacturers. Beecher had called for "Domestic Economy" to be taught as a scientific subject. By the early 1900s, Home Economics was taught in many colleges and universities, at MIT by Richards, and at Columbia University by Balderston. Is it chauvinistic to suggest that the success of domestic engineering was due largely to the fact that it was carried out by women? Who else had the intimate, firsthand knowledge of the problems? Who else would have addressed this long-neglected subject? And who else would have done so in such a straightforward and practical way?

Of course, these early pioneers of efficiency in the home—Gilbreth, Frederick as well as their precursor Beecher—were remarkable women.* But they were by no means alone. One comes across many later books on the subject—all by women. The sloganeering titles explain themselves: *The Business of the Household*, *The Business of Being a Woman*, *The Home and Its Management*. Did the movement for more efficient housekeeping assume that the woman's place was in the home? Of course it did; it could not separate itself from the reality of the time, and in any case it did not try to. But it should not be judged by what "might have been" but by what had been before . . . and by what followed. The reduction of hours necessary to do housecleaning, or cooking, or laundry, would eventually make it possible for women to free themselves, once and for all, from their domestic isolation. That neither Catherine Beecher nor Christine Frederick had this in mind does not alter the outcome. Indeed, the events of the last fifty years have vindicated the correctness of their fundamental rethinking of domestic comfort. The home has continued to be a place of work; the increased number of working mothers— and the sharing of housework between husbands and wives— has done nothing to change that. So many aspects of the modern home that we take for granted date from this period—the small size of the house, the correct height for work counters, the placement of major appliances to save needless steps, the organization of storage. Anyone who works comfortably at the kitchen counter, or takes dishes out of a dishwasher and places them in a convenient overhead shelf, or dusts the house in an hour, not a day, owes something to the domestic engineers.

---

* Catherine Beecher, who wrote several books, also established the first American college for women, in Hartford in 1821. Lillian Gilbreth not only had a long professional career as an industrial engineer, consultant and writer but also raised twelve children. Christine Frederick wrote and lectured widely on consumer affairs during the Twenties and Thirties; she also founded the Advertising Women of America, after being refused entry into the all-male Advertising Club.

Chapter Eight

Maurice Dufrène, *Chambre de Dame* (1925)

Style and Substance

A house is a machine for living in . . . an arm-chair is a machine for sitting in and so on.

—LE CORBUSIER

TOWARDS A NEW ARCHITECTURE

One might have expected the various inventions that contributed to human comfort at the turn of the century to have had a profound impact on the appearance of the home. Surprisingly, this was not the case. Even as the home was becoming more efficiently organized for domestic work—and in spite of the growing number of mechanical devices that were required to do this—its interior decor remained largely unaffected. It was not that decor remained unchanged, but rather that the changes that did occur were due to fashion and popular taste, and hardly at all to technology. Although there is some evidence that gasoliers, and later electric lamps, had an effect on room decoration, for example, brighter interiors did not become fashionable because of technology, but because of a Scandinavian influence, which had more to do with sunniness than with electricity. It is similarly difficult to relate the vogue for the all-white room, popularized by interior decorators such as Syrie Maugham and Elsie de Wolfe, to anything but fashion.

There was no reason it should have been otherwise. It is a modern conceit that machinery, or houses incorporating machines, should look different from their preindustrial antecedents. The statement that "form follows function" (originally coined by the American architect Louis Sullivan) has *173* been quoted so often that it is easy to forget that it was a slogan and not a rule. It had demonstrably not been true during the nineteenth century. The Victorians, who were, after all, great engineers, and who were the first to glorify the idea of progress, never felt the need to develop what might be called an engineering aesthetic. The interiors of steamships, trains, and tramways—extraordinary inventions—always took comfortingly familiar forms. The stateroom of a liner resembled a suite at the Ritz. Train compartments were designed to look like small parlors; wealthy businessmen had their own railway carriages, whose interiors were finished like plush smoking rooms, with paneled walls, easy chairs, and tasseled drapery. Tramway cars assumed the visual language and ornamentation of the horse-drawn carriage. Although people admired Paxton's soaring Crystal Palace and attached similar cast-iron and glass conservatories to their own homes, such utilitarian constructions did not affect the rest of the house; it did not occur to them—as it would to architects in the early 1900s—to build entire buildings out of glass.

It was taken for granted that interiors of houses—as indeed their exteriors—should be decorated in a period style. Of course, at the time, this did not seem any more anachronistic than does wearing a tie (that offspring of the seventeenth-century lace cravat) today. Nor did it necessarily demonstrate any particular interest in history. Eighteenth-century classicism (which had been motivated by an authentic curiosity about the past) had been replaced by several period styles, and after 1820, rooms could be decorated and furnished in neo-Rococo, neo-Greek, neo-Gothic, neo-anything-you-fancied. Inevitably, this lead to eclecticism, which was deplored by purists but allowed imaginative architects and interior decorators—these were now separate professions—a great deal of leeway in fashioning, interpreting, and even combining various styles.

One historian has distinguished between the "creative" and

"historical" revivals that coexisted during the nineteenth century.[1] Creative revivals were not concerned with historical accuracy, but merely used traditional motifs and forms, often in a highly original way. The French Antique style that was popular in America before the Civil War was an amalgam of the three Louis styles, often freely adapted. Historical revivals, on the other hand, were an attempt to more or less faithfully imitate the appearance of a particular historical style. They were based on scholarly study of the past and usually reflected an admiration not only for the furnishings, but for the mores of the period in question. The Colonial revival of the 1870s and the Georgian revival of the early 1900s were both historical revivals. But historical revivals came later and were rare; the earliest revivals—like neo-Gothic—tended to be creative.

That most nineteenth-century revivals were creative instead of historical greatly facilitated innovation. Since form was not expected to follow function—only tradition, and then loosely—it was not difficult to introduce devices such as gasoliers or electric lamps into the home. Either they were fitted into familiar shapes—hence the gas or electric chandelier—or, if this was not possible, they were treated in a "traditional" manner. As it was not necessary to adhere strictly to historical precedents, this was not difficult. A bit of swag here, some encrusted flowers there, and the ventilating tube or the bathtub was readily incorporated into the overall decor of the room. It is easy to scoff at the way that the Victorians made new devices conform to old, nonmechanical tastes—that criticism is the staple of many books on industrial design. But it was precisely the absence of any perceived contradiction between tradition and innovation that accounted for the rapidity of change during this period. The ornate kerosene lamps, chandelier-style gasoliers, and richly decorated ceiling fans that collectors prize so highly today are a reminder of how effortlessly—and frequently how gracefully—the new was combined with the old. Whatever new invention came along, however innovative it might be, the Victorians felt comfortably at home with it.

There were some difficulties with period styles, however. A room in the Roman style was intended to look grand in a decadent, imperial way; a room done up in neo-Gothic was supposed to be brooding and melancholy. The servantless household, however, required, above all, a reduction in the *size* of rooms. Since most of the historical styles had originally been developed for large houses—palaces, really—it was not always easy to adapt them to the smaller houses that were being built by the middle class at the end of the century. Few of the period styles were suited to the decoration of small rooms. Even Louis XIV boudoirs and salons required a certain amount of elbow room; Rococo furniture was meant to be seen in uncluttered, spacious surroundings. Some tried all the same to decorate their modest homes in the grand manner; usually the intended effect was not achieved, however, and the result could be slightly ridiculous. The "Roman-style" bathroom or the "baronial" dining-room set was a poor caricature of the original.

The difficulties of adapting historical styles to small homes were not limited to decor. The symmetry of a neo-Classical floor plan was a constraint in arranging a small house, even in the hands of the most skillful architect. If there were not enough rooms, the required spatial effect was lost; and if the rooms themselves were irregularly shaped and designed for efficiency rather than effect, it might be impossible to combine them in the correct classical manner. The formality of Georgian planning was also ill suited to the more relaxed way of life that was being adopted. What was needed was a more intimate domestic style. The seventeenth-century Dutch had built small houses that were both cozy and comfortable, and a "Dutch revival," had one occurred, would have offered one solution. In the event, the development of the small, efficient, servantless home was made easier by the appearance, in 1870, of a different, but not unrelated, eighteenth-century style— Queen Anne.

The originator of the Queen Anne style and one of its most vocal proponents was the same J. J. Stevenson who wrote that practical guide *House Architecture*. Stevenson felt that neither the neo-Gothic nor the neo-Greek and neo-Roman styles were particularly suitable for homes; what he was looking for was a more domestic approach. He based his designs, very loosely, on seventeenth-century English domestic architecture. His houses were typically built out of unplastered red brick, and the façades incorporated little or no applied classical detail. They were far from plain, however, for the exterior consisted of varied fenestration, dormers, chimneys, metalwork, shutters, and bay windows, disposed in an irregular way with no attempt at symmetry. Stevenson called his style "Free Classic." This name never caught on; instead, it became known as "Queen Anne" (Queen Anne ruled from 1702 to 1714) a not very historical appellation, but then it was not a very historically accurate style. Therein lay its appeal; the words most often used to describe Queen Anne homes are "charming" and "picturesque," attributes that quickly endeared it to the general public.

The interior of a Queen Anne home was furnished with little regard for historical accuracy. Stevenson's own home, Red House, included not only contemporary furniture, but also a mixture of Chippendale, Rococo, and eighteenth-century Dutch pieces. The intention of a Queen Anne interior was to produce a picturesque effect, which was done by mixing eighteenth- and nineteenth-century furniture in as "artistic" a way as possible. In that sense a Queen Anne room exhibited "a harmony less of style than of treatment."[2] While this usually produced a crowded interior, it did have the virtue of allowing a much greater degree of freedom to the householder than the more restrictive historical styles. The other advantage lay in planning. Since irregularity was admired, rooms could be planned according to the activities that they contained, they could assume different shapes and sizes and be combined in different ways, and the heights of their ceilings could vary. The use of fireside inglenooks, window seats, and alcoves enhanced the cozy and informal atmosphere. This is not to say that Queen Anne was by any means a functional style—its aspirations were primarily visual—but it unintentionally made it much easier to plan smaller and more convenient homes. Equally fortuitously, since the main architectural feature of a Queen Anne house was a multitude of white-painted, small-paned windows, interiors tended to be brighter than in the past.

In America, a parallel to the Queen Anne style developed which the historian Vincent Scully has termed the Shingle Style. Influenced by early Colonial domestic buildings, the Shingle Style was popularized in several East Coast mansions by the New York architectural firm McKim, Mead and White. Their houses incorporated many Queen Anne features—irregular gables, bays, and windows—as well as porches, but were usually built of wood and covered in shingles. Although it was first used in large houses, this vocabulary proved extremely flexible, so that the individual elements of the Shingle Style could be adapted to small homes—the Cape Cod cottage, for example. Eventually, it ceased to be a style altogether and became, instead, an American suburban vernacular, with more or less ornament as the budget allowed, with and without shingles, sometimes architecturally impressive (as in the hands of a young Frank Lloyd Wright) and, happily, more often plain and straightforward.

With the popularization of Queen Anne and the Shingle Style, the problem of how to arrange a satisfactory small house was solved. The Chicago house that Christine Frederick illustrated in *Household Engineering* was a Shingle Style variant and incorporated a relaxed plan that allowed the combination of various rooms of different sizes as required by function and need. Its inglenook and alcoves, the irregularly disposed porches, and the windows of different size were all vestiges of Queen Anne, filtered through an American sensibility. It was typical of the houses of that period, which were efficiently planned to take advantage of all the comforts and conveniences offered by domestic technology. At the same time, its interior appearance was not significantly different from what had come before. Some rooms were changed—the kitchen and the bathroom, above all—but the living room maintained the cozy domesticity that people were accustomed to. Fireplaces were no longer a functional necessity, but still symbolized the family hearth. Historical decoration had been simplified—most people could not afford it—but vestiges remained. Classical columns supported the porch, vaguely Georgian wainscoting gave some elegance to the dining room, ornamental light fixtures lit the hall. Although the rooms were greatly reduced in size, a feeling of comfort was achieved by adapting elements derived from seventeenth-century cottages—window seats, bay windows, glazed inside doors—and these coexisted happily with electric lights, central heating, and a rapidly growing number of household appliances.

We have arrived—very nearly—at the modern home. Until the beginning of the twentieth century, the story of comfort is one of a gradual evolution. It was an evolution that was undisturbed even by the arrival of electricity and household management. It managed to survive the disappearance of servants, and the reappearance of the small family home. It was resilient enough to absorb not only new technology, but also a new way of life. But this easy balance between innovation and tradition was about to be upset by a rupture in the evolution of domestic comfort which would drastically alter the appearance of the domestic interior.

• • •

The Exposition Internationale des Arts Décoratifs et Industriels Modernes that was held in Paris in the summer of 1925
was an elaborate affair, located in the center of the city and
lasting six months. Unlike earlier world exhibitions, this one
focused on a single subject—the decorative arts—and it was
intended to display the latest ideas in furniture and interior
decoration. More than seventeen European countries took
part, as well as Japan, Turkey, and the Soviet Union. Only
Germany and the United States were noticeable by their ab-
sences. (Germany was not invited for political reasons; American failure to participate has not been explained.) It was the
first (and indeed the last) time that the domestic interior was
the subject of an international exhibition of this size. There
was no single great structure in the 1925 Exposition—no
Crystal Palace or Eiffel Tower. Instead, nearly two hundred
buildings covered a seventy-five-acre site that stretched from
the Invalides across the Seine to the Grand Palais. The Exposition was intended to reestablish France as the European
leader in interior decoration—a position then held by Aus-
tria—and, in addition to the buildings representing each
country, there were special pavilions erected by prominent
manufacturers as well as by the largest French department
stores. In them were displayed room settings, furniture. ce-
ramics, glass, printed materials, rugs, wallpaper, and ironwork.

The stars of the show were without question the French
ensembliers—a term that was used to describe a sort of master
decorator, a couturier of the domestic interior. The most
famous was Jacques-Emile Ruhlmann, a furniture designer
and manufacturer, who had his own pavilion, the Hôtel du
Collectionneur, made to resemble the house of a wealthy art
collector. The art displayed was contemporary and included
work by many of the best-known French artists and craftsmen
whose painted panels, sculptures, glass chandeliers and wrought
ironwork were combined with Ruhlmann's furniture into an

elegant decor. The main salon, whose predominant colors were purple and blue, was lit by tall windows with straight-falling folds of gauze drapery. The space was dominated by an immense drum-shaped, glass-beaded chandelier; over the peach-blossom marble fireplace was a large painting by Jean Dupas—*The Parakeets*—whose gray-black-and-blue color scheme, with a touch of vivid green, was the focus of the room. The chairs and sofas were upholstered in Beauvais tapestry. The dark Macassar ebony of the furniture was relieved by tracings of inlaid ivory and silver bronze, which, like the occasional gilt, reflected the light and added sparkle to the otherwise severe room. The Ruhlmann pavilion was widely acclaimed as an exemplary piece of modern design, and when a traveling exhibition of selected material from the International Exposition was brought to the United States the following year and displayed at the Metropolitan Museum of Art in New York (as well as in museums in eight other major cities), the centerpiece of the show was the "House of a Collector." *

The rooms displayed at the Exposition were celebrations of visual richness and delight. Here is a contemporary description of a lady's bedroom designed by Maurice Dufrène, an *ensemblier* who worked for the elegant Parisian department store Galeries Lafayette. It was written by an English journalist obviously captivated by the delightful setting: "He has lit this wonderful room from an oval recess in the ceiling, in which waving lines in pale tones of fawn interlace to a design. But a more marked innovation is the luminous ornament that undulates in clean, yet suave sweeps, about a great circular mirror opposite the bed. This *chambre de dame* is a truly successful harmony of softly graceful curves among

---

* The traveling exhibit had a powerful—and lingering—influence on American design; the interior of the Radio City Music Hall in New York, completed in 1933, bears a striking resemblance to Ruhlmann's salon.

which the eye wanders luxuriously till it comes to rest on the foot-high dais enthroned in the alcove's withdrawal. The alcove itself is walled by spraying, radiating forms of silver, a final statement of the femininity that pervades the whole. Ah! am I forgetting the enormous white bear skin that covers half the floor? A rope of silver, thick and tasseled, is knotted about the muzzle. How one figures to oneself the rose and ivory of madame's exquisite feet sinking softly, gracefully into the whiteness of the stupendous fur!"[3] Whether it was Dufrène's voluptuous boudoir or Paul Follot's more serious gold-and-black library, the French interiors were decorated in the same striking style, which one historian has described as "jazz-modern," and which eventually derived its name from the Exposition itself—Art Deco.

Art Deco was the final in a line of creative styles, each less historical than the last. The Arts and Crafts movement in England had begun by developing the so-called English Cottage style, which, like Queen Anne, was based on earlier domestic architecture, but was freer and more original in its interior decoration. This led to the even more creative Art Nouveau style. Although there were precedents for Art Nouveau, both in England and America, it emerged first in Brussels, a well-defined, creative style, uninfluenced by history. During its short life—it lasted less than a decade, from 1892 to 1900—it spread over Europe, where it was known by a variety of names: *Jugendstil*, Liberty, *il stile floreale*, and Modern Style. It was first and foremost an *interior* style, and Art Nouveau rooms were characterized by sinuous ornament based on forms drawn from nature, by an absence of clutter, and by the stylistic consistency of the furniture, fabrics, and carpets. The reasons for its rapid demise are unclear. Perhaps people tired of its extravagance, perhaps it was so perfect and fully formed that it could not develop further, or perhaps its "breath of decadence" (Praz's phrase) doomed it from the beginning. In any case, it encouraged further experimentation, and closed the door, or so it seemed, on period decor. In its final variation in Vienna, where it was known as the Secession style, it shed much of its floral character, and thanks to designers like Josef Hoffmann it acquired a more abstract, and geometrical, appearance.

Art Deco came to the attention of the general public at the International Exposition, but this French style had its beginning earlier. It was triggered by the arrival in Paris of Serge Diaghilev's Ballets Russes in 1909. The music of Rimsky-Korsakov and the dancing of Nijinsky had an electrifying effect on Parisian society, but the sensuous decor and costumes of Leon Bakst made as great an impression. They were exotic and flamboyant, and a radical departure from what people were used to. After seeing the ballet *Sheherazade*, leading couturiers like Paul Poiret introduced feathered turbans, colored silk stockings, harem pants, and other oriental fashions. The new look, glamorous and sexy, was an enormous success. The full curves of the Belle Epoque were replaced by slim layered skirts, and corsets were replaced by straight cocktail dresses (eventually quite short) and small bosoms. As had happened so often in the past, clothing influenced decor. Gold lamé needed an appropriate setting—neither the quaint Cottage style nor the strict Viennese Secession would do. Looser and freer clothing produced a more relaxed posture; people began lounging—oriental fashion—on piles of loose cushions. In 1911, Poiret opened his own interior-decorating business—anticipating Ralph Lauren by more than half a century—and extended the languorous luxury of his clothes to the room itself. Art Deco was born.

After the First World War, in the heady atmosphere of the Twenties, Art Deco flourished and became the predominant Parisian style. It had always had a whiff of sinfulness, which now, if anything, increased. It continued to be influenced by dance, but now it was by the cabaret revues of Josephine Baker, by the sultry tango, and the Black Bottom. Art Deco apartments—it was always an urban style, hence its glossy toughness—incorporated African influences with zebra and leopard skins and tropical woods.

By 1925, it was pretty much taken for granted, at least in France, that comfortable interiors could be designed without any specific reference to the past. The organizers of the International Exposition had explicitly insisted that there should not be any period interiors at all—everything was to be "new and modern." It was felt necessary to redecorate the interior of the Grand Palais, which had been built only twenty-five years before for an earlier exhibition, in order to camouflage its neo-Classical appearance. But the modernism of Ruhlmann and Dufrène did not constitute a denial of the past. Delight, and comfort, continued to be evident. Craftsmanship and rich materials figured prominently in their work, as did ornamentation, even if it tended to be geometrical instead of figurative. The elements of the past were there—chandeliers, friezes, ornate paneling—but they were reworked according to a different aesthetic. Nor was Art Deco uninterested in technology. Lighting was a major preoccupation of the *ensembliers*. For Suzanne Talbot, a Paris couturier, Eileen Gray designed an apartment with a floor built entirely out of silvered mat glass, lit from below. Jacques Dunand's windowless smoking room, which was displayed at the Exposition, had a stepped, silvered ceiling concealing both indirect electric lighting and ventilation outlets. Pierre Chareau, a decorator and engineer who three years later would build his famous glass house, the *Maison de Verre*, built a study-library at the Exposition with an overhead dome of palm-tree wood that could be opened at night to disclose an illuminated ceiling consisting of several layers of thick white glass. Another innovative designer, Rob. Mallet-Stevens, also used multilayered glass—gray-green—to diffuse and color the light. More than any style of that time, Art Deco showed an aesthetic

appreciation for modern materials and devices; for these designers technology was fun.

As a result of the International Exposition, Art Deco was
seen by a great number of people. Like Queen Anne the new
style had no scholarly pretensions, and it was popular with
the general public, although not with avant-garde artists and
intellectuals. Nor with traditionalists; "It is not for the lover
of maple and pine," an American critic warned her readers,
"not for the partisan of cotton and horsehair. It would be
impossible to travel much further away from the American
Colonial."[4] Part of the attraction of Art Deco was its atmosphere of glamour. The main patrons of the new style
were wealthy couturiers such as Jacques Doucet, Jeanne Lanvin, and Talbot. They could afford lighting fixtures of veined
alabaster, a dining room faced in lapis lazuli, or furniture
inlaid with shagreen and amboyna wood, all of which were
featured, and admired, in the Paris show. Although a few
critics muttered about "this frank appeal to the class of privilege," most people, including most of the public, accepted
the wealthy style on its own terms. The war to end all wars
had been fought and forgotten, postwar prosperity was in
full swing, and the jazz-modern style seemed just right. The
consensus was that the Paris exhibition was a great success.
The "modernest of modern" styles was sometimes strange,
often exotic, but all agreed it was the coming thing.

Although the work of even such progressive designers as
Chareau and Mallet-Stevens was appreciated, the taste for
modernism had its limits. "While the password is Simplicity
and Rationalism," wrote the critic for the American *Architectural Record*, "the effect in many instances is cold and
dismal and occasionally preposterous."[5] The most contro-
versial building at the Exposition was undoubtedly the Soviet
pavilion. It was designed in the Constructivist manner that
was then favored by the new revolutionary state, and its stark,

plain, geometrical appearance, of unpainted wood, shocked many, as it was intended to do. The (apocryphal) story was that when the pavilion was being erected on the Exposition site, the packing crates in which it had arrived from Russia had been incorporated in the building by mistake.[6]

Some distance from the Soviet pavilion was a site that had been entrusted to one of the innumerable small art magazines then being published in Paris. The pavilion was called *Esprit Nouveau* (New Spirit)—that was the name of the magazine—and it was probably what an American correspondent had in mind when he complained about certain designs that exhibited the "prosaic literalness of a cold storage warehouse cube."[7] That was not altogether unfair for it was roughly box-shaped, and its plain exterior was white, relieved only by enormous, twenty-foot-high letters painted on one wall—EN. The official encyclopedia of the Exposition called it an "oddity," and assured the reader that despite its strange appearance, it was not something from another planet.[8] As for the public, it seems to have been largely uninterested. The "strange Slavonic conceptions" of the Russian pavilion attracted attention, but few of the visitors that hurried by spared the New Spirit house a glance. None of the extensive articles on the Exposition that appeared in the American and English architectural press mentioned it by name. Yet this building, not even worth criticizing, was to prove more influential in the development of the home than any of its lauded and illustrious neighbors.

The pavilion had been designed by the Jeanneret cousins, Charles-Edouard and Pierre. The former, who was the editor of *L'Esprit Nouveau*, was to become better known by his recently assumed *nom de plume*, Le Corbusier. Why did this building, designed by a man who would become arguably the most famous architect of the twentieth century, receive so little attention? The Swiss-born Le Corbusier was not altogether unknown; he had lived in Paris for eight years. With

the painter Fernand Léger he had founded an art movement—
Purism—and, although he had built little, his ideas had received considerable public exposure in his magazine, in several exhibitions, and lately in his book *Towards a New
Architecture.* The widely accepted explanation for the neglect
accorded to the New Spirit pavilion, suggested by Le Corbusier himself, was that there was a concerted effort by the
Exposition organizers to sabotage his pavilion.* A simpler
reason was that most people simply did not cotton to the
New Spirit.

Visitors to the pavilion would have found the interior as
bare and unfinished as the exterior. There were no ornaments,
no draperies, no wallpaper. There was no mantelpiece to
display the family photographs, no paneling in the study.
There was no polished wood, let alone lapis lazuli. The color
scheme was stark: predominantly white walls contrasted with
a blue ceiling; one wall of the living room was painted brown;
the storage cabinets that served as room dividers were painted
bright yellow. The effect was distinctly unhomey, and was
heightened by the staircase, which was made out of steel pipes
and looked as if it had been plucked directly from a ship's
boiler room. The industrial atmosphere was echoed in the
window frames, which were not wood, but steel, of a type
commonly known as factory sash. There were some strange
transpositions—the kitchen was the smallest room in the house,
the size of a bathroom, and the bathroom, which was intended to double as an exercise room and had one entire wall
built out of glass blocks, was almost as big as the living room.
Even more surprising was the furniture. Not only was there

---

*Le Corbusier claimed that the authorities erected a twenty-foot-high wall
around the pavilion to hide it. Recent evidence suggests that the infamous
wall had a different function; because of last-minute financial difficulties,
construction of the New Spirit pavilion was begun only on the night before
the Exposition was to open, and the wall was needed to hide the unsightly
construction work, which continued for three months.[9]

little of it, it seemed intentionally lackluster: a couple of non-descript leather armchairs, side chairs of a common variety usually found in popular restaurants, and tables consisting of slabs of plain wood mounted on tubular steel frames. Compared to the syncopations of jazz-modern, the New Spirit was a one-note tune played on a penny whistle.

The drabness of this interior was not the result of budgetary limitations—although these had posed problems—but was intentional. Nor was it done *pour épater les bourgeois*—to shock the public—although Le Corbusier's plan, displayed in the pavilion, to raze the center of Paris and replace it with sixty-story high-rises is hard to take seriously except as a monumental *blague*. But the New Spirit was no joke. Over the next five years Le Corbusier built a series of villas whose interiors followed strictly in the footsteps of "the cold storage warehouse cube," and indeed, as a perspicacious French critic foresaw, the ideas that only five years before had seemed outlandish were, by 1930, beginning to gain ascendancy.[10]

What did the New Spirit consist of? First, the complete rejection of decorative art. This meant, obviously, the rejection of the ornament that characterized the historical revival styles, which Le Corbusier scornfully called Louis A, B, and C. But it also meant rejecting such creative revivals as Arts and Crafts and the Secession style, and avoiding even the abstract decoration of Art Deco. That would leave the interior rather bare, wouldn't it? And what was wrong with that? asked Le Corbusier. You could always hang a painting on the wall. In fact, the pavilion contained works by several avant-garde Parisian artists—Picasso, Gris and Lipschitz. But what about furnishings? Although Le Corbusier deplored the bourgeois habit of collecting furniture—he derided their homes as "labyrinths of furniture"—he had to admit that some pieces—tables and chairs—were necessary. But he had the answer to that as well: New Spirit homes would no longer contain *furniture*, instead they would be furnished with *equip-*

ment. "Decorative art is equipment," he wrote, "beautiful equipment."[11]

Only the metal storage cupboards, which resembled filing cabinets and were built by a manufacturer of office equipment, were made especially for the pavilion. Lacking enough funds, and time, to design original pieces, Le Corbusier was obliged to use ready-made furniture. He could have used any variety of inexpensive, mass-produced domestic furniture that was available, but he chose instead to use bentwood restaurant chairs inside and common cast-iron Parisian park furniture on the terrace. Laboratory jars served as flower vases; cheap bistro glasses replaced cut crystal. Instead of chandeliers or decorative lighting fixtures there were spotlights, wall-mounted shop-window lamps, or bare bulbs.

To most visitors, the pipe railings and restaurant furniture appeared crude and makeshift. To them there was nothing attractive about cheap bistro glasses or industrial lighting fixtures. The blank white walls were uninviting and bare, the harsh colors and the factory-made objects seemed cold and impersonal. The tall living room with its enormous window resembled a workshop or an artist's studio, its Spartan furnishings and hard bright finishes more suited to a common commercial establishment than to a home.* The cramped kitchen had all the charm of a tiny laboratory. In an exhibition devoted to the decorative arts, Le Corbusier's pavilion contained neither decoration nor, it seemed to most, artistry.

Was the reason for these drastic changes, as Le Corbusier claimed, the requirements of a "new mechanical age"? In "The Manual of the Dwelling," published two years before, Le Corbusier had offered advice to the prospective home-owner.[13] Surprisingly, little of it concerned domestic tech-

---

* According to Le Corbusier, the inspiration for the two-story-high living room, overlooked by a gallery and lit be a large window—which he repeated in many houses—was a Parisian truckers' café.[12]

nology. Heating was not mentioned. Ventilation was hardly touched on. He offered nothing more mechanical than openable windows in every room. His proposal that the kitchen be at the top of the house to avoid smells was quaint—and impractical. As for domestic appliances, the best he could do was suggest a vacuum cleaner and a gramophone—hardly revolutionary devices. The pavilion demonstrated little interest in such technical details as the convenient location of electric outlets and lamps. "The house is a machine for living in" was one of his most famous sayings, but judged from a purely mechanical perspective the New Spirit offered little that was—well, new.

Yet one cannot help sympathizing with Le Corbusier's efforts to come to grips with the problems of modern living, something that set his plain pavilion apart from the sumptuous interiors of the Art Deco *ensembliers*. He was trying, however awkwardly, to make the home a more efficient place, and to deal with everyday life, instead of with the esoteric, almost outdated problems of decor. In this regard he shared many of the goals of the American domestic engineers. Like Frederick and Gilbreth, Le Corbusier had read F. W. Taylor's book on scientific management, but he seemed to have applied Taylor's ideas only to the construction of houses, not to housework itself.[14] If his attempts at efficient domestic planning seem crude, that was also an indication of how advanced American domestic design was compared to Europe. Combined living rooms, built-in closets, shower baths, and concealed lighting, which he presented as "new" ideas, had been commonplace in American homes for decades. When Ellen Richards wrote that "the house as a home is merely outer clothing, which should fit as an overcoat should, without wrinkles and creases that show their ready-made character," she was anticipating—by twenty years—Le Corbusier's statement that "one can be proud of having a house as serviceable as a typewriter."[15]

But there was a telling difference in their choice of metaphors: clothing and machinery. The aim of scientific management in the factory was to discover efficient and standardized work procedures. When they applied these theories to the home, the domestic engineers realized that they were dealing with activities that were more complex, and more personal. They also recognized that there was more than one "correct" way of doing things, and their aim was to help people discover solutions that would suit their individual needs—that was why Richards imagined the house as clothing, which should be fitted to the individual. Lillian Gilbreth's flow process charts and micro-motion transfer sheets were intended to enable the housewife to organize the home according to *her own* work habits. She continually reminded her readers that there was no ideal solution; the height of a kitchen counter must be adjusted to the height of the person, and the most useful layout of appliances would vary from one household to the next. Her first two rules for improving the layout of the home were "Be guided by convenience, not convention" and "Consider the personalities and habits of your family, yourself included." [16]

When Gilbreth referred to "standards" she meant the personal norms that each family decided for itself; once these were established, the technique of scientific management could be applied to find the most efficient way of achieving them. For Le Corbusier, on the other hand, standards were something that was imposed from without. According to him, human needs were universal and could be uniformalized, and consequently his solutions were prototypical, not personal. He visualized the home as a mass-produced object (a typewriter), to which the individual should adapt. The job of the designer was to identify the "correct" solution; once it was found, it was up to people to accustom themselves to it. For Le Corbusier, the ideal furniture was office furniture, which, like the typewriter, was based on "prototypes" and which, through mass production, was repeated on a large scale. In a book he published just after the International Exposition he illustrated this by showing an exemplary interior—the City-National Bank in Tuscaloosa, of all places—in which desks and office chairs with identical fans, telephones, lamps—and typewriters—are neatly lined up one behind the other.[17]

The idea of standardization, useful though it might be in banks, is ill suited to the complicated and varied activities that are contained by the home. Because of this, Le Corbusier's ideas about domestic planning were less sophisticated than those of the domestic engineers. The cramped kitchen in the New Spirit house, with its minimal counter space, was poorly conceived, its relation to the dining room inconvenient. The open study would have been noisy and impractical. The one room which could have benefited from standardization, the bathroom, was treated sculpturally, to little benefit. Not only was Le Corbusier's design not a "servantless house," it was not even, despite his admiration for efficiency, particularly small. In addition to the large outdoor terrace, the three-bedroom home had an area of 2,500 square feet. This was more than twice as big as Catherine Beecher's model house, and much larger than Von Holst's "efficient home," which had included a family room, four bedrooms, and two porches, and which had been designed fifteen years before.

Another difference between Le Corbusier and the domestic engineers concerned the question of what the efficient home should look like. Richards's, Frederick's, and Gilbreth's attitude to the appearance of the home can only be described as cheerfully pragmatic; they were concerned with function, not appearance. They took it for granted that people would want to decorate their homes in different ways, and they saw no reason to claim that one was better than another. Gilbreth stressed the importance of color in workrooms, but added that this was an individual choice, and that what was pleasing for one was depressing for another. Frederick recommended the "modern" Viennese fashion as an inexpensive alternative to Louis XIV, but did not insist on this, and went on to discuss Colonial and other revival styles. Neither saw any conflict between traditional decor and efficient housekeeping, which was the reason that their teaching met with public acceptance.

This was where Le Corbusier parted company with the domestic engineers. He was still, in a sense, a nineteenth-century architect, fighting the battle of the styles. That was what the New Spirit was all about—a new style, a style suited to the twentieth century, a style for the Machine Age, a style for more efficient living. His was not simply a modern home, but a home that *looked* modern. He was right about the need for domestic efficiency, even if that was not always evident in practice, but he was wrong about its effect on the appearance of the home. Efficiency did not depend on what the interior of the home looked like, but on how work was organized within it. If the kitchen was planned according to the principles of scientific management, it really did not matter if the cupboards had colonial trim or flowered porcelain handles, just as long as things were in the right place and not too far apart. And if people felt more comfortable, and worked better, with patterned tiles or cheery curtains, well, that was efficiency too. It was not the absence of wallpaper and ogee trim that made a house "modern," it was the presence of central heating and convenient bathrooms, electric irons and washing machines. Like most architects, Le Corbusier did not understand, or would not accept, that the advent of domestic technology and home management had put the whole question of architectural style in a subordinate position.

Chapter Nine

Marcel Breuer, Wassily Chair (1925–26)

Austerity

> . . . *we shared what had once been a dressing-room and had been changed to a bathroom twenty years back by the substitution for the bed of a deep, copper, mahogany-framed bath, that was filled by pulling a brass lever heavy as a piece of marine engineering; the rest of the room remained unchanged; a coal fire always burned there in the winter. I often think of that bathroom—the water colors dimmed by steam and the huge towel warming on the back of the chintz armchair—and contrast it with the uniform, clinical, little chambers glittering with chromium-plate and looking-glass, which pass for luxury in the modern world.*
>
> —EVELYN WAUGH
>
> *BRIDESHEAD REVISITED*

When Angelo Donghia was engaged by Ralph Lauren and his wife to renovate their New York duplex, the fashionable interior decorator assumed that the comfortable man in Levi's who was also the originator of the Vanderbilt look would want his home to look like "either the Harvard Club or a very prosperous ranch."[1] To his surprise—and ours—it turned out to be neither. None of the ten rooms has so much 195 as a shred of swag, patterned fabric, or flowered prints—not a square inch of paisley in the entire place. One looks in vain for flocked paper and Aubusson tapestries. They are not there; there are no carpets or rugs to disfigure the stripped and varnished floors, no draperies to mar the plain white walls. The window shades are simple bamboo blinds. There are a few, enormous plants; there is very little furniture—none of it is antique. A commercial-looking stainless-steel work island is the most prominent feature of the kitchen; an upholstered leather sofa-table command post with built-in controls for the home entertainment system forms the focus of the media room. The bathroom is dominated by a severe, laboratory-like counter and resembles the scrubroom of a prosperous hospital; of course, it contains no watercolors, let alone a chintz armchair. Waugh would have hated it.

The Laurens' duplex is what designers call "deceptively simple." In other words, it doesn't look decorated at all. The man who wants to house America in tattersalls, foulards, and chambray has chosen something much more fashionable for himself—Minimal decor. According to the strict rules of this genre, not only are all decorative architectural elements stripped away, but all personal possesions are made invisible as well. The lights are hidden in the ceiling, books and children's toys are hidden in the cupboards, even the cupboards are hidden behind smooth, usually mat-white, doors. Dining rooms resemble monastic refectories. Kitchens look as bare as the other rooms—refrigerator, oven, pots and pans, spoons and spatulas are out of sight. In one extreme case of Minimal design—the flat of an art dealer in London—even the beds are hidden, for they consist of cotton futons that are rolled up and put away during the day. In the same home the bathroom is so pristine that it is not provided with shelves or cabinets—the owner is obliged to carry the toothbrush and soap with her in what she calls a "wet-pack." If this sounds awkward, we are assured that she "cheerfully insists that the minor inconveniences of her disciplined way of living are worth putting up with for the sake of a highly refined way of life."[2]

How fashion has changed. In 1912, when the great Paris couturier Jacques Doucet sold his collection of eighteenth-century art and replaced it with Cubist and Surrealist paintings, he commissioned Paul Iribe to design an appropriately up-to-date decor. The glamorous result—Iribe later designed movie sets for Cecil B. De Mille—is generally considered to have been the first Art Deco interior. When Ralph Lauren wants glamour, he settles for bare walls and potted plants. Sixty years ago, the owner of the London flat would have been living in a concoction of silver-and-black-lacquered walls and leopard skins, such as was designed by Eileen Gray for Suzanne Talbot. She would have been reclining on angora in a "Pirogue" chaise longue, not sleeping on a cotton mat on the floor.

Minimal decor has been facetiously described as "conspicuous austerity."[3] It is like the expensive versions of certain automobiles that can be ordered from the manufacturer without model markings, or like the native costumes worn by Saudi politicians at international conferences. It represents a subtle form of snobbism, which achieves singularity by avoiding the familiar; in the case of interiors, this means decor without decoration. But it is also an example of the current taste for reducing the clutter and crowd of objects in a room. Every period, sometimes even every decade, has its own visual taste, just as it has its own culinary taste. During the 1970s, for example, there was an appreciable shift in American eating away from bland food toward a spicier cuisine—ethnic food such as tart Szechwan and hot Tex-Mex became popular. Today, *nouvelle cuisine* has replaced Escoffier, and the palate seems ready for a simpler diet. So also in interiors; the number of patterns and objects and the degree of visual richness and diversity in rooms vary.

Peter Thornton has termed this quality of interiors "density."[4] The ebb and flow of density varies—like fashion, like the length of women's skirts and men's hair. It is a function of how much patterning and clutter the eye can stand. This is not just a question of historical periods or styles, for even within one period density can change. An English neo-Palladian interior in 1720 was denser than one twenty years later; on the other hand, mid-Victorian rooms were not nearly as cluttered as were those in the 1870s, especially if they were Queen Anne. After 1920, there was a decided shift in popular taste, and rooms became less dense, a trend that reached its culmination with the Minimalism of the 1970s. Since then, according to Thornton, there has been a perceptible shift toward greater fussiness and more patterns, exemplified by a renewal of interest in the previously ignored Victorian interior.

Conspicuous austerity—it is a curious, antipodean term. It well describes the contradictions of modern decor: marble kitchen counters and bamboo window shades, painted plasterboard walls and fitted oak doors, a Matisse on the wall and a sleeping mat on the floor—a domestic atmosphere which is both highly regimented and clumsily improvised. The decor is artless, but it is a studied, refined artlessness. The bathroom looks like an ordinary white tiled bathroom, until you realize that it has been so dimensioned that not a single tile has been cut; perfect and pristine, they all fit in place. The oak floor looks straightforward enough, but every piece of wood is exactly the same length. The simplicity too is deceptive—it is not easy to design cupboards that disappear into the wall, or doorways without frames. The precision with which materials are joined is severe; its perfection intimidates and accuses at the same time. No wonder everything must be put away. It is not only clutter that has been removed from this interior, but all signs of sloppiness and human frailty, and even of design itself.

This process of stripping away, which is so characteristic

of modern interiors, began with the Viennese architect Adolf Loos. In 1908, he had written a disputatious essay entitled "Ornament and Crime" which advocated the abolition of all ornament from everyday life, including from architecture and from interior decoration. Loos argued that what had been necessary in the past was no longer appropriate in a modern industrialized world. He equated the urge to ornament with primitivism, and he offered bathroom graffiti and tattoos as examples of what he considered to be deviational decoration. The "crime" of ornament was that it wasted society's resources, both money and people's time, on what, in Loos's opinion, was both unnecessary and archaic.

As early as 1904, Loos was designing villas with plain white unornamented plastered walls, flat roofs without cornices, and rectangular windows unrelieved by any trace of a frame or molding—the first "cold storage warehouse cubes." But Loos was a reformer, not a revolutionary. He was an opponent of ornament, but not of decoration, and the interiors of his cubes did not resemble the exteriors in the least. The rooms were finished in rich materials, marble cladding and parquetry, and contained comfortable, traditional furniture—he was an admirer of Chippendale and Queen Anne. Loos's interiors exhibited all the solid, comfortable, bourgeois domesticity that he and his Viennese clients expected in a home.

Loos's vociferous attack on ornament, which he was later to regret, opened the door to a wholesale questioning of traditional values. Moreover, since he had established a moral basis for this questioning it soon acquired the rhetoric, and the self-assurance, of a crusade. For the French, German, and Dutch avant-garde, the elimination of ornament was just the beginning. They turned Loos's ideas inside out, and the interiors of their houses became just as white and blank as the exteriors. All vestiges of the past were removed. If ornament was a crime, so was luxury. No more rich materials, no more extravagance, no more frills. It was not long before even bourgeois ease itself came under attack. Wallpaper, paneling, and wainscoting were replaced by unpainted plaster, brick, and concrete. The more austere the better. Walls were undecorated, floors were bare, and lighting was harsh.

Next, the very idea of domesticity itself came under attack. Coziness had to go, the moralists were clear about that. Which was why their interiors, unlike those of Loos, had no snug alcoves or fireside inglenooks. Loos had argued that if something was practical it should be used, no matter how old it was—he frequently had copies made of Windsor chairs for his clients. But for the crusaders, bourgeois furnishings, like bourgeois ornament, were to be avoided. That was why they shunned period furniture and used commercial chairs, or designed furniture that looked like industrial equipment.* That was why cupboards were made to look like filing cabinets and stairs like ships' ladders. The home was being remade in a new image, stripped of its bourgeois traditions and bereft of easeful intimacy and well-established ideas of comfort. The more radical architects were open about it. Extreme measures were required to "prevent us from falling prey to dullness, to habit, *and to comfort*" (emphasis added).[6] It is reasonable to ask how such an unlikely—and on the surface, at least, unpopular—agenda could ever have succeeded. It was the result of a series of accidents, coincidences, and historical forces, none of which could have been foreseen in the summer of 1925, when the New Spirit pavilion stood neglected and ignored, the cheerless harbinger of a future that, apparently, nobody wanted.

---

* Loos was living in Paris at the time of the International Exposition, and he represented an Austrian firm which was to have supplied furniture for the New Spirit pavilion. Although he was the first Modern architect to have used bentwood chairs—in 1899—he did so in a café, and felt that Le Corbusier's use of restaurant chairs in a home was "unfortunate."[5]

. . .

To begin with, the Crash of 1929 and the Great Depression put a damper on the Art Deco style. Most of the private patrons who had supported the *ensembliers* in the past could no longer afford to pay for the craftsmanship and the fine materials; those who could preferred to spend their money in more discreet ways. Art Deco did not die out altogether—the interiors of the famous French ocean liner *Normandie*, launched in 1935, were Art Deco—but it ceased to be a domestic style; it had always in any case been too expensive for most people. It did continue in large buildings, especially those that were required to appeal to the public, and as a decor for restaurants, shops, and hotels it reigned supreme for the next twenty-five years. Most American cities had at least one Art Deco movie theater, whose glamorous atmosphere seemed tailor-made for Hollywood's products. Cities like Miami Beach and Los Angeles practically adopted Art Deco as a municipal style. But authentic Art Deco was for elegant aesthetes, not for the masses, and in its public transformation it was rarely as refined as it had been in its heyday; it became a coarsened and sanitized version of its original risqué self.

The unglamorous warehouse cube style, on the other hand, was well suited to post-Depression sobriety; it was also more adaptable to small budgets and limited resources—all you needed was enough white paint. But it was more than a question of economics. During the 1920s, the only government to (briefly) endorse the anti-bourgeois style had been that of the Soviet Union—Le Corbusier's first large commission was in Moscow—for the ideology of the anti-bourgeois crusaders was appealing to revolutionary socialists. The new Nazi powers in Germany, on the other hand, were staunchly traditionalist—at least as far as architecture was concerned—and wanted nothing to do with what they considered to be a bolshevik style. Since neo-Classicism was favored by dictators—by both Hitler and Mussolini, and, as it turned out, by Stalin—the austere architecture of the modernists came, by default, to represent antifascism and antitotalitarianism.

The new, socialist postwar governments in England, Germany, Holland, and the Scandinavian countries responded favorably to the left-leaning rhetoric of the Modern school. In the United States, where many of the Modern German architects had sought refuge from the Nazis, the Modern style was similarly well received, not because of its socialist teachings, but because, given its origins, it was considered to be sophisticated and avant-garde. Just as in 1925, when Americans had visited the International Exposition to admire Art Deco, so, ten years later they were learning about another new European style. This time they were doing so at first hand, however, from two of the foremost German Modern architects—Walter Gropius and Mies van der Rohe. They were feted, exhibited, put in charge of their own schools of architecture and provided with commissions. With the active support of socialite patrons, museums, universities, and architectural critics, their approach to architecture became preeminent.[7] Its antitotalitarian reputation also helped, and it became a "Free World" style, representing democracy and America in the Cold War. In this role it was not seen as just another architectural style; not only white in appearance, it was morally unblemished as well. It was a break with the past, a past that was increasingly seen as worthless and immoral, at least architecturally speaking. According to this view Art Deco had been lewd, the Victorian revivals were decadent, let-them-eat-cake Rococo was the worst—only white austerity was virtuous. Decoration was bad for the soul; it had to be stripped away. People would feel happier discarding the baggage of period decor. If that was not always easy, or agreeable, it was, at least, like medicine, good for you.

The endorsement of European politicians or New York intellectuals would not have counted for much, however, if the new architecture had not had some major practical advantages of its own. The reconstruction of Europe, and the American postwar economic boom, required a fast and inexpensive way of building that would be suited to mass production and industrialization. Both the historical revival styles as well as Art Nouveau and Art Deco involved expensive craftsmanship, as well as costly materials. The architecture of plain walls and undecorated rooms required neither—indeed, it made a virtue of standardization—and for that reason alone, at least as far as businessmen were concerned, it was attractive. The public's reaction was less enthusiastic. Given the choice, most people would have preferred something a bit cozier, Queen Anne or Colonial, say, but they were not consulted. Buildings in the stripped-down style were grudgingly accepted on the assumption that they were "functional" and "efficient." They were even admired—especially if they were tall—but they were not loved. Although the architectural profession and its supporters extolled the moral virtues of the New Spirit, to the man on the street it was just another unpleasant, but inevitable by-product of modern life, like traffic jams or plastic forks.

Interior decoration followed architecture. Architects had learned their lesson, and they were not going to lose control over the insides of buildings, as they had done in the nineteenth century. The arrangement of the interior was no longer left to the whims of the owner; nor was it allowed to fall into the hands of interior decorators. A modern building was a total experience; not only the interior layout but also the finish materials, the furnishings, the accessories, and the location of chairs were planned. The result was rooms of a visual consistency not seen since the Rococo. This was not the product of a team of craftsmen sharing a common formal vocabulary, however. The most admired interiors were those where everything was designed by a single architect—including lights, door handles, and ashtrays.* And of course the furniture, especially the furniture.

Furniture tells all. Just as a paleontologist can reconstruct a prehistoric animal from a fragment of jawbone, one can reconstruct the domestic interior, and the attitudes of its inhabitants, from a single chair. A Louis XV *fauteuil* reflects not only the decor of the room for which it was intended, but also the delightful elegance of the period. A gleaming mahogany Georgian Windsor chair, with its gracefully carved stickwork, is the essence of gentlemanly restraint. An over-stuffed Victorian armchair, with its deeply tufted, rich fabrics and lace antimacassars, represents both the conservatism of that period and its desire for physical ease. An Art Deco chaise longue, upholstered in zebra skin and encrusted with mother-of-pearl, exhibits a tactile and voluptuous enjoyment of luxury.

The Wassily armchair, designed by Marcel Breuer in 1925–26, is considered to be a classic. Like Mies van der Rohe's Barcelona chair of the same period, it exemplifies the ideals of contemporary chair design: it is lightweight, it uses machined materials, and it contains no ornament. It is a structure of bent, chromed-metal tubing, across which unpadded leather is stretched to form the seat, back, and armrests. It looks, as the saying goes, untouched by human hands. Its stark beauty is not derived from decoration, but from the explicit and

---

* Adolf Loos had disagreed with the "master designer" approach. "I am an opponent of the trend that considers it to be especially desirable that a building has been designed along with everything in it—down to the coal scoop—by the hand of one architect. I am of the opinion that the building can have a rather monotonous appearance as a result."[8] This appeared in a collection of his essays which he published in 1921 under the apt title *Spoken into the Void.*

structurally expressive way the materials are combined—the tubing in compression, the fabric in tension. Like all modern chairs it makes no reference to period furniture; its associations are contemporary, and intentionally everyday. The bent metal pipe recalls a bicycle frame, the hard leather resembles a barber's razor strop. When it was designed it was unlike any chair that anyone had ever seen—even sixty years later it still looks more like an exercise machine than an armchair. Hence the first reaction to sitting in the Wassily chair is favorable; one is surprised that it is possible to sit at all in this unlikely montage of intersecting pipes and planes.

A well-designed easy chair must accommodate not only relaxed sitting, but also having a drink, reading, conversation, bouncing babies on the knee, dozing, and so on. It must permit the sitter to shift about and adopt a variety of positions. This changing of postures has a social function—so-called body language. It should be possible to lean forward (to express concern) or to recline backward (to indicate pensiveness); one should be able to sit primly (to show respect) or to lounge (to communicate informality or even disrespect). The ability to change positions also has an important physical function. The human body is not designed to stay in one position for extended periods; prolonged immobility adversely affects body tissues, muscles, and joints. Changes of position—crossing the legs, tucking one, or both, up under the body, even hanging a leg over the armrest—shift the weight from one part of the body to another, relieve the pressure and stress, and relax different muscle groups. Even the most perfectly designed seat will soon feel uncomfortable if such movement is restricted—as all airline passengers well know. Engineers call this tendency of the body to change positions motility. Lying motility has been extensively studied, with regard both to sleeping comfort and to hospital beds, in which lack of motility quickly causes bedsores.[9] Sitting motility is less well understood, but there are indications that it is equally important in providing a feeling of comfort.* [10]

One way to accommodate motility is for the chair itself to move. This is what a traditional rocking chair does; its main purpose is not to rock continuously, but to permit the sitter to shift positions and to alleviate stresses, both in the legs and in the back. This is why rocking chairs are often prescribed for people with back problems. Beginning in the middle of the nineteenth century, mainly in America, there appeared a variety of furniture in which sitting comfort was achieved not by upholstery and padding as in the past, but by movement—flexing, rolling, tilting, and swiveling. Unlike the rocking chair, however, this moving furniture was mechanical. Today mechanical furniture has become associated with offices and stenographer's chairs, or with specialized seating such as barber's and dentist's chairs, but its origins are domestic. The first tilting and swiveling armchair on casters, which was patented in 1853, was intended for the home. [11] The Victorian family used many "machines for sitting in": flexible chairs for sewing, adjustable invalid couches, swivel chairs for writing and playing the piano, mechanical rockers and adjustable easy chairs.

Mechanical furniture not only permits motility, it also solves a problem that has always plagued furniture designers: the human body comes in a variety of shapes and sizes, and no chair can suit them all. In that sense, traditional furniture has always been a compromise; the best that could be done was to provide different sizes of chairs (usually smaller ones for women, broader and heavier versions for men) and enough upholstery and padding to make up the difference. The mechanical chair, on the other hand, can be designed to be

---

* The variety of adjustments that is now offered in many automobile seats is not only to accommodate different drivers, but to allow changes of position by the same driver during long trips.

adjustable, not only as far as seat height is concerned, but for the angle and height of the back support as well. Tilting mechanisms permit various postures within the same chair, and the pressure can be calibrated to take into account different body weights.

Domestic mechanical chairs have never attracted the attention of architects and designers; they scorn the adjustable lounge chair or "La-Z-Boy"—a nineteenth-century survivor—as hopelessly lowbrow.* The Wassily chair, like all modern domestic furniture, does not include any mechanical devices which would allow the sitter to adjust it to suit his or her requirements. Moreover, the steeply inclined angle of the seat makes it impossible to sit in any position except all the way back; if one tries to move forward to reach a coffee cup, for example, one finds oneself balanced unpleasantly on the unyielding edge of the seat. If one turns sideways, the armrests offer little support. The flat back and seat discourage movement; one soon begins to feel restless. If the knees are bent, the thighs are no longer supported by the taut seat, which also prevents one from stretching the legs out full-length. Before long, the edge of the hard leather begins to cut painfully into the underside of the thighs, and the double-stitched edges of the armrests rub unpleasantly along the elbow. This is an easy chair in which one cannot relax for more than thirty minutes at a time.

How can an uncomfortable chair also be a "classic"? Is it its historical importance, given the fact that Breuer designed this chair in 1926? One can admire the earliest bicycle, for example, awkward as it is, simply for the leap of invention

---

* One of the rare attempts to improve the La-Z-Boy, which is large and clumsy in appearance, is a reclining chair designed by Ferdinand Porsche. The fact that an automobile designer interests himself in mechanical furniture is not surprising, for the best car seats exhibit a degree of comfort and adjustability unmatched by any domestic chairs and only equaled by some office furniture.

that it represents. But the Wassily chair is hardly the first easy chair, even if it was the first to be constructed out of metal tubing. In any case, the "penny-farthing" has been consigned to a museum, and Breuer's chair is still being manufactured and sold—and sat in. It is not unfair to single out this chair for criticism, for it is a much-admired paragon of modern design, as is also the elegant Barcelona easy chair, designed by Mies van der Rohe, which continues to grace lobbies, museums, and living rooms. The Barcelona easy chair, too, offers limited comfort. Its thin cushions are too flat to offer proper support, its absence of arms makes sitting down and getting up awkward, and its slippery leather seat and back are unable to keep the sitter from sliding. This same slipping problem can be encountered in other chairs, such as the famous leather lounge chair designed by Charles Eames. Several critics have pointed out the "operational failure" of the ingenious Hardoy chair, also known as the Butterfly chair, whose popularity and reputation become more mysterious the longer one sits in it.[12] It would be an exaggeration to claim that all recent domestic furniture is uncomfortable, but it is a fact that many of what are generally considered to be outstanding examples of modern chair design demonstrate little concern for human comfort.*

It has been suggested that the ergonomic failure of contemporary furniture is due to a disregard for the traditional conventions of sitting comfort.[14] It is not easy to reinvent the wheel—or a chair—especially if one insists that the wheel should be anything but round. It had taken a long time for eighteenth-century furniture makers to find the correct seat and back angles and the appropriate curves, shapes, and ma-

---

* The Barcelona chair, the Eames lounge chair and the Hardoy chair were all included in a 1957 list of the "one hundred greatest products" chosen by a large sample of designers, critics and teachers.[13]

terials for sitting comfort. These advances were incorporated in a series of prototypes such as the padded wing chair, the tub chair, and the splatted dining chair, which became the functional paradigms for successful seating. Pattern books, like those of Hepplewhite and Chippendale, provided the detailed information that described the paradigm, and also suggested various formal possibilities that could be combined with it. The dimensions of the functional paradigm were detailed and explicit, and ensured sitting comfort. The formal alternatives were usually undimensioned, and left more to the imagination of the individual furniture maker. He was expected to produce original pieces, but always within the context of the paradigm; furniture design consisted of endless variations on a set number of themes.

This practice continued well into the twentieth century. Art Deco designers shared the eighteenth century's regard for commodity and delight, and although their furniture was smaller—to suit smaller rooms—it generally followed tradition, at least in its general form. When Ruhlmann designed an armchair, he took as his starting point the fully upholstered Victorian tub chair, with padded back and sides, and a loose cushion on the seat. In the nineteenth century it would have been ornamented; Ruhlmann's version was plainer, unpatterned velvet with slender dark ebony legs and a thin wooden band defining the shape of the chair. Although a Ruhlmann sofa recalled its French Empire antecedent, its use of burr walnut with silver and ivory inlays was also unmistakably Art Deco. A spoon-backed side chair by Louis Süe and André Mare, which in its details and its appearance was modern, continued to follow the Rococo tradition of a broad front, a bombé padded seat, and a gently curved and shaped back. It was not that the snobbish Art Deco designers placed such a high premium on comfort—they were primarily concerned with sumptuous surface effects—but they were content to observe the conventions of the past as they played their jazzed-up versions of the old standards.

Contemporary designers are not interested in variations; they want a brand-new score. They want to develop solutions on their own, without the aid of paradigms, and so their work has come to be judged primarily according to its novelty. This has led to a "cult of originality," as Allan Greenberg has called it, in which "What's new?" is more frequently asked than "What's better?"[15] Hepplewhite and Chippendale had offered dozens of examples of alternative chair designs for any particular model. Each modern chair, on the other hand, is considered to be unique—a new paradigm, but one which should never be copied. An Italian fills a bag with polystyrene pellets—an ingenious idea—and that avenue is closed for good; no designer will touch plastic pellets again. The next breakthrough is awaited—will it be chairs made out of corrugated cardboard, or out of expanded plastic mesh? Since each paradigm "belongs" to its designer, it can never be improved by other furniture makers—one finds less-expensive imitations of famous chairs but these are almost never improvements. Under such circumstances gradual evolution becomes impossible; to adapt someone else's design is to be accused of a lack of imagination, and to improve one's own is to admit that it was not perfect in the first place.

The problem of comfort is further compounded by the wish of designers to make furniture out of industrialized materials and to use new techniques. It is not the desire to experiment that is at fault—that much was shown a century ago by the inventors of mechanical furniture—but rather the search for novelty. Even when they work with wood, most designers avoid time-tested functional models and look instead for altogether new solutions. When they do use traditional methods and materials, the results are almost always beneficial. The back and seat of the popular Breuer side chair are made out of shaped wood and woven rattan, and like Georgian side chairs in these materials, the Breuer chair is pleasant to sit in. The Weissenhof chair, designed by Mies van der Rohe, is more comfortable than the Wassily chair, because the tubular frame is covered in handwoven cane—a seventeenth-century technique. The Eames lounge chair achieves its imperfect comfort not from its innovative plywood shell, but by being stuffed with feathers and down.

A well-known British architect James Stirling once described some favorite furniture as follows: "I like [the chairs] in an intellectual way. They aren't awfully comfortable to sit on, although of course you can sit in them for an hour or so without danger of collapse."[16] So that is what we can expect, an hour without cardiac arrest? Hardly a ringing endorsement. As it happens, Stirling was talking about the furniture of Thomas Hope, an early-nineteenth-century dilettante, who designed eccentric-looking chairs in a neo-Egyptian style, but the attitude is revealing nonetheless. Sitting comfort is no longer the main consideration in judging the worth of a chair; it may now be appreciated intellectually. Or aesthetically. Philip Johnson, a protégé of Mies van der Rohe, told his students at Harvard, "I think that comfort is a function of whether you think a chair is good-looking or not."[17] With characteristic wit, he went on to suggest that people who liked the appearance of the Barcelona chairs in his home would enjoy sitting in them, even though, by his own admission, these are "not very comfortable chairs."

There is something charmingly naïve about this belief in the power of art to overcome physical reality. It is, of course, wishful thinking. The people slumped in a Barcelona chair, or struggling to get out of an Eames lounge chair, do not feel comfortable, they are simply willing to put up with discomfort in the name of art—or prestige—which is not the same thing. We expect our interiors, and our furniture, to be comfortable, not merely to look attractive. Before the eighteenth century, a chair might have been considered successful even if it was not pleasant to sit in. When a chair looked beautiful, or grand, or impressive, it was "good." Our grandparents wore whale-bone corsets and starched high collars, and felt stylish and elegant—they had pinched waists and chaffed necks, but it could be argued that dressed this way they also felt "good." But if we exchanged our jeans and sweatshirts for a similar attire we would only feel awkward. We have come to take it for granted that however clothes look, they should offer freedom of movement, just as we expect that furniture, however it looks, will support us in ease and comfort.

And what does the twentieth-century chair offer us? It shows an optimistic belief in technology and the efficient use of materials. It shows a concern for fabrication, not crafts-manship in the traditional sense, but in precise and exact assembly. It is a purposeful object, without frivolity or frills. It offers status; you can buy a used car for less than many modern chairs. It exhibits lightness and movability, and it invites admiration for these qualities—just as a well-made camp cot does. But it does not ask to be sat in, or at least not for long. The Rococo chair invites conversation, and the Victorian chair invites after-dinner naps, but the Modern chair is all business. "Let's get this sitting over with and get back to something useful," it commands. It is about many things, this chair, but it is no longer about ease, leisure, or, if truth be told, about comfort.

Two hundred years ago, when people came to buy chairs or side tables at Thomas Chippendale's shop in St. Martin's Lane in London, they did not consider that they were pur-chasing classics, nor could they have imagined that much later these pieces would be sought after by collectors. They bought

Chippendale's chairs because his designs, although they were nominally Louis XV, neo-Gothic, or Chinese, were new and because they wanted to furnish their homes in the most up-to-date fashion. In 1977, on the other hand, when *Better Homes and Gardens* magazine surveyed its readers, only 15 percent preferred furniture in the "latest modern style."[18] What the majority wanted, and continue to want, was old-fashioned—not necessarily old—furniture and traditional decor, exactly what Ralph Lauren is offering in "Thoroughbred" and "New England." If department stores or home-decorating magazines are any indication, most people's first choice would be to live in rooms that resemble, as much as their budgets permit, those of their grandparents.

No one finds this peculiar. But, as Adolf Loos pointed out, such nostalgia is absent from other aspects of our everyday lives. We do not pine for period cuisine. Our concern for health and nutrition has altered the way that we eat, as well as what we eat; our admiration for the slim physique would be puzzling to the corpulent nineteenth century. We have changed our way of speaking, our manners, and our public and private behavior. We do not feel the need to revive the practice of leaving visiting cards, for example, or of indulging in extended, chaperoned courtship. A return to eighteenth-century decorum would ill suit our informal way of life. Unless we are collectors, we do not drive antique cars. We want automobiles that are less expensive to operate, safer, and more comfortable, but we do not imagine that these improvements can be achieved by resurrecting car models from previous periods. We would feel as odd in a Model T as we would in plus fours or a hooped skirt, yet although we would not think of dressing in period clothes, we find nothing strange in dressing our homes in period decor.

One writer has suggested an explanation for this nostalgia: "Americans may be fascinated with the future, but they don't want to live in it." [19] This sounds cogent, but it is inaccurate. For one thing it implies that resistance to innovation in the home is an American tradition, whereas in fact the enormous changes that took place in the home during the end of the nineteenth century and the introduction of efficient home management by the domestic engineers were both largely un- opposed. And there has never been any opposition to "fu- turistic" appliances, whether they are portable phones, Jacuzzi baths, home computers, or big-screen video. For another, the "future" that people seem unwilling to live in—white walls, pipe railings, and steel-and-leather furniture—is hardly shockingly new. The New Spirit is now more than sixty years old, and there has been plenty of time to get used to it.

Nostalgia for the past is often a sign of dissatisfaction with the present. I have called the modern interior "a rupture in the evolution of domestic comfort." It represents an attempt not so much to introduce a new style—that is the least of it —as to change social habits, and even to alter the underlying cultural meaning of domestic comfort. Its denial of bourgeois traditions has caused it to question, and reject, not only lux- ury but also ease, not only clutter but also intimacy. Its em- phasis on space has caused it to ignore privacy, just as its interest in industrial-looking materials and objects has led it away from domesticity. Austerity, both visual and tactile, has replaced delight. What started as an endeavor to rationalize and simplify has become a wrong-headed crusade; not, as is often claimed, a response to a changing world, but an attempt to change the way we live. It is a rupture not because it does away with period styles, not because it eliminates ornament, and not because it stresses technology, but because it attacks the very idea of comfort itself. That is why people look to the past. Their nostalgia is not the result of an interest in archaeology, like some Victorian revivals, nor of a sympathy for a particular period, like Jeffersonian classicism. Nor is it a rejection of technology. People appreciate the benefits of central heating and electric lighting, but the rooms of a Colonial country home or of a Georgian mansion—which had neither—continue to attract them, for they provide a measure of something that is absent from the modern interior. People turn to the past because they are looking for something that they do not find in the present—comfort and well-being.

Chapter Ten

Norman Rockwell (1946)

Comfort and Well-being

. . . lately I have been thinking how comfort
is perhaps the ultimate luxury.

—BILLY BALDWIN

as quoted in THE NEW YORK TIMES

Domestic well-being is a fundamental human need that is deeply rooted in us, and that must be satisfied. If this need is not met in the present, it is not unnatural to look for comfort in tradition. In doing so, however, we should not confuse the idea of comfort with decor—the external appearance of rooms—nor with behavior—how these rooms were used. Decor is primarily a product of fashion, and its longevity is measured in decades or less. A decorating style like Queen Anne lasted at the most thirty years; Art Nouveau barely more than a decade; Art Deco even less than that. Social behavior, which is a function of habits and customs, is more durable. The male practice of withdrawing to a special room to smoke, for example, began in the mid-nineteenth century and continued well into the twentieth. As late as 1935, the steamship *Normandie* was provided with a smoking room, although by then women were beginning to smoke in public. Public smoking has lasted about forty years, but it is likely that before long it will cease altogether, and we will return to the time when it was considered impolite to smoke in the company of others. Cultural ideas like comfort, on the other hand, have a life that is measured in centuries. Domesticity, for example, has existed for more than three hundred years. During that time the "density" of interior decoration has varied, rooms have changed in size and function and have 217 been more or less crowded with furniture, but the domestic interior has always demonstrated a feeling of intimacy and hominess.

Changes in fashion occur more frequently than changes in behavior; cultural ideas, because they last so long, are more resistant to change, and consequently tend to constrain both behavior and decor. Although new fashions are often called revolutionary, they are rarely that, for they can only alter social customs slightly, and traditional culture not at all. Long hair, that symbol of 1960s rebellion, was heralded as a major cultural shift; it turned out to be what we should have known it was all the time—a short-lived fashion. When fashion does attempt to change social behavior, it does so at its peril. Paper clothing, for example, another fad of the 1960s, could not satisfy people's traditional use of dress as status symbol, and did not last long. The power of culture to constrain behavior is evident when foreign customs are borrowed from abroad. The Japanese hot tub, for example, is currently an American fashion—it may eventually become a custom—but the traditions of bathing in Japan and America are tremendously different. The hot tub has consequently been turned from an oriental semireligious, contemplative ritual to a western social recreation. This adaptation occurs in both directions, and just as the hot tub has been westernized, the Japanese have altered our domestic customs to suit their own habits and culture.*

Borrowing from the past must similarly accommodate itself to contemporary customs. That is why period revivals, even when they were not outright inventions, were never intended to be authentic recreations of the past; they were always, in

---

* According to George Fields, an Australian marketing consultant, appliances such as washing machines and refrigerators have a higher "psychological positioning" for the Japanese, who attach the same importance to these utilitarian devices as Americans do to furniture; in a Japanese home, the refrigerator is just as likely to be placed in the living room as in the kitchen.[1]

the strict sense of the word, "superficial." When the Gothic style returned to favor in the eighteenth century it affected room decoration, but it was not meant to revive the "big house," or the medieval lack of privacy—the basic arrangement of the Victorian house remained intact. When Renaissance interiors became fashionable in America in the 1880s, there was no attempt to turn back the clock; the style was always used selectively, and only in specific rooms. There were no Renaissance kitchens, for example—the idea of convenient and efficiently planned work areas was by then too strong a part of domestic culture.

One cannot recapture the comfort of the past by copying its decor. The way that rooms looked made sense because they were a setting for a particular type of behavior, which in turn was conditioned by the way that people thought about comfort. Reproducing the former without the latter would be like putting on a play and only building the stage set, but forgetting the actors and script. It would be a hollow and unsatisfying experience. We can appreciate the interiors of the past, but if we try to copy them we will find that too much has changed. What has changed the most is the reality of physical comfort—the standard of living—largely as the result of advances in technology. Technological changes have affected the evolution of comfort throughout history, of course, but ours is a special position. The evolution of domestic technology that has been traced in the preceding chapters demonstrates that the history of physical amenities can be divided into two major phases: all the years leading up to 1890, and the three following decades. If this sounds outlandish, it is worth reminding ourselves that all the "modern" devices that contribute to our domestic comfort—central heating, indoor plumbing, running hot and cold water, electric light and power and elevators—were unavailable before 1890, and were well known by 1920. We live, like it or not, on the far side of a great technological divide. As John Lukacs reminds us, although the home of 1930 would be familiar to us, it would have been unrecognizable to the citizen of 1885.[2] Until then, recreating the past was plausible—even if it was rare—after 1920 it became an eccentricity.

Comfort has changed not only qualitatively, but also quantitatively—it has become a mass commodity. After 1920, especially in America (somewhat later in Europe), physical comfort in the home was no longer the privilege of a part of society, it was accessible to all. This democratization of comfort has been due to mass production and industrialization. But industrialization has had other effects—it has made handwork a luxury (in that regard Le Corbusier's analysis was correct). This, too, separates us from the past. As the Art Deco designers discovered, a reliance on craftsmanship was expensive and meant an extremely limited clientele. We can admire Mrs. Lauder's Louis XV office, but how many could afford even good reproductions, let alone authentic antiques? If we insist on Rococo we must be content with ersatz—a poor imitation that is neither commodious nor delightful. Only the wealthy or the very poor can live in the past; only the former do so by choice. If one has enough money—and enough servants—a Georgian country home is just the ticket. But the reality of small, servantless households makes it impossible for most people to undertake such wholesale restorations: who will dust all those pretty moldings, who will shake the carpets and polish the brass?

The current fashion for decorating interiors with bits and pieces of traditional-looking ornament, without adhering to any particular historical style, seems, at least on the surface—and it is mostly surface—to be an acceptable alternative. It is an inexpensive if halfhearted compromise—neither outright revivalism nor unadulterated modernism. But so-called postmodernism has missed the point; putting in a stylized strip of molding or a symbolic classical column is not really the issue. It is not watered-down historical references that are missing from people's homes. What is needed is a sense of domesticity, not more dadoes; a feeling of privacy, not neo-Palladian windows; an atmosphere of coziness, not plaster capitals. Postmodernism is more interested in (mostly obscure) architectural history than in the evolution of the cultural ideas that history represents. Moreover, it is reluctant to question any of the basic principles of modernism—it is aptly named, for it is almost never antimodern. Despite its visual wit and fashionable insouciance, it fails to address the basic problem.

What is needed is a reexamination not of bourgeois styles, but of bourgeois traditions. We should look at the past not from a stylistic point of view, but regarding the idea itself of comfort. The seventeenth-century Dutch bourgeois interior, for example, has much to teach us about living in small spaces. It suggests how simple materials, appropriately sized and placed windows, and built-in furniture can create an atmosphere of cozy domesticity. The way that Dutch homes opened up onto the street, the careful variety of types of windows, the planned gradient of increasingly private rooms, and the sequence of small sitting places are architectural devices that are applicable still.[3] The Queen Anne house offers similar lessons in informal planning. The Victorians were faced with technical devices more innovative than our own, and the ease with which they incorporated new technology into their homes without sacrificing traditional comforts is instructive. The American home of 1900 to 1920 shows that convenience and efficiency can be dealt with effectively without in any way creating a cold or machinelike atmosphere.

Reexamining bourgeois traditions means returning to house layouts that offer more privacy and intimacy than the so-called open plan, in which space is allowed to "flow" from one room to another. This produces interiors of great visual interest, but there is a price to be paid for this excitement. The space flows, but so also does sight and sound—not since the Middle Ages have homes offered as little personal privacy to their inhabitants. It is difficult for even small families to live in such open interiors, especially if they are using the large variety of home entertainment devices that have become popular—televisions, video recorders, audio equipment, electronic games, and so on. What is needed are many more small rooms—some need not be larger than alcoves—to conform to the range and variety of leisure activities in the modern home.

It also means a return to furniture that is accommodating and comfortable; not chairs that make an artistic statement, but chairs that are a pleasure to sit in. This will involve going both forward and backward—backward, to recover the eighteenth century's knowledge of ergonomics, and forward to devise furniture which can be adjusted and modified to suit different individuals. It means returning to the idea of furniture as practical rather than aesthetic object, and as something enduring rather than a passing novelty.

Another tradition that should be reexamined is that of convenience. In many parts of the house, the pragmatism of the early domestic engineers has been lost in the emphasis on visual appearance. Aesthetics, not practicality, predominate. The modern kitchen, in which everything is hidden in artfully designed cabinets, looks well organized, like a bank office. But a kitchen does not function like an office; if anything, it is more like a workshop. Tools should be out in the open where they are accessible, near those places where the work is done, not secreted below counters or in deep, difficult-to-reach cupboards. The need for different work-surface heights was identified a long time ago, but kitchens continue to have uniform counters, of standardized height and width, finished in the same material. This neatness and uniformity follow the modern dictum requiring lack of clutter and visual simplicity, but they do little to improve working comfort.

The small standardized bathroom (whose layout is unchanged since the 1850s) looks efficient, but it is ill suited to the modern home. The combination of tub and shower is awkward, the fixtures are neither particularly comfortable nor safe nor even easy to clean. For functional and hygienic reasons the water closet would be better separated, as it is in Europe. When houses contained many more rooms, bathrooms could be small. Today, the bathroom must accommodate activities which previously took place in dressing rooms, nurseries, and boudoirs (even washing machines are now located in bathrooms). In small houses, the bathroom may be the only totally private room, and although bathing may not be a ritual in America as it is in Japan, it is certainly a form of relaxation, and yet this activity takes place in a room that is devoid of both charm and commodity. The modern kitchen is also too small. Early studies of kitchen efficiency focused on reducing the amount of walking done during food preparation. This has produced the tiny, so-called efficient kitchen—often without windows—in which there is little countertop area, but where one can work almost without moving. If such an arrangement was ever convenient, which is arguable, it has outlived its usefulness. There is not enough space for the large number of appliances—mixers, blenders, pasta makers, and coffee grinders—required by the time-conscious housekeeper.

Ever since the seventeenth century, when privacy was introduced into the home, the role of women in defining comfort has been paramount. The Dutch interior, the Rococo salon, the servantless household—all were the result of women's invention. One could argue, with only slight exaggeration, that the idea of domesticity was principally a feminine idea. So was the idea of efficiency. When Lillian Gilbreth and Christine Frederick introduced management and efficiency to the home, they took it for granted that this work would be done by a woman whose main occupation would be taking care of the family. Domestic management may have been more efficient, but housework was still a full-time job—the woman's place was in the home. The desire of women for careers—and not just for economic reasons—has changed all that. This does not mean that domesticity will disappear, although it may mean that the home will cease to be "the woman's place." The scarcity of servants in the early 1900s prompted an interest in machines that would help the home-maker and reduce the tedium of housework; the reduced presence of women in the home requires machines that can do chores on their own. Most recently developed home appliances, such as automatic clothes washers, ice-cube makers, self-cleaning ovens, and frost-free refrigerators, are intended to replace manual operations with self-regulating mechanical ones—they are all partially automated. This development—from tools to machines to automatons—is a characteristic of all technologies, in the home no less than in the workplace.[4] The drying rack leads to the manual- and then the machine-driven wringer, which is replaced by the automatic dryer. The availability of inexpensive microchips is hastening the day when full-scale automation will enter the home in the form of domestic robots—mechanical servants.

A reexamination of the bourgeois tradition of comfort is an implicit criticism of modernity, but it is not a rejection of change. Indeed, the evolution of comfort will continue. For the moment, this evolution is dominated by technology, though to a lesser degree than in the past. This need not dehumanize the home, any more than effective fireplaces or electricity did in the past. Can we really have coziness and robots? That will depend on how successful we are in turning away from modernism's shallow enthusiasms, and developing a deeper and more genuine understanding of domestic comfort.

What is comfort? Perhaps the question should have been asked earlier, but without a review of the long evolution of this complex and profound subject the answer would almost certainly have been wrong, or at least incomplete. The simplest response would be that comfort concerns only human physiology—feeling good. Nothing mysterious about that. But this would not explain why, although the human body has not changed, our idea of what is comfortable differs from that of a hundred years ago. Nor is the answer that comfort is a subjective experience of satisfaction. If comfort were subjective, one would expect a greater variety of attitudes toward it; instead, at any particular historical period there has always been a demonstrable consensus about what is comfortable and what is not. Although comfort is experienced personally, the individual judges comfort according to broader norms, indicating that comfort may be an objective experience.

If comfort is objective, it should be possible to measure it. This is more difficult than it sounds. It is easier to know when we are comfortable than why, or to what degree. It would be possible to identify comfort by recording the personal reactions of large numbers of people, but this would be more like a marketing or opinion survey than a scientific study; a scientist prefers to study things one at a time, and especially to measure them. It turns out that in practice it is much easier to measure *dis*comfort than comfort. To establish a thermal "comfort zone," for example, one ascertains at which temperatures most people are either too cold or too hot, and whatever is in between automatically becomes "comfortable." Or if one is trying to identify the appropriate angle for the back of a chair, one can subject people to angles that are too steep and too flat, and between the points where they express discomfort lies the "correct" angle. Similar experiments have been carried out concerning the intensity of lighting and noise, the size of room dimensions, the hardness and softness of sitting and lying furniture, and so on. In all these cases, the range of comfort is discovered by measuring the limits at which people begin to experience discomfort. When the interior of the Space Shuttle was being designed, a cardboard mock-up of the cabin was built. The astronauts were required to move around in this full-size model, miming their daily activities, and every time they knocked against a corner or a projection, a technician would cut away the offending piece. At the end of the process, when there were no more obstructions left, the cabin was judged to be "comfortable." The scientific definition of comfort would be something like "Comfort is that condition in which discomfort has been avoided."

Most of the scientific research that has been carried out on terrestrial comfort has concerned the workplace, since it has been found that comfortable surroundings will affect the morale, and hence the productivity, of workers. Just how much comfort can affect economic performance is indicated by a recent estimate that backaches—the result of poor working posture—account for over ninety-three million lost workdays, a loss of nine billion dollars to the American economy.[5] The modern office interior reflects the scientific definition of comfort. Lighting levels have been carefully controlled to fall within an acceptable level for optimal reading convenience. The finishes of walls and floors are restful; there are no garish or gaudy colors. Desks and chairs are planned to avoid fatigue.

But how comfortable do the people feel who work in such surroundings? As part of an effort to improve its facilities, one large pharmaceutical corporation, Merck & Company, surveyed two thousand of its office staff regarding their attitudes to their place of work—an attractive modern commercial interior.[6] The survey team prepared a questionnaire that listed various aspects of the workplace. These included factors affecting appearance, safety, work efficiency, convenience, comfort, and so on. Employees were asked to express their satisfaction, or dissatisfaction, with different aspects, and also to indicate those aspects that they personally considered to be the most important. The majority distinguished between the visual qualities of their surroundings—decoration, color scheme, carpeting, wall covering, desk appearance—and the physical aspects—lighting, ventilation, privacy, and chair comfort. The latter group were all included in a list of the ten most important factors, together with size of work area, safety, and personal storage space. Interestingly, none of the purely visual factors was felt to be of major importance, indicating just how mistaken is the notion that comfort is solely a function of appearance or style.

What is most revealing is that the Merck employees expressed some degree of dissatisfaction with *two-thirds* of the almost thirty different aspects of the workplace. Among those about which there was the strongest negative feelings were the lack of conversational privacy, the air quality, the lack of visual privacy, and the level of lighting. When they were asked what aspects of the office interior they would like to have individual control over, most people identified room temperature, degree of privacy, choice of chair and desk, and lighting intensity. Control over decor was accorded the lowest priority. This would seem to indicate that although there is wide agreement about the importance of lighting or temperature, there is a good deal of difference of opinion about exactly how much light or heat feels comfortable to different individuals; comfort is obviously both objective and subjective.

The Merck offices had been designed to eliminate discomfort, yet the survey showed that many of the employees did not experience well-being in their workplace—an inability to concentrate was the common complaint. Despite the restful colors and the attractive furnishings (which everyone appreciated), something was missing. The scientific approach assumes that if background noises are muffled and direct view controlled, the office worker will feel comfortable. But working comfort depends on many more factors than these. There

must also be a sense of intimacy and privacy, which is produced by a balance between isolation and publicness; too
much of one or the other will produce discomfort. A group
of architects in California recently identified as many as nine
different aspects of workplace enclosure that must be met in
order to create this feeling.[7] These included the presence of
walls behind and beside the worker, the amount of open space
in front of the desk, the area of the workspace, the amount
of enclosure, a view to the outside, the distance to the nearest
person, the number of people in the immediate vicinity, and
the level and type of noise. Since most office layouts do not
address these concerns directly, it is not surprising that people
have difficulty concentrating on their work.

The fallacy of the scientific definition of comfort is that it
considers only those aspects of comfort that are measurable,
and with not untypical arrogance denies the existence of the
rest—many behavioral scientists have concluded that because
people experience only discomfort, comfort as a physical phenomenon does not really exist at all.[8] It is hardly surprising
that genuine intimacy, which is impossible to measure, is
absent in most planned office environments. Intimacy in the
office, or in the home, is not unusual in this respect; there
are many complicated experiences that resist measurement.
It is impossible, for example, to describe scientifically what
distinguishes a great wine from a mediocre one, although a
group of wine experts would have no difficulty establishing
which was which. The wine industry, like manufacturers of
tea and coffee, continues to rely on nontechnical testing—
the "nose" of an experienced taster— rather than on objective
standards alone. It might be possible to measure a threshold
below which wine would taste "bad"—acidity, alcohol content, sweetness, and so on—but no one would suggest that
simply avoiding these deficiencies would result in a good wine.
A room may feel uncomfortable—it may be too bright for

intimate conversation, or too dark for reading—but avoiding such irritations will not automatically produce a feeling of well-being. Dullness is not annoying enough to be disturbing, but it is not stimulating either. On the other hand, when we open a door and think, "What a comfortable room," we are reacting positively to something special, or rather to a series of special things.

Here are two descriptions of comfort. The first is by a well-known interior decorator, Billy Baldwin: "Comfort to me is a room that works for you and your guests. It's deep upholstered furniture. It's having a table handy to put down a drink or a book. It's also knowing that if someone pulls up a chair for a talk, the whole room doesn't fall apart. I'm tired of contrived decorating."[9] The second is by an architect, Christopher Alexander: "Imagine yourself on a winter afternoon with a pot of tea, a book, a reading light, and two or three huge pillows to lean back against. Now make yourself comfortable. Not in some way which you can show to other people, and say how much you like it. I mean so that you *really* like it, for *yourself*. You put the tea where you can reach it: but in a place where you can't possibly knock it over. You pull the light down, to shine on the book, but not too brightly, and so that you can't see the naked bulb. You put the cushions behind you, and place them, carefully, one by one, just where you want them, to support your back, your neck, your arm: so that you are supported just comfortably, just as you want to sip your tea, and read, and dream."[10] Baldwin's description was the result of sixty years of decorating fashionable homes; Alexander's was based on the observation of ordinary people and ordinary places.* Yet

---

* Baldwin, until his death in 1983, was generally considered to be the foremost high-society decorator; his clients included Cole Porter and Jacqueline Kennedy. Alexander is the author of the iconoclastic *A Pattern Language*, a critique of modern architecture.

they both seem to have converged in the depiction of a domestic atmosphere that is instantly recognizable for its ordinary, human qualities.

These qualities are something that science has failed to come to grips with, although to the layman a picture, or a written description, is evidence enough. "Comfort is simply a verbal invention," writes one engineer despairingly.[11] Of course, that is precisely what comfort is. It is an invention—a cultural artifice. Like all cultural ideas—childhood, family, gender—it has a past, and it cannot be understood without reference to its specific history. One-dimensional, technical definitions of comfort, which ignore history, are bound to be unsatisfactory. How rich, by comparison, are Baldwin's and Alexander's descriptions of comfort. They include convenience (a handy table), efficiency (a modulated light source), domesticity (a cup of tea), physical ease (deep chairs and cushions), and privacy (reading a book, having a talk). Intimacy is also present in these descriptions. All these characteristics together contribute to the atmosphere of interior calm that is a part of comfort.

This is the problem with understanding comfort and with finding a simple definition. It is like trying to describe an onion. It appears simple on the outside, just a spheroidal shape. But this is deceptive, for an onion also has many layers. If we cut it apart, we are left with a pile of onion skins, but the original form has disappeared; if we describe each layer separately, we lose sight of the whole. To complicate matters further, the layers are transparent, so that when we look at the whole onion we see not just the surface but also something of the interior. Similarly, comfort is both something simple and complicated. It incorporates many transparent layers of meaning—privacy, ease, convenience—some of which are buried deeper than others.

The onion simile suggests not only that comfort has several layers of meaning, but also that the idea of comfort has developed historically. It is an idea that has meant different things at different times. In the seventeenth century, comfort meant privacy, which lead to intimacy and, in turn, to domesticity. The eighteenth century shifted the emphasis to leisure and ease, the nineteenth to mechanically aided comforts—light, heat, and ventilation. The twentieth-century domestic engineers stressed efficiency and convenience. At various times, and in response to various outside forces—social, economic, and technological—the idea of comfort has changed, sometimes drastically. There was nothing foreordained or inevitable about the changes. If seventeenth-century Holland had been less egalitarian and its women less independent, domesticity would have arrived later than it did. If eighteenth-century England had been aristocratic rather than bourgeois, comfort would have taken a different turn. If servants had not been scarce in our century, it is unlikely that anyone would have listened to Beecher and Frederick. But what is striking is that the idea of comfort, even as it has changed, has preserved most of its earlier meanings. The evolution of comfort should not be confused with the evolution of technology. New technical devices usually—not always—rendered older ones obsolete. The electric lamp replaced the gasolier, which replaced the oil lamp, which replaced candles, and so on. But new ideas about how to achieve comfort did not displace fundamental notions of domestic well-being. Each new meaning added a layer to the previous meanings, which were preserved beneath. At any particular time, comfort consists of *all* the layers, not only the most recent.

So there it is, the Onion Theory of Comfort—hardly a definition at all, but a more precise explanation may be unnecessary. It may be enough to realize that domestic comfort involves a range of attributes—convenience, efficiency, leisure, ease, pleasure, domesticity, intimacy, and privacy—all of which contribute to the experience; common sense will do the rest. Most people—"I may not know why I like it, but I know what I like"—recognize comfort when they experience it. This recognition involves a combination of sensations—many of them subconscious—and not only physical, but also emotional as well as intellectual, which makes comfort difficult to explain and impossible to measure. But it does not make it any less real. We should resist the inadequate definitions that engineers and architects have offered us. Domestic well-being is too important to be left to experts; it is, as it has always been, the business of the family and the individual. We must rediscover for ourselves the mystery of comfort, for without it, our dwellings will indeed be machines instead of homes.

Notes

Chapter One

1. Fred Ferretti, "The Business of Being Ralph Lauren," *New York Times Magazine*, September 18, 1983, pp.112–33.
2. *New York Times*, April 17, 1973, p.46.
3. David M. Tracy, vice-chairman of J. P. Stevens Company, quoted in Ferretti, "Ralph Lauren," p.112.
4. Hugh Trevor-Roper, "The Invention of Tradition: The Highland Tradition of Scotland," from Eric Hobsbawm & Terence Ranger, eds., *The Invention of Tradition* (New York: Cambridge University Press, 1983).
5. Peter York, "Making Reality Fit the Dreams," London *Times*, October 26, 1984, p.14.
6. Quoted in Ferretti, "Ralph Lauren," p.132.
7. Ibid., p.132.
8. Quoted in ibid., p.133.
9. *New York Times*, April 17, 1973, p.46.
10. *Fortune*, April 2, 1984.
11. William Seale, *The Tasteful Interlude: American Interiors Through the Camera's Eye, 1860–1917* (Nashville: American Association for State and Local History, 1982), p.21.
12. Judith Price, *Executive Style: Achieving Success Through Good Taste and Design* (New York: Linden Press/Simon & Schuster, 1980), pp.20–23.
13. Ibid., pp.168–71.

Chapter Two

1. Quoted in Martin Pawley, "The Time House," in Charles Jencks and George Baird, eds., *Meaning in Architecture* (London: Cresset Press, 1969), p.144.
2. Jean Gimpel, *The Medieval Machine: The Industrial Revolution of the Middle Ages* (New York: Penguin, 1980), pp.237–38.
3. Ibid., pp.43–44.
4. J. H. Huizinga, *The Waning of the Middle Ages: A Study of the Forms of Life, Thought and Art in France and the Neth-* 233

erlands in the Dawn of the Renaissance, trans. F. Hopman (Garden City, N.Y.: Doubleday Anchor, 1954), p.250.

5. Ibid., p.248.

6. Martin Pawley, *Architecture vs. Housing* (New York: Praeger, 1971), p.6.

7. Philippe Ariès, *Centuries of Childhood: A Social History of the Family*, trans. Robert Baldick (New York: Knopf, 1962), p.392.

8. John Lukacs, "The Bourgeois Interior," *American Scholar*, Vol. 39, No. 4 (Autumn 1970), pp.620–21.

9. Joan Evans, *Life in Medieval France* (London: Phaidon, 1969), pp.30–43.

10. John Gloag, *A Social History of Furniture Design: From B.C. 1300 to A.D. 1960* (London: Cassell, 1966), p.93.

11. Siegfried Giedion, *Mechanization Takes Command: A Contribution to Anonymous History* (New York: Norton, 1969), pp.270–72.

12. Ibid., pp.276–78.

13. Evans, *Medieval France*, pp.61–62.

14. Colin Platt, *The English Medieval Town* (New York: David McKay, 1976), p.73.

15. From a poem by Prince Ludwig of Anhalt-Kohten (1596), quoted in Gloag, *Social History*, p.105.

16. Mario Praz, *An Illustrated History of Interior Decoration: From Pompeii to Art Nouveau*, trans. William Weaver (New York: Thames and Hudson, 1982), p.81.

17. Gimpel, *Medieval Machine*, pp.3–5.

18. Lawrence Wright, *Clean and Decent: The History of the Bath and the Loo* (London: Routledge & Kegan Paul, 1980), pp.19–21.

19. Platt, *Medieval Town*, pp.71–72.

20. Quoted in Evans, *Medieval France*, p.51.

21. Wright, *Clean and Decent*, pp.29–32.

22. Ibid., p.31.

23. Madeleine Pelner Cosman, *Fabulous Feasts: Medieval Cookery and Ceremony* (New York: Braziller, 1976), p.45.

24. Ibid., p.69.

25. Quoted in Praz, *Interior Decoration*, pp.52–53.

26. Giedion, *Mechanization*, p.299.

27. Lewis Mumford, *The City in History: Its Origins, Its Trans-*

formations and Its Prospects (New York: Harcourt, Brace & World, 1961), p.287.

28. Cosman, *Fabulous Feasts*, pp.105–8.
29. Ibid., p.83.
30. Barbara W. Tuchman, *A Distant Mirror: The Calamitous 14th Century* (New York: Ballantine, 1979), pp.19–20.
31. Huizinga, *Middle Ages*, pp.249–50.
32. Ibid., p.27.
33. Ibid., pp.109–10.
34. Lukacs, "Bourgeois Interior," p.622.
35. Ibid., p.623.
36. Fernand Braudel, *The Structures of Everyday Life: Civilization and Capitalism, 15th–18th Century*, Vol. 1, trans. Miriam Kochan, rev. Sian Reynolds (New York: Harper & Row, 1981), pp.310–11.
37. Jean-Pierre Babelon, *Demeures parisiennes: sous Henri IV et Louis XIII* (Paris: Editions de temps, 1965), p.82.
38. Braudel, *Everyday Life*, pp.300–302.
39. Ibid., pp.310–11.
40. Wright, *Clean and Decent*, pp.42–44.
41. Babelon, *Demeures parisiennes*, p.96.
42. Ibid., pp.96–97.
43. I have drawn considerably on ibid., pp.69–116, for the description of seventeenth-century Parisian houses.
44. Ibid., pp.96–97.
45. Ibid., p.111.
46. Wright, *Clean and Decent.*, p.73.
47. Quoted in Terence Conran, *The Bed and Bath Book* (New York: Crown, 1978), p.15.
48. Braudel, *Everyday Life*, p.310.
49. Ibid., p.196.
50. Ibid., pp.189–90.
51. Ibid., p.196.
52. Praz, *Interior Decoration*, pp.50–55.
53. Odd Brochmann, *By og Bolig* (Oslo: Cappelans, 1958), translated and quoted in Norbert Schoenauer, *6,000 Years of Housing*, Vol.3, *The Occidental Urban House* (New York: Garland, 1981), pp.113–17.
54. Ariès, *Childhood*, pp.391–95.
55. Ibid., p.369.

Chapter Three

1. G. N. Clark, *The Seventeenth Century* (Oxford: Clarendon Press, 1929), p.14.
2. Steen Eiler Rasmussen, *Towns and Buildings: Described in Drawings and Words*, trans. Eve Wendt (Liverpool: University Press of Liverpool, 1951), p.80.
3. Charles Wilson, *The Dutch Republic and the Civilization of the Seventeenth Century* (New York: McGraw-Hill, 1968), p.30.
4. "Our national culture is bourgeois in every sense you can legitimately attach to that word." J. H. Huizinga, "The Spirit of the Netherlands," in *Dutch Civilization in the Seventeenth Century and Other Essays*, trans. Arnold J. Pomerans (London: Collins, 1968), p.112.
5. J. H. Huizinga, "Dutch Civilization in the Seventeenth Century," in ibid., pp.61–63.
6. N.J. Habraken, *Transformations of the Site* (Cambridge, Mass.: Awater Press, 1983), p. 220.
7. Paul Zumthor, *Daily Life in Rembrandt's Holland*, trans. Simon Watson Taylor (New York: Macmillan, 1963), pp.45–46.
8. Ibid., p.135.
9. Ibid., p.100.
10. Ariès, *Childhood*, p.369.
11. Bertha Mook, *The Dutch Family in the 17th and 18th Centuries: An Explorative-Descriptive Study* (Ottawa: University of Ottawa Press, 1977), p.32.
12. Petrus Johannes Blok, *History of the People of the Netherlands* Part IV, trans. Oscar A. Bierstadt (New York: AMS Press, 1970), p.254.
13. Rasmussen, *Towns*, p.80.
14. William Temple, *Observations upon the United Provinces of the Netherlands* (Oxford: Clarendon Press, 1972), p.97.
15. Wilson, *Dutch Republic*, p.244.
16. Quoted in Madlyn Millner Kahr, *Dutch Painting in the Seventeenth Century* (New York: Harper & Row, 1982), p.259.
17. Quoted in Zumthor, *Daily Life*, p.137.
18. Huizinga, *Dutch Civilization*, p.63.
19. Temple, *Observations*, p.80.
20. Blok, *History*, p.256.

21. Quoted in Zumthor, *Daily Life*, pp.53–54.
22. Ibid., pp.139–40.
23. Temple, *Observations*, p.89.
24. Zumthor, *Daily Life*, p.41.
25. Ibid., p.138
26. Lukacs, "Bourgeois Interior," p.624.

Chapter Four

1. Bernard Rudofsky *Now I Lay Me Down to Eat* (Garden City, N.Y.: Anchor Press/ Doubleday, 1980), p.62.
2. Braudel, *Everyday Life*, pp.288–92.
3. Ibid., pp.283–85.
4. Gervase Jackson-Stops, "Formal Splendour: The Baroque Age," in Anne Charlish, ed., *The History of Furniture* (London: Orbis, 1976), p.77.
5. Nancy Mitford, *Madame de Pompadour* (New York: Harper & Row, 1968), p.111.
6. Pierre Verlet, *La Maison du XVIIIe Siècle en France: Société Décoration Mobilier* (Paris: Baschet & Cie, 1966), p.178.
7. Ariès, *Childhood*, p.399.
8. Michel Gallet, *Stately Mansions: Eighteenth Century Paris Architecture* (New York: Praeger, 1972), p.115.
9. Quoted in Mitford, *Pompadour*, p.171.
10. Peter Collins, "Furniture Givers as Form Givers: Is Design an All-Encompassing Skill?" *Progressive Architecture*, No.44 (March 1963), p.122.
11. Jacques-François Blondel, *Architecture françoise* (Paris: Jombert, 1752), p.27. Translation by author.
12. Braudel, *Everyday Life*, p.299.
13. Verlet, *Maison*, p.106.
14. Wright, *Clean and Decent*, pp.74-75.
15. Giedion, *Mechanization*, p.653.
16. Wright, *Clean and Decent*, p.72.
17. Verlet, *Maison*, p.61.
18. Ibid., pp.247–59.
19. J. H. B. Peel, *An Englishman's Home* (Newton Abbot, Devon: David & Charles, 1978), pp.161–62.
20. Michel Gallet, *Demeures parisiennes: l'époque de Louis XVI* (Paris: Le Temps, 1964), pp.39–47.
21. Allan Greenberg, "Design Paradigms in the Eighteenth and

Twentieth Centuries," in Stephen Kieran, ed., *Ornament* (Philadelphia: Graduate School of Fine Arts, University of Pennsylvania, 1977), p.67.

22. Joseph Rykwert, "The Sitting Position—A Question of Method," in Charles Jancks & George Baird, eds., *Meaning in Architecture* (London: Cresset Press, 1969), p.234.

Chapter Five

1. Paige Rense, ed., *Celebrity Homes II* (Los Angeles: Knapp Press, 1981), pp.113–19.

2. Marilyn Bethany, "A House in the Georgian Mode," *New York Times Magazine*, April 24, 1983, pp.96–100.

3. John Martin Robinson, *The Latest Country Houses* (London: Bodley Head, 1984).

4. Quoted in Peel, *Englishman's Home*, p.20.

5. Nikolaus Pevsner, *European Architecture* (Harmondsworth, Middlesex: Penguin, 1958), p.226.

6. Peter Thornton, *Authentic Decor: The Domestic Interior 1620–1920* (New York: Viking, 1984), p.102.

7. Quoted in ibid., p.140.

8. Giedion, *Mechanization*, pp.321–22.

9. John Kenworthy-Browne, "The Line of Beauty: The Rococo Style," in Charlish, *History of Furniture*, p.126.

10. Ralph Dutton, *The Victorian Home* (London: Orbis, 1976), pp.2-3.

11. Mark Girouard, *Life in the English Country House* (New Haven: Yale University Press, 1978), p.235.

12. Thornton, *Authentic Decor*, p.150.

13. Praz, *Interior Decoration*, p.60.

14. Alice Hepplewhite & Co., *The Cabinet-Maker and Upholsterer's Guide*, 3rd ed. (London: Batsford, 1898). Originally published 1794.

15. Gallet, *L'époque de Louis XVI*, p.97.

Chapter Six

1. Robert Kerr, *The Gentleman's House: How to Plan English Residences, from the Parsonage to the Palace*, 3rd ed. (London: John Murray, 1871), p.278.

2. Girouard, *English Country House*, p.256.

3. Quoted in Lawrence Wright, *Warm and Snug: The History*

of the Bed (London: Routledge & Kegan Paul, 1962), p.144.

4. C. S. Peel, *The Stream of Time: Social and Domestic Life in England 1805–1861* (London: Bodley Head, 1931), p.114.

5. Girouard, *English Country House*, p.4.

6. Jill Franklin, *The Gentleman's Country House and Its Plan 1835–1914* (London: Routledge & Kegan Paul, 1981), p.114.

7. Hepplewhite & Co., *Guide*, plates 81, 82 and 89.

8. Ibid., p.7, plates 35 and 36.

9. C. J. Richardson, *The Englishman's House: From a Cottage to a Mansion*, 2nd ed. (London: John Camden Hotten, 1860), p.405.

10. John J. Stevenson, *House Architecture*, Vol. II, *House-Planning* (London: Macmillan, 1880), pp.229–35.

11. Girouard, *English Country House*, p.295.

12. Mark Girouard, *The Victorian Country House* (Oxford: Clarendon, 1971), p.146.

13. Douglas Galton, *Observations on the Construction of Healthy Dwellings*, 2nd ed. (Oxford: Clarendon, 1896), p.52.

14. W. H. Corfield, *Dwelling Houses: Their Sanitary Construction and Arrangements* (London: H. K. Lewis, 1885), p.16.

15. John S. Billings, *The Principles of Ventilation and Heating and Their Practical Application* (London: Trubner, 1884), p.41.

16. Stevenson, *House Architecture*, p.236.

17. Quoted in Wright, *Clean and Decent*, p.122.

18. Stevenson, *House Architecture*, p.248.

19. Franklin, *Gentleman's Country House*, p.110.

20. Stevenson, *House Architecture*, pp.212–13.

21. Andrew Jackson Downing, *The Architecture of Country Houses* (New York: Da Capo, 1968), p.472. Originally published 1850.

22. Catherine E. Beecher, *A Treatise on Domestic Economy: For the Use of Young Ladies at Home and at School* (New York: Harper, 1849), p.281.

23. H. M. Plunkett, *Women, Plumbers and Doctors: Or Household Sanitation* (New York: Appleton, 1885), p.56.

24. J. G. Lockhart, *Life of Scott*, quoted in Girouard, *Victorian Country House*, p.17.

25. Stevenson, *House Architecture*, p.254.

26. T. K. Derry and Trevor I. Williams, *A Short History of Technology* (Oxford: Oxford University Press, 1979), p.512.

27. C. S. Peel, *A Hundred Wonderful Years: Social and Domestic Life of a Century, 1820–1920* (London: Bodley Head, 1926), pp.45– 46.

28. Reyner Banham, *The Architecture of the Well-Tempered Environment* (London: Architectural Press, 1969), p.56.

29. Ibid., p.55.

30. Ibid., p.55.

31. Stefan Muthesius, *The English Terraced House* (New Haven: Yale University Press, 1982), p.52.

32. Ibid., pp.53-54.

33. Giedion, *Mechanization*, p.539.

34. Girouard, *Victorian Country House*, p.188.

Chapter Seven

1. Kerr, *Gentleman's House*, p.278.

2. J. Drysdale and J. W. Hayward, *Health and Comfort in Home Building*, 2nd ed. (London: Spon, 1876), pp.54–58. The Hayward house is also described in Banham, *Well-Tempered Environment*, pp.35–39.

3. Henry Rutton, *Ventilation and Warming of Buildings* (New York: Putnam, 1862), p.37.

4. Stevenson, *House Architecture*, p.280.

5. Edith Wharton and Ogden Codman, Jr., *The Decoration of Houses* (London:Batsford, 1898), p.87.

6. Stevenson, *House Architecture*, p.212.

7. Giedion, *Mechanization*, pp.540–56.

8. Lydia Ray Balderston, *Housewifery: A Manual and Text Book of Practical Housekeeping* (Philadelphia: Lippincott, 1921), p.128.

9. Matthew Sloan Scott, "Electricity Supply," in *Encyclopaedia Britannica* (Chicago: University of Chicago, 1949), Vol. 8, pp.273–74.

10. Christine Frederick, *Household Engineering: Scientific Management in the Home* (Chicago: American School of Home Economics, 1923), p.238.

11. Ibid., pp.158–59.

12. Beecher, *Treatise*, p.261.

13. Alba M. Edwards, "Domestic Service," in *Encyclopaedia*

Britannica (Chicago: University of Chicago, 1949), Vol.7, pp.515–16.

14. Frederick, *Household Engineering*, p.377.
15. Domestics' salaries are based on Peel, *Hundred Wonderful Years*, p.185 and Frederick, *Household Engineering*, p.379.
16. Ellen H. Richards, *The Cost of Shelter* (New York: Wiley, 1905), p.105.
17. Mary Pattison, *Principles of Domestic Engineering: Or the What, Why and How of a House* (New York: Trow Press, 1915), p.158.
18. Frederick, *Household Engineering*, p.391.
19. Balderston, *Housewifery*, p.240.
20. Giedion, *Mechanization*, pp.516–18.
21. Beecher, *Treatise*, p.259.
22. Ibid., p.263.
23. Douglas Handlin, *The American Home: Architecture and Society 1815–1915* (Boston: Little, Brown, 1979), p.522, fn.33.
24. For a history of other domestic pioneers, see Dolores Hayden, *The Grand Domestic Revolution: A History of Feminist Designs for American Homes, Neighborhoods, and Cities* (Cambridge, Mass.: MIT Press, 1983).
25. Catherine E. Beecher and Harriet Beecher Stowe, *The American Woman's Home* (New York: J. B. Ford, 1869), pp.23–42.
26. Ibid., p.25.
27. Beecher, *Treatise*, p.259.
28. Beecher and Stowe, *American Woman's Home*, p.34.
29. Richardson, *Englishman's House*, pp.373–88.
30. Hermann Valentin van Holst, *Modern American Homes* (Chicago: American Technical Society, 1914).
31. Beecher and Stowe, *American Woman's Home*, pp.61–62.
32. Frederick, *Household Engineering*, pp.471–77.
33. Balderston, *Housewifery*, p.9.
34. Richards, *Cost of Shelter*, p.71.
35. Frederick, *Household Engineering*, p.8.
36. Christine Frederick, *The New Housekeeping: Efficiency Studies in Home Management* (Garden City, N.Y.: Doubleday, Page, 1914).
37. Lillian Gilbreth, *Living with Our Children* (New York: Norton, 1928), p.xi.

Chapter Eight

1. Seale, *Tasteful Interlude*, p.15.
2. Girouard, *Sweetness and Light*, p.130.
3. Vernon Blake, "Modern Decorative Art," *Architectural Review*, Vol. 58, No. 344 (July 1925), p.27.
4. F. L. Minnigerode, "Italy and People Play Loto Once a Week," *New York Times Magazine*, October 25, 1925, p.15.
5. W. Franklyn Paris, "The International Exposition of Modern Industrial and Decorative Art in Paris," Part II, "General Features," *Architectural Record*, Vol. 58, No. 4 (October 1925), p.379.
6. Ibid.
7. Ibid., p.376.
8. *Encyclopédie des Arts Décoratifs et Industriels Modernes au XXème Siècle*, Vol.2, *Architecture* (Paris: Imprimerie Nationale, 1925), pp.44–45.
9. Stanislaus von Moos, *Le Corbusier: Elements of a Synthesis* (Cambridge, Mass.: MIT Press, 1979), p.339, fn.55.
10. George Besson, a contemporary art critic, quoted in ibid., p.165.
11. Charles-Edouard Jeanneret, *L'Art décoratif d'aujourd'hui* (Paris: Crès, 1925), p.79.
12. Charles-Edouard Jeanneret, *Le Corbusier et Pierre Jeanneret: Oeuvre Complète de 1910–1929* (Zurich: Editions d'Architecture Erlenbach, 1946), p. 31.
13. Charles-Edouard Jeanneret, *Towards a New Architecture*, trans. Frederick Etchells (London, John Rodker, 1931), pp.122–23.
14. Brian Brace Taylor, *Le Corbusier et Pessac* (Paris: Fondation Le Corbusier, 1972), p.23.
15. Richards, *Cost of Shelter*, p.45; Jeanneret, *Towards a New Architecture*, p.241.
16. Lillian M. Gilbreth, Orpha Mae Thomas and Eleanor Clymer, *Management in the Home: Happier Living Through Saving Time and Energy* (New York: Dodd, Mead, 1954), p.158.
17. Jeanneret, *L'Art décoratif*, pp.92–93.

Chapter Nine

1. Quoted in Marilyn Bethany, "Two Top Talents Seeing Eye to Eye," *New York Times Magazine*, July 13, 1980, p.50.

2. Doris Saatchi, "Living in Zen," *House and Garden*, Vol. 157, No. 1 (January 1985), p.110.

3. Joan Kron, *Home-Psych: The Social Psychology of Home and Decoration* (New York: Clarkson N. Potter, 1983), p.178.

4. Thornton, *Authentic Decor*, pp.8–9.

5. Quoted in Burkhard Rukschcio and Roland Schachel, *Adolf Loos: Leben und Werk* (Salzburg: Residenz Verlag, 1982), p.308.

6. Adolf Behne, quoted in Ulrich Conrads and Hans G. Sperlich, *Fantastic Architecture* (London: Architectural Press, 1963), p.134.

7. For a humorous retelling of this period, see Tom Wolfe, *From Bauhaus to Our House* (New York: Farrar, Straus & Giroux, 1981), pp.37–56.

8. Adolf Loos, "Interiors in the Rotunda," in *Spoken into the Void: Collected Essays 1897–1900*, trans. Jane O. Newman and John H. Smith (Cambridge, Mass.: MIT Press, 1982), p.27. Originally published 1921.

9. Henry McIlvaine Parsons, "The Bedroom," *Human Factors*, Vol. 14, No. 5 (October 1972), pp.424–25.

10. P. Branton, "Behavior, Body Mechanics and Discomfort," *Ergonomics*, Vol. 12 (1969), pp.316–27.

11. Giedion, *Mechanization*, pp.402–3.

12. Rykwert, "The Sitting Position," pp.236–37.

13. Ralph Caplan, *By Design* (New York: McGraw-Hill, 1982), pp.91–92.

14. Greenberg, "Design Paradigms," p.80.

15. Ibid.

16. "James Stirling at Home," *Blueprint*, Vol. 1, No. 3 (December 1983–January 1984).

17. Philip Johnson, *Writings* (New York: Oxford University Press, 1979), p.138.

18. Kron, *Home-Psych*, p.177.

19. Ibid.

Chapter Ten

1. George Fields, *From Bonsai to Levi's: When West Meets East, an Insider's Surprising Account of How the Japanese Live* (New York: Macmillan, 1983), pp.25–26.

2. John Lukacs, *Outgrowing Democracy: A History of the United States in the Twentieth Century* (Garden City, N.Y.: Doubleday, 1984), p.170.

3. Many of the patterns described in Christopher Alexander et al., *A Pattern Language: Towns, Buildings, Construction.* (New York: Oxford University Press, 1977), are derived from seventeenth-century interiors.

4. See the author's *Taming the Tiger: The Struggle to Control Technology* (New York: Viking, 1983), p.25.

5. J. Douglas Phillips, "Establishing and Managing Advance Office Technology: A Holistic Approach Focusing on People," paper presented to the annual meeting of the Society of Manufacturing Engineers, Montreal, September 16–19, 1984, p.3.

6. S. George Walters, "Merck and Co., Inc. Office Design Study, Final Plans Board," unpublished report (Newark, N.J.: Rutgers Graduate School of Management, August 24, 1982).

7. Alexander, *Pattern Language*, pp.847–52.

8. Henry McIlvaine Parsons, "Comfort and Convenience: How Much?" paper presented to the annual meeting of the American Association for the Advancement of Science, New York, January 30, 1975, p.1.

9. Quoted in George O'Brien, "An American Decorator Emeritus," *New York Times Magazine: Home Design*, April 17, 1983, p.33.

10. Christopher Alexander, *The Timeless Way of Building* (New York: Oxford University Press, 1979), pp.32–33.

11. Parsons, "Comfort and Convenience," p.1.

Index

Adam, Robert, 117, 147
advertising, 1–6, 8, 11, 71*n*, 80
agriculture, 23
Albert Edward, Prince of Wales, 141
Alexander, Christopher, 229–230
American Chippendale style, 119–20
American Telephone and Telegraph Building, 102
American Woman's Home, The (Beecher and Stowe), 161
antechambers, 109, 110
Antonello da Messina, 43–44
appliances:
electric, 144, 151–52, 153, 155, 157–58
"labor-saving," 154–55, 157
apprentices, 45, 48
Architectural Record, 185
architecture:
amateur, 125–26
antitotalitarian, 202–203
domestic technology vs., 145–148, 160, 166–67, 179, 189–93
external, 167
French, 89, 90
historical revivalism in, 101–104, 174–77
interior decoration vs., 127–128, 130, 131
moral basis of, 201–203
"naturalness" in, 118–19, 121
as visual approach, 147–48, 167
see also individual architectural styles
Architecture française (Blondel), 90
Architecture of Country Houses, The (Downing), 137, 160
arc lamps, 150
Argand, Ami, 138
Argand lamps, 138–39, 151
Ariès, Philippe, 45, 60
armchairs, 83, 95, 97, 98, 204–205, 206
Armstrong, William, 147, 151
Art Deco style, 5, 102, 180–85, 190, 197, 202, 203, 209–210, 217, 220
artisans, 48
Art Nouveau style, 182–83, 203, 217
Arts and Crafts style, 188

Astral lamps, 139
Austen, Jane, 111–13, 120–21,
    125, 131

back problems, 206, 226
back-stools, 15, 18–19, 40,
    123
Baker, Josephine, 183
Bakst, Leon, 183
Balderston, Lydia Ray, 157,
    166*n*, 170
Baldwin, Billy, 229–30
Ballets Russes, 183
Balzac, Honoré de, 112
Barcelona chair, 204, 208, 211
Baroque style, 101
bathing:
    in Japan, 218, 223
    medieval, 28–29, 30
    in seventeenth century, 42, 46
    in sixteenth century, 36
    Victorian, 135
bathrooms, 46, 56, 65, 91–92,
    125, 129–30, 143*n*
    arrangement of, 164, 222–23
    modern, 192, 193
baths, public, 36–37, 65
bathtubs, 91–92, 164
    full-length, 92
    portable, 164–65
bedpresses, 159, 161
bedrooms, 42–43, 94
    English, 110
    master, 45
    parents', 165
    small, 161
    state, 82–83
beds:
    built-in, 62–63, 159
    four-poster, 39, 62
    medieval, 28
bedsores, 205

Beecher, Catherine E., 137, 155–
    162, 170, 171, 192, 231
Belle Epoque style, 183
benches, 26, 27, 32, 123
"bended-back" chairs, 114
Better Homes and Gardens, 213
bicycles, 107, 207–208
Billings, John S., 134, 137
Blondel, Jacques-François, 90–
    91, 92, 127*n*, 147
Blondel, Jean-François, 89, 90
Bok, Edward, 166
bombé shape, 97, 98–99, 209
bookcases, 16, 39
boots, leather, 118
Bosse, Abraham, 40
Boucher, François, 76, 93
boudoirs, 85, 86, 88
Bramah, Joseph, 128–29
Bramah Valve Closet, 128–29,
    130
Braudel, Fernand, 79, 91
Breuer, Marcel, 194, 204, 207,
    208, 210–11
Breuer chair, 210–11
Brideshead Revisited (Waugh), 9
broom closets, 164
Brummell, George "Beau," 118
Brun family, 44–49, 72
bureaus, 39, 85
burgesses, 24
Butterfly chair, 208

cabinetmakers, 95, 96, 119, 125,
    147
cabinets, 38, 39, 42
cabinets, medicine, 164
Calvinism, 54, 65
camphine, 139
candles, 36
    beeswax, 138, 141
    light from, 141–42, 231

tallow, 138, 141, 142
wax, 138
Cape Cod cottages, 178
Carcel, Bernard, 139
Cardin, Pierre, 4
Carlyle, Thomas, 22
carpets, 124, 149
oriental, 116
carpet sweepers, 149
cesspits, 29
cesspools, 37, 128
chairs:
in ancient times, 26, 80, 81,
84, 95
arm-, 83, 95, 97, 98, 204–
205, 206
Art Deco, 209–10
back support of, 96, 225
cabriole, 114
ceremonial uses of, 26, 32,
81, 83
comfortable, 97, 99, 205–
207, 208–12
director's, 81
easy, 81, 95, 123, 205, 207
ergonomic design of, 26, 95–
96, 205–209, 222
etiquette for, 83
figurative, 81–82
French styles of, 82–84, 95–
98
front rail of, 96
function of, 77–84
Greek, 80, 81, 84, 95
lounge, 207, 208, 211
medieval, 25, 81, 95
modern designs for, 203–13
padding on, 95–96, 97
posture and, 78, 81, 84
side, 40, 210–11
sitting motility of, 205–206
straight-backed, 40

swivel, 206–207
as symbols of authority, 26,
32, 81
tub, 209
types of, 97–98
upholstered, 95–97
see also individual types
chaises longues, 95, 97, 204
chamber pots, 37, *56n*, 125, 130
Chambre de Dame (Dufrène),
172
chambres, 38, 42, 43
Champs-Elysées, 61
Chardin, Jean, 93
Chareau, Pierre, 184, 185
Chaucer, Geoffrey, 31
Cheney House, 166
chests, 25
cheval glass, 98
Chicago World's Fair (1893),
153
chimneys, 36, 91
design of, 131–32
Chippendale style, 114–15,
119–20, 125–26, 199, 209,
210, 212–13
chivalry, 34
Choisy hunting lodge, 86
Cistercian monastic order, 29
cisterns, 161
City-National Bank (Tuscaloosa,
Ala.), 192
Classical Revival style, 101
cleanliness, 64–66, 74–75
close stool, 41, 92
closets, 164
clothing:
layers of, 58–59
medieval rules for, 32–33
paper, 218
ready-to-wear, 4
for warmth, 19

clothmakers' guilds, 55
coal gas, 140, 141
coat closets, 164
coats, short, 118
Collins, Peter, 89
Colonial revival style, 175, 185
colors, meaning of, 35
colza oil, 139
comfort:
　advertising of, 1–3
　bourgeois notions of, 221–22
　as concept, 20–22, 32, 77–
　　78, 90, 121n, 158, 224–32
　discomfort vs., 225–26, 227
　as efficiency, 166, 170–71,
　　192, 193
　English notion of, 106–107,
　　125
　in fashion, 1–4
　historical development of, 22,
　　31–32, 49, 118, 230–31
　in home furnishings, 4–13
　in Middle Ages, 31–32, 33,
　　35
　modern design and, 189–93
　modern notion of, 200, 205–
　　212, 214–15
　nostalgia and, 2–3, 218–20
　Onion Theory of, 230–31
　physical, 93, 219, 225
　privacy and, 227–28, 231
　scientific research on, 226–27
　spaciousness and, 162–63,
　　179
　subjective, 227, 228–30
　technology and, 147–48, 224
　well-being and, 215, 217–32
　in workplace, 226–28
　zone for, 225
computers, 21, 170
Constructivist style, 185–86
Corfield, W. H., 134
corridors, 41, 47, 119

Cost of Shelter, The (Richards),
　156
cottages, 46, 178
couches, 84
coziness, 21, 120–21, 179
credenzas, 63, 91
Crystal Palace, 174
cuisine, 30–31, 32, 73
cupboards:
　accessible, 222
　book, 124
　plate, 63
　sleeping, 159
curtains, window, 57, 124
customs, medieval, 33–34

de Boisregard, Andry, 96
de Brosse, Salomon, 39, 40–41
de Hooch, Pieter, 67, 70
de Parival, Jean-Nicolas, 64
desks, writing, 18, 39, 123–
　124
de Witte, Emanuel, 50, 67–71,
　73, 75, 111, 113
de Wolfe, Elsie, 102, 173
Diaghilev, Serge, 183
dining rooms, 42, 43, 85, 88,
　109, 117, 160
Dior, Christian, 3
dishwashers, 151–52
domesticity, 75, 217, 223–24
Donghia, Angelo, 195–96
Doucet, Jacques, 185, 197
Downing, Andrew Jackson, 137,
　155, 160, 164
drawing rooms, 109, 117, 161
duchesse, 95
ducts, air, 135–36, 145–46
Dufrène, Maurice, 172, 181,
　184
dumbwaiters, 87
Dunand, Jacques, 184
Dupas, Jean, 181

Dürer, Albrecht, 14, 15–16, 18–19, 20, 28, 43–44, 123, 124

Eames, Charles, 208, 211
Easton, David Anthony, 103–104
Edison, Thomas, 150–51
efficiency, 166, 170–71, 192, 193
electric lighting, 142–43, 147, 150–51, 165, 231
enfilade arrangement, 41, 69, 86
engineers, 147–48
  domestic, 167, 169–70, 171, 214
English Cottage style, 182, 183
Englishman's House, The (Richardson), 159, 162–63
ensembliers, 180, 184, 190
Esprit Nouveau, L', 186
etiquette, 30–33, 38, 74, 108
Exposition Internationale des Arts Décoratifs et Industriels Modernes (1925), 180–93, 200*n*, 202

fans:
  ceiling, 152, 175
  electric, 151, 152
fashion:
  advertisements for, 1–2, 6, 8, 11
  changes in, 218
  comfort in, 1–4
  haute couture, 3–4
  invented traditions and, 7*n*, 9–12
  literary allusions in, 10–11
  nostalgia and, 2–3, 7, 9, 13, 213–14
  twenties-influenced, 3
  women's influence on, 93–95

fireplaces, 19, 91, 161
  improvements in, 130–32, 136, 148
  mantled, 36
  open, 147
Fitch, James Marston, 159
Forbes, Malcolm S., 12, 13
Frederick, Christine, 156–57, 163–67, 178, 190, 192, 223, 231
Frederick, George, 168
Free Classic style, 177
French Antique style, 175
furnaces, 161, 165
furniture:
  American, 115, 119–20
  Arabic, 84
  "architectural," 84–85
  arrangement of, 40
  as artificial vs. natural, 80–81
  built-in, 163
  Chinese, 78*n*, 79
  comfort in, 80, 81, 84, 225–226
  as concept, 26
  cultural influences on, 79–80
  decorative aspect of, 95
  design and construction of, 12, 81, 124, 125–26
  Dutch, 62–64, 69–70
  ecclesiastical vs. secular, 27
  eighteenth-century, 125–26
  English vs. French, 104–106, 116–17, 119
  as equipment, 27, 188–89, 200
  feminine vs. masculine, 97, 99
  history of, 81, 83, 124
  Indian, 79
  Japanese, 79
  mass produced, 125–26, 189, 191–92, 200, 203
  mechanical, 206–207

furniture *(cont.)*
  medieval, 15–16, 25
  modern, 203–13
  movable, 26–27, 84, 85, 90, 104–105
  office, 191
  ownership of, 124
  period styles in, 101–102, 103
  serial production of, 125–26
  upholstered, 95–97, 124
  utility of, 34–35, 98
  variety of, 40, 79
  see also individual pieces and styles

Galeries Lafayette, 181
Galton, Douglas, 134, 137, 149*n*
garderobes, 29
garde-robes, 38, 39, 42, 43
gaslight, 36, 130, 139–43, 145, 146, 148, 149, 150, 165
gasoliers, 140–43, 145, 151, 173, 175
Gentleman and Cabinet-Maker's Director, The (Chippendale), 116
Gentleman's House, The (Kerr), 145, 158
Georgian revival style, 175
Georgian style, 104, 105–21, 124, 176, 220
Gesner, Abraham, 139
Giedion, Siegfried, 31, 92, 143, 158, 159
Gilbreth, Frank, 168, 169–70
Gilbreth, Lillian, 169–70, 171*n*, 190, 191, 192, 223
Girl Embroidering (Kersting), 100, 111–12
Girouard, Mark, 129
Gray, Eileen, 184, 197
Gropius, Walter, 202

halls, central, 25, 26–27, 47, 108
Hamilton, George, 102–103
Handlin, Douglas, 159
hand-washing, 29, 30, 35, 74, 92–93
Hardoy chair, 208
Harington, John, 129
Hayward, John, 146
hearths, 46–47
heating:
  central, 137, 152, 193
  Dutch methods of, 58–59
  electric, 150, 152–53
  fuels for, 58
  improvements in, 126, 130–132, 148
  in Middle Ages, 19–20
  in seventeenth century, 46–47, 49, 91
  in sixteenth century, 19
Hepplewhite style, 114–15, 116, 120, 125–26, 209, 210
Hermitage, 88, 93
Hitler, Adolf, 35*n*, 202
Hoffmann, Joseph, 183
Hogarth, William, 5
home:
  in art, 15–16, 66–71
  children and, 48–49, 59–60, 165–66
  as concept, 24, 62
  family and, 24, 35, 39, 47–48, 49, 51, 60, 77
  female vs. male conceptions of, 160–61
  feminization of, 72–75
  "hominess" in, 16–17, 43
  intimacy and, 15, 39, 43–44, 47–48, 64, 69, 74–75, 77, 86, 110–12, 228
  marriage and, 47–48
  as middle-class institution,

24–25, 40, 42, 45, 48, 63, 86
women's role in, 29–30, 70–71, 72–75, 117, 156, 160–161, 223–24
see also houses
home economics, 158, 170
Hope, Thomas, 211
Hôtel de Liancourt, 40–41
Hôtel du Collectionneur, 180–181
Hôtel Lambert, 41, 42
hôtels, 40–41, 42, 105, 118, 165–66
House Architecture (Stevenson), 146–47, 177
Household Engineering (Frederick), 163–67, 169, 178
houses:
American, 161–67, 178–79
compact, 155, 159–62
country, 104, 105
domestic arrangements in, 26–27, 47–48, 49, 56, 73–75, 77, 161–62, 179
Dutch, 55–59, 61–62, 67–71, 113, 160, 162, 221, 231
"efficient," 166, 192
furnishings for, 4–13
historical periods in, 103–105
housecleaning of, 29–30, 65–66, 73, 145–71
illumination of, 126, 130, 138–43, 145
interiors of, 35–36, 51
irregular arrangement of, 177–78
mechanization in, 19, 153–55
medieval, 22–36
of nobility, 40–41
period styles of, 101–106, 174–77
of poor, 23–24, 29, 79

removal of shoes in, 64, 66
rented accommodations in, 39, 59
scientific management of, 167–71, 191, 193, 214, 223–24
in seventeenth century, 38–49
small, 59, 155, 159–63, 178–179, 192
zoning in, 165–66
Housewifery (Balderston), 157, 166*n*
housewives, 29–30
Huizinga, J. H., 23, 34, 54, 65
hygiene, 28–30, 37, 56*n*–57*n*, 64–66, 74–75

interior design:
architecture vs., 127–28, 130, 131
austerity in, 214–15
bourgeois, 199–200, 201
density in, 197–98, 217–18
domestic technology vs., 147–148, 173–74
exterior decoration vs., 89
in France, 52, 180–81
historical verisimilitude in, 11–13
"master designer" approach to, 203–204
modern, 11–13, 173–93, 195–215, 222
of offices, 12–13
Scandinavian influence in, 173
Viennese influence in, 180, 183, 193
Interior with a Woman Playing the Virginals (de Witte), 50, 67–71, 73, 111
I quattro libri di architettura (Palladio), 114
Iribe, Paul, 197

irons:
    electric, 153–54
    flat-, 153
    gas-heated, 148–49

"Jamaica" collection, 6–7, 8n, 9
Jeanneret, Charles-Edouard, 186–93, 200n, 201, 220
Johnson, Philip, 211
Jones, Inigo, 114

kerosene lamps, 139–40, 175
Kerr, Robert, 145, 158, 160, 162n
Kersting, Georg Friedrich, 100, 111–12
kitchens, 45, 46, 47, 88, 161, 190
    Dutch, 73–74
    layout of, 163–64, 169, 171, 193, 222, 223
klismos, 26

"ladder-back" chairs, 97, 114
Ladies' Home Journal, 166, 169, 170
lamps:
    electric, 147, 150, 173, 175
    gas, 140–43, 145, 151, 173, 175
    kerosene, 139–40, 175
    oil, 36, 138–39, 142
Lanvin, Jeanne, 185
Lauder, Estée, 12, 98, 103, 220
Lauren, Ralph, 1–3, 5–12, 183, 195–96
La-Z-Boy chair, 207
Le Corbusier, 186–93, 200n, 201, 220
Léger, Fernand, 187
Le Sueur, Eustache, 42
libraries, 109, 110, 118
lighting, 19–20

electric, 142–43, 147, 150–151, 165, 231
gas, 36, 130, 139–43, 145, 146, 148, 149, 150, 165
linen closets, 164
living rooms, 165, 179
"Log Cabin" collection, 6, 7, 11, 12
Loos, Adolf, 199, 200, 204n, 213
Louis XIV style, 41–42, 82–83, 102, 176
Louis XV style, 83–84, 86, 92–98, 102, 105, 106
Love Letter, The (Vermeer), 71
Lukacs, John, 35, 36, 75, 219–220

McKim, Mead and White, 178
Mallet-Stevens, Rob., 184, 185
manners, 30–33, 38, 74, 108
Mansfield Park (Austen), 111–112
"Manual of the Dwelling, The" (Le Corbusier), 189–90
Mare, André, 209
"Mariner" collection, 8, 11
Maugham, Syrie, 173
Merch & Co., 226–27
Metsu, Gabriel, 67
miasmatic theory, 134–35
Mies van der Rohe, Ludwig, 202, 204, 208, 211
Minimal style, 195–215
Modern style, 195–215
Morris, William, 101
Mumford, Lewis, 31
Mussolini, Benito, 202

Nash, John, 147
neo-Classic style, 202
neo-Georgian style, 104
neo-Gothic style, 175, 219

Netherlands:
    bourgeois society in, 53–54
    government of, 51–54, 58
    houses in, 55–59, 61–62, 67–
        71, 113, 160, 162, 221,
        231
    hygiene in, 64–66, 74–75
    role of women in, 70–71, 72–
        75
"New England" collection, 6, 7,
    213
"New Housekeeping, The"
    (Frederick), 169
New Spirit style, 186–93, 200,
    203, 214
"night soil," 29, 56n–57n
Nijinsky, Waslaw, 183
Northanger Abbey (Austen), 131
nostalgia:
    comfort and, 2–3, 218–20
    fashion and, 2–3, 7, 9, 13,
        213–14

"Ornament and Crime" (Loos),
    199
ornamentation, 43, 89, 188,
    198–200
ovens, cooking, 131

paintings, 66–71, 84
Palais de Luxembourg, 39
Palladian architecture, 114, 117,
    118, 127n
Palladio, Andrea, 114, 127n
pandemayne, 31
Parakeets, The (Dupas), 181
Parliament, Houses of, 135–36,
    140, 151
pattern books, 114–15, 116,
    120, 125–26, 209
Pattern Language, A (Alex-
    ander), 229
Pattison, Mary, 156, 169

Paxton, Joseph, 174
Peel, J. H. B., 93
playrooms, 165
plumbing, 124, 129–30
Poiret, Paul, 183
Pompadour, Jeanne Antoinette
    Poisson, Marquise de, 87n,
    88, 94, 104, 112
porches, sleeping, 163
postmodernism, 102, 220–22
posture, 25, 26, 78, 81, 84,
    205–206, 226
Praz, Mario, 43, 120, 182
*Principles of Domestic Engineer-
    ing, The* (Pattison), 156,
    169
privacy:
    comfort and, 227–28, 231
    as concept, 18, 26–27, 28,
        221–22
    English notion of, 107–108
    French cultivation of, 87, 88
    history of, 39, 49, 118
    as separation, 165–66
    as valued by Dutch, 57, 59,
        60, 63–64, 66, 77
    in Victorian households, 165
    visual, 227
privies, 29, 37, 38, 47, 56
pumps, hand, 73

Queen Anne style, 10, 177–79,
    182, 185, 198, 217, 221

Rambouillet, Catherine de Vi-
    vonne de Savelli, Marquise
    de, 42–43, 94
Randolph, Benjamin, 120
Rasmussen, Steen Eiler, 61
Reagan, Ronald, 98
Red House, 177
refrigerators, 151
Rembrandt van Rijn, 52

revivalism, historical, 101–104,
174–77
Richards, Ellen H., 156, 167,
170, 190, 191, 192
Richardson, C. J., 132, 159,
162–63
Ricket's globes, 146
Rimsky-Korsakov, Nikolai, 183
rocking chairs, 115
Rockwell, Norman, 67, 216
Rococo style, 89, 93–99, 101,
104–105, 106, 114, 147,
166, 176, 202, 212
roofs, gabled, 58
rooms:
breakfast, 109
ceremonial, 90
common, 108–109, 110
private, 90
reception, 90
size of, 179, 222, 225
specialized functions of, 18,
42–43, 85–86, 109–10,
124
row houses, 55–56, 113
Rudofsky, Bernard, 77–78, 80
Ruhlmann, Jacques-Émile, 180–
181, 184, 209
Rumford, Count (Benjamin
Thompson), 131–32
Ruskin, John, 22
Rutton, Henry, 146
Ruyter, Michel Adriaanszoon de,
72

"Safari" collection, 8, 11
St. Jérôme in His Study (Dürer),
14, 15–16, 18–19, 20, 28,
43–44
Saint Laurent, Yves, 3
salles, 38, 39, 86
salles à manger, 43, 86

salons, 85–86, 88, 110
saloons, 110
sanitation, 28–30, 37, *56n–57n,*
64–66, 74–75
Sartre, Jean-Paul, 21
Scott, Walter, 20, 31, 35, 112,
140
Scully, Vincent, 178
Secession style, 183, 188
secretaries, 39
servants, 39, 86–87
Dutch, 59, 72, 73
need for, 124, 126, 141, 160,
164–65, 220
scarcity of, 220, 223, 224,
231
sleeping quarters of, 41, 42,
45, 49
in U.S., 155–57
Shaw, Norman, 147
Sheraton, Thomas, 125
"shield-back" chairs, 97, 114
Shingle Style, 178–79
Singer, Isaac, 151
sinks, 73, 164
sitting, squatting vs., 78–81, 96
*Smoke Nuisance and Its Rem-
edy, The* (Richardson), 132
smoking, 74, 131–32
smoking rooms, 133, 217
sofas, 84, 118, 123
soot, 141, 149
Soviet pavilion, 185–86, 201
Space Shuttle, 226
steam engines, 148
steamships, 174
Steen, Jan, 67
Stevenson, John James, 136–37,
146–47, 148, 162*n,* 177
Stirling, James, 211
stools, 15, 18–19, 40, 84, 123
stoops, 56, 64

stoves:
  cast-iron, 138
  coal-burning, 143
  Dutch, 73
  gas, 143, 148
  glazed earthenware, 36
  for heating, 47, 58, 91, 137
  porcelain, 91
  radiating, 137
Stowe, Harriet Beecher, 159,
  161
studies, 15–20, 86, 123, 124–
  125, 192
Süe, Louis, 209
Swan, Joseph, 147, 150

table manners, 30–31
tables, 15, 27, 85, 109, 118
Talbot, Suzanne, 184, 185, 197
Taylor, Frederick Winslow,
  167–68, 169, 190
technology:
  comfort and, 147–48, 224
  domestic, 126, 127, 130–32,
    145–71, 173–74, 179,
    189–93
  mass, 142–43
  medieval, 21, 22–23
Temple, William, 61, 65–66, 74
terrace houses, 73
Tesla, Nikola, 151
Thorigny, Jean-Baptiste Lambert
  de, 41, 42
Thornton, Peter, 117, 197–98
"Thoroughbred" collection, 6, 7,
  9, 10–11, 12, 213
toilets, 92, 128–29
Toky, Richard, 28
Towards a New Architecture (Le
  Corbusier), 187
townhouses, 24–25
  English, 105–106

in Paris, 37–39, 40–41, 60
*Treatise on Domestic Economy,
  A* (Beecher), 137, 158–62
tubs, 30, 218

upholsterers, 127–28, 130, 131,
  147–48

vacuum cleaners, 149, 151, 154,
  190
valve closets, 128–29
van Heusden, Adriana, 72
van Holst, H. V., 166, 192
Vaux, Calvert, 145
ventilation, 126, 130, 132–38,
  145–46, 148, 152
Verberckt, Jacques, 92–93
Vermeer, Jan, 52, 67, 71, 75,
  111, 113
Versailles, 82–83, 87, 88, 91,
  92–93, 104
Victoria, Queen of England, 7n,
  133
Victorian style, 101, 165, 174,
  175–76, 198, 202, 212,
  221
Villas and Cottages (Vaux), 145
Villa Trianon, 102
Vitruvius, 90
Vogue, 3

washing machines, 149, 151–52
washstands, 30, 85
Wassily chair, 194, 204–205,
  207–208, 211
water closets, 92, 128–29, 161,
  164, 223
water supply, 37, 46, 49, 129–
  130, 161, 164
Water Witch, 149
Waugh, Evelyn, 9, 196
Weissenhof chair, 211

Westinghouse, George, 151, 152, 153
Westminster Palace, 30
whale oil, 139, 141
windows:
    curtains for, 57, 124
    in Dutch houses, 57–58
    glazed, 36, 123, 146
    location and size of, 119
    sash, 57–58, 113, 187
    ventilation from, 137

Windsor chair, 115–16, 200, 204
women:
    domestic role of, 29–30, 70–71, 72–75, 117, 156, 160–161, 223–24
    fashion influenced by, 93–95
Wright, Frank Lloyd, 166, 178
writing, 17–19, 39, 42, 123–24

Yellow Oval Room, 98